GOOD LIVES

Good Lives

GEORGE R. STEWART

illustrated with photographs

HOUGHTON MIFFLIN COMPANY BOSTON
1 9 6 7

TO ANNA

CONTENTS

ILLUSTRATIONS

all following page
146

Effigy of the Marshal on the tomb in
the Temple Church, London

Schliemann, about the time of his first
excavations at Troy

Tresguerras, probably about 1810

The Carmen Church, Celaya

Tresguerras's bridge over the Río Laja

Prince Henry in middle age

Sagres Point, the southern tip of Europe

The Bidwells in 1894

FOREWORD

THAT PHRASE, "the good life," seems to have come over the horizon at some time during the twentieth century. Its origin is not associated with the sayings or writings of any particular person. It is not a frequenter of the books of quotations.

The reason why the phrase must be considered of anonymous source is doubtless that its words are too common. In the course of the centuries they must have been linked a countless number of times. Only in recent years, however, have they attained a special meaning, so that the living or attainment of "the good life" has become a widespread and even a conscious aspiration.

Even so, just what the words, thus linked, may be taken to mean — all this seems to remain uncertain in people's minds, even when they say the syllables. As often, however, we may make some beginning of a definition by lopping off the areas to which the phrase is not generally considered applicable.

The good life does not seem to be conceived, first of all, in religious terms. It does not mean merely living in strict accordance with the dogmas of any church.

Moreover, it does not refer to a person who is devoted to the doing of good deeds and the service of others. Such a one may be said, curiously, to have lived "a good life," but not "the good life."

On the other hand, the term possesses a certain idealistic

quality. It is not to be applied to someone who has merely attained a high degree of pleasure and satisfaction from eating, drinking, and sleeping — whether alone or in company.

A positive description is more difficult, and will be attempted as a conclusion, not here at the beginning. The primary method of this book will be to present six exemplars or candidates. These, it is maintained, managed to live the good life, in one way or another, and from their demonstrations of it some conclusions may possibly, at the end, be established.

The reasons for my choices, however, call for brief explanation. On the whole, I may say, to attain the good life does not seem to me to be an especially rare phenomenon. I myself have known some people who seem to me to have done so, and from the annals of biography I would have had no difficulty in selecting a large number.

But the six that I have chosen to present here share certain qualities. First, they have been old favorites of mine, and were not artificially dredged up for the immediate purpose. My interest in William the Marshal, for instance, dates from 1921. I thus did not decide to write about the good life and then look around for people to exemplify it. Instead, I have followed what may be called an inductive method, attempting to derive the principles from the individual instances. Granted the instances, some generalization could logically follow.

Second, biographical data for my purposes had to be available, although in two instances it proved to be extremely scant. Moreover, this material had to be available in languages that I could read.

Third, the candidate had to be a person of some achievement, so as to be of general interest. But, at the same time, he must not be a person universally known. I saw no reason to add another essay on Franklin or Jefferson.

The basic method, however, is to present, not an abstraction or theory of the good life, but some concrete examples of people who may have attained it. The shorter the introduction, therefore, the better. I begin.

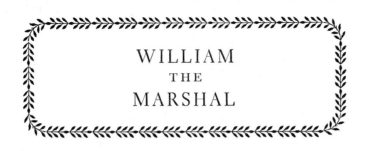

WILLIAM
THE
MARSHAL

During the spring of the year 1219, at Caversham in Oxfordshire, a man lay dying. He was old, and it was time. He was ready.

All was as it should be. His wife, his sons and daughters, his knights and squires, his chaplains, attended him.

Of few deathbeds is the story better preserved, or more moving. But, before we can appreciate the death, we must know something of the life. . . .

This man was called William, that is, Guillaume, in the language of the Norman lords of England, of whom he was one. He had received from his father the hereditary office of King's Marshal, and so he was known as William the Marshal. Besides, he had won more titles and honors than can well be listed. He was knight, knight-banneret, Lord of Leinster, Lord of Longueville, Earl of Striguil, Earl of Pembroke, Regent of England.

Great though he was, as he lay there dying at Caversham, he had been of comparatively humble origin, and the year of his birth is not surely known. Shortly after his death, an official biography was compiled, in 19,214 lines of Norman-French verse. But the biographer did not know the precise age of the great earl, and in one passage made him state that he was eighty years old. From various bits of evidence, historians have concluded that he must have been, at his death, about seventy-five.

His birth date, then, would have been 1144, and there have been few more turbulent years in which to be born in England. Stephen and Matilda were fighting for the throne, and the whole realm was full of tumult and rapine.

In those bad years there was a minor nobleman of southern England named John and called "the Marshal." His father, also "the Marshal," had been named Gilbert, and that is all that is known of the family.

This John Marshal was in all the tumult and rapine, up to his ears. Apparently, he thrived on it. He held castles at Marlborough and Ludgershall, and from these bases he went around plundering. He was of King Stephen's party, but in those times every man had to be, first of all, for himself.

Eventually the pressure was too much for John Marshal. In those troubled waters the big fish were eating the little fish, and he was not much more than a minnow. From the south, his powerful neighbor, Patrick, Earl of Salisbury, closed in on him. In such circumstances, as compared with lands, and even life, a theoretical allegiance to Stephen could not stand. John went over to Matilda, made his peace with Patrick, and took Patrick's sister in marriage. Before he could do the last, he had to divorce the wife that he already had, or just send her home to her family — since people cannot be squeamish and stick to the letter of canon law in such times.

It sounds a sordid business and a marriage and environment out of which no good could come. But the second child and son was called William, and he grew up to refute all such expectations. Moreover, he was to be throughout his life notable for his loyalty, equanimity, stability, magnanimity, and love of justice, and these are qualities that point to the securest of secure early years.

Perhaps we exaggerate the sense of danger. His childhood

within the walls of Marlborough castle, where he was probably born and grew up, may have been quiet and warm during years when the strong hands of his father and uncle kept
the fighting at a distance.

Then there was his mother. We know little of her except
that her name was Sybile. Yet we should remember that
William's biographer, nearly a century later, liked to quote
the proverb, "Of good tree comes good fruit!" Lady Sybile
may well have been such a good tree, whether she gave
staunch qualities to her son by blood or by warmth of love
afterwards.

Probably the father had little to do with his earliest upbringing. John was generally away killing someone or burning someone's house. Yet perhaps we should not merely write
of him as the stereotyped "rough baron." He had, surpris-
ingly, a gift of wit (rough wit, as you would expect) and two
of his *mots* have even been preserved.

Once when Matilda's army was flying in rout, and John
was trying to get her to ride faster, he cried out, "Lady, it is
time to spread your legs!" He meant, of course, that she
should quit riding side-saddle.

The other saying involves his son William, who had now
reached the small-boy stage. By this time he would have
spoken French, with a Norman accent, as his usual language,
but had probably been around with nursemaids and grooms
and other servants sufficiently to pick up English, in a broad
southern dialect that said "vox" for "fox" and "hull" for "hill."

What happened at this point we know only from the
way William himself told the story, years later.

The father, again, had suffered bad luck in the fortunes
of the long-continuing civil war, and found it expedient to
offer a hostage to King Stephen, a common practice. John

3

Marshal, by this time, had four sons, two by each marriage. William was the youngest, and therefore was, by feudal thought, the least valuable. He was given as hostage.

John Marshal at once broke his side of the bargain by reinforcing Newbury castle. The King, realizing that he had been hoodwinked, was naturally incensed, and laid siege. He also sent a message to John Marshal to reconsider the matter and surrender Newbury, or else the life of the hostage would be forfeited.

The father replied, with seeming brutality but still with a well-turned phrase, "I'm not concerned about it. I still have the hammers and the anvils to forge even better children." Quite possibly, he was gambling that Stephen, knowing the game already lost, would not take revenge on the child.

The King immediately ordered William to be led out to the nearest tree, and he himself escorted him with a guard. Not knowing what it was all about, the child went along cheerfully. He happened to see a certain earl brandishing an attractive throwing-spear, and in his childish voice asked for the gift of it. The King, suddenly breaking at these innocent words, took the child in his arms, and reprieved him.

During two months (one can imagine an old earl telling the story half a century later) the child remained in Stephen's camp before Newbury. As the besiegers continued to endure hardships, some of them, vindictively, urged the death of the hostage.

Once, as if trying to fit the punishment to the crime, some of these men persuaded the king that he should have William put into one of the siege-engines, and thrown into the castle. But the little boy, seeing the engine, cried out, "What a swing! I should have a swing in it!" Again the kind-hearted King relented.

Once William played with the King at a game in which each took a flower and tried to snap off the head of the other's flower. William won, to his great delight. Again, we can imagine him telling the story to his own sons — perhaps, or perhaps not, adding the moral, "You see, even as a child I could hold my own against a king, or even get a little the better of him."

We ourselves, if the child is father to the man, may see in William's naïveté a presage of the later frankness and integration of spirit that inspired confidence in others, and carried him through many straits. Moreover, throughout his life he evinced a remarkable, and apparently unconscious, charm of personality.

Fortunately for young William, his term as hostage came just at the end of the civil war. Matilda's son, Henry Plantagenet, finally won the decision, and took the throne as Henry II. In the general settlement William went back to his family. He stayed with them a few years more.

Throughout his childhood he enjoyed, presumably, almost nothing in the way of what we would consider education. He did not learn to read — at least, not readily. The biographer once mentions his receiving a letter and having a clerk read it to him. In those times, however, a gentleman generally expected to employ a clerk for such matters, just as a businessman now expects to have a secretary do his typing. Few books were available, but the pleasures of literature were not lacking. William was probably brought up with a taste for good professional oral renditions of *The Song of Roland* and *The Four Sons of Aymon*. At the chimney-corner he heard the crones telling ghost stories and all about Wade and his wonderful boat, so that later generations could have the phrase, "an old wives' tale."

A baron's son in those raw years was sure to be taught the handling of weapons. He also learned about horses and horsemanship. The life, however, might have been an idle one, and rather boring in the times when a boy had to keep inside the walls. But again, we can maintain, it must have been a good childhood, to turn out the man that it did.

When William was about twelve, John Marshal decided to send him away, to get what would pass for an education, and, at the same time, to seek his fortune. Promising lad though he was, he remained, after all, only a younger son. So he set out with two attendants, taking no more worldly goods than could be carried behind the saddles, and doubtless with the understanding that this was his patrimony. He rode to the coast, and then, for the first of many times, voyaged across the channel. He reported, as had been arranged, to his father's cousin, who was Chamberlain of Normandy, and held a hilltop castle at Tancarville, overlooking the broad reaches of the lower Seine.

There William spent eight years, learning the profession of arms. He could not have done so at a better time. The days of the crude baron were ending; the days of the courtly knight were about to begin. The *chanson de geste* was yielding to the romance; Roland, to Lancelot. A young squire still learned how to don armor, how to leap into the saddle, how to handle lance and sword. But he also was instructed in much else that would have made William the Conqueror, or even John Marshal, think that the world was going soft. The squire learned manners; he learned to love poetry, or even to write it; he learned to sing; he learned how to talk to a lady acceptably — and, not infrequently, to make love to her acceptably. Eleanor of Aquitaine was Queen of England, and her daughter Marie was Countess of Champagne, and all through the South the troubadours were singing madly, and it was one of the better times in all history to be young.

Whether William mastered all these arts, we are not sure. Certainly he learned to wield arms and to sing. But, from the little we know (and, again, it must have come from the old man's telling), these years were the time when William showed off to least advantage. All that happened, we should guess, was that he was passing through an unusually awkward adolescence, so that he was growing fast and his feet seemed too big for him. All he wanted to do, as the story tells us, was to drink and eat and sleep. People nicknamed him Wastemeat. There was danger that he might eliminate himself in the competition, and never become a knight.

But the Chamberlain stuck by his young cousin, perhaps for family loyalty, but more likely because he saw what was happening. And he was right. William, as was only to be expected, came out of adolescence. Finally, after serving as squire for about eight years, he was judged ready for the next step. The Chamberlain himself girded the sword of knighthood on, "with which," as the biographer stops to comment proudly, "he later struck many a blow."

As for William's person, the biographer lets us know that he had brown hair, and beautiful hands and feet, but otherwise takes refuge in superlatives and generalities, as by assuring us that his hero looked fit to be emperor of Rome. The conclusion must be that William, though handsome, lacked unusual physical traits. If, for instance, he had been very tall, the biographer would have noted it. From the record of William's exploits as a knight we can be certain that he was at least above the average in size and strength, and that in coordination and dexterity he must have been the equivalent of a decathlon champion.

The long years of his squirehood had been generally peaceful, but war between Louis VII of France and Henry II of England flared up in 1167, with Normandy a part of Henry's holdings. In fact, we can assume, the outbreak of hostilities was the occasion for William's being knighted.

One morning the counts of Flanders and Boulogne came pouring over the Norman border with their men, and threatened the town of Drincourt. The Chamberlain, though outnumbered, went to the rescue.

Sir William, overeager in his first fight, pressed forward to the front, and the Chamberlain had to reprimand him, telling him to give precedence to his elders. But when the fight was joined, William was in it. Breaking his lance, he laid about him with his sword. There was charge and countercharge through the streets of the town. The French, rather ungallantly, brought some foot soldiers in.

One of these seized William with a large hook, and dragged him from his horse. Keeping his feet and fighting the foot soldiers off, William got clear, but his horse was killed.

In the end the Chamberlain and his men drove the invaders off, and held the town.

William, fighting always for honor, had distinguished himself, but he faced anticlimax. Old-timers in war knew that they must make a profit at it. But William had not stopped to take possession of the armor and horses of the men he had overcome, or to hold them as prisoners for ransom.

At the victory banquet, that evening, some of the older knights twitted William. He had captured nothing, and had lost his war horse, an essential and very expensive piece of equipment. But William may have been happy enough. If a man wins honor in his first fight, he can rest assured that some lord will give him another horse.

8

A peace was soon concluded, and the Chamberlain, after keeping William on tenterhooks for a while, did give him another horse, so that he could take part in a tournament that was to be held shortly.

In those fine years, we may say, a battle was almost a tournament, and a tournament was almost a battle. As William had had underscored for him in his first fight, the object in battle was not to kill people but to capture them. In both battle and tournament the knights used the same equipment and fought in the same manner. About the only difference was that a tournament was held at a stated time and place, usually in a field specified as lying between two villages.

Having learned that honor could be combined with profit, William attended to business in his first tournament, captured three knights, and became possessed of their expensive weapons and armor, and also of their war horses, palfreys, and pack horses. It was a highly profitable day for a landless younger son.

Naturally, he was off to another tournament as soon as possible. The Chamberlain could not go, but he did not stand in the way of his young cousin, and granted permission. William thus became what was known as a *knight-errant*. He did not ride about like Lancelot and Gawain, rescuing damsels and killing giants, but he made the round of what we might call the tournament-circuit.

Some time in the year William asked permission to go to England. The Chamberlain said that England was a dull country where no good tournaments were held, and that William should hurry back. Normandy and Brittany were the places!

William's father, that salty old baron, had died, and so had two elder brothers. Only one brother stood between William

9

and the family lands. But they did not amount to very much, and William could think himself better off serving the Chamberlain and playing *knight-errant*.

Then a revolt broke out in ever-restless Poitou against the authority of King Henry. That wide-ruling monarch summoned his vassals of England to help him put down his vassals of Poitou. Earl Patrick of Salisbury, William's uncle, was one of those who crossed to the continent, and William went with him.

Well on in 1168 the Count was in Poitou, having been given special charge of the person of Queen Eleanor. The revolt had been put down, generally speaking. But the Poitevins were proverbially discontented and unreliable, and of all the Poitevins the five Lusignan brothers were the worst.

One day Count Patrick was riding along, escorting the Queen. Everything was supposed to be peaceful, and the knights were mounted on their palfreys and not wearing their armor.

Suddenly they looked up to see an armed band spurring down on them. By the banners and shields anyone could see it was the Lusignans.

The Count reacted as a good soldier. He ordered the Queen to hurry on to a nearby castle. He yelled for his warhorse and armor, and turned to cover the Queen's escape.

There was no time! The attackers were upon them. The Count, unarmored and just springing to his horse, was stabbed in his defenseless back and fell dead.

William had had time to mount, and had slipped into a short coat of chain-mail, but had no helmet on. Wild at the dastardly killing of his uncle, he spurred in, and with his spear thrust one man from his saddle. Then his own horse went down.

Making a dash for it, William got his back against a hedge,

and dared them, with a fine epic taunt, "Come on, anyone who wants to try his strength!" They came, but William struck down horse after horse, until the bodies lay like a barricade in front of him. The biographer can only lose himself in simile, declaring that the young knight fought like a lion or like a boar against hounds.

Finally, a Poitevin got behind the hedge, and thrust a spear clear through William's thigh. He yielded then.

When the spear was drawn out, the wound bled badly. But Lusignans were anxious to make their getaway. They bundled their prisoner onto a horse, and started.

William was in a bad fix — his worst since King Stephen had held him as hostage. He was weak from loss of blood, badly wounded, and in great pain from having to ride. Besides, he was a prisoner, and Earl Patrick was dead. His uncle, under whom he had been serving, would have been the one to furnish ransom for him.

The next few weeks were black ones. The Lusignans shifted warily, dragging William along, in spite of his sufferings from an almost untended wound.

But the vigor of his own youthful body soon began to get the better of the wound. Besides, in one respect he was in luck. If you are going to be wounded and captured, at least you can be happy that it has happened when you have just made a great fight in defense of a queen — especially when the queen is Eleanor.

Not only was she Queen of England but she was also, in her own right, Duchess of Aquitaine, and, even beyond that — she was Queen of Love and Lady of Chivalry. Naturally she must ransom a brave and handsome young knight who had been wounded in her defense.

So William was freed, and came to whatever place Eleanor was holding court at the time, and she started him in life again. She gave him "horses and arms and money and fine clothes."

Whether she gave him anything more personal — ? Eleanor was forty-six, and William was twenty-two. But in the theories of Courtly Love, which Eleanor had propagated, the lady was often the older. Still, the theories also demanded a long and formal courtship, and not a quick yielding to infatuation. So it is unlikely.

The curious thing is that a ballad, *Queen Eleanor's Confession,* turns upon a love affair between Eleanor and the Earl Marshal, and that was William's title in later life. At first thought, as the saying goes, "It makes you wonder." But, then, the ballad cannot be dated before the seventeenth century, and there would seem to be no possibility that the ballad-maker knew anything about such a delicate matter.

In any case, handsome young men being what they always have been and twelfth-century feudal society being far from Puritanical, we cannot suppose that William passed through his bachelorhood as a Galahad. In fact, the story of Galahad was not even to be invented for some time, and it would certainly have struck William and his contemporaries as very odd.

Having once made this direct contact with the royal family, William never lost it. Except for a few interludes, he served the House of Anjou until his death.

William's prowess at tournaments and his fight against the Poitevins made him a widely talked-about young man. As a result, some time during the next year, he must have received a summons to attend upon King Henry himself, to be interviewed, so to speak, for a job. That great monarch, whose domain swept from the Roman wall to the Pyrenees, was contemplating a most serious move — the coronation of his eldest son, who would thus come to be known as the Young

King. The advantage of the action would be to insure the proper succession.

This prince was only fifteen years old. The coronation would put him into a difficult and somewhat false position, since he would have the title but no power. Obviously his father needed to supply him with good advisors, and he did his best. The older Henry, as modern historians note, had a gift for choosing the right man. On this occasion, to be a kind of elder brother and a tutor in chivalry, the King chose William. (Queen Eleanor may well have sent a word of recommendation; after all, the Young King was her son, and she might have had something to say in the matter.)

The promotion was nothing short of dazzling. William remained a young and landless knight, but he became a man of importance, close to the seat of power, and enjoying many perquisites.

By this time he seems to have been generally called "the Marshal." Not being head of the family, he did not hold that office, but the title must have been given him in courtesy, being almost a family name.

The first three years were a honeymoon period. The Young King was only a squire in the chivalric rating. While he was sixteen and seventeen, he could look with admiration and awe upon that ideal of knighthood who was eleven years older.

But sons of Henry and Eleanor matured early, in so much as they matured at all. By 1173 young Henry had a mind of his own, and had quarreled with his father about prerogatives to such a degree that he went to war, allying himself with the French king. This son-against-father war is shocking to moderns, but the people who were involved in it were not so much concerned.

War was their way of life, and any war was better than just going to tournaments. War would mean, they conceived, a lot of racing and chasing over the fair fields of France, with bold young knights doing chivalrous deeds, and no more of them killed than would just lend a slight titillation of danger to the whole affair.

The Marshal cannot greatly have liked the idea of war, much as the prospect of it must have excited him. He was by nature a person of calm judgment, and he would have been torn two ways. Duty and interest and a tie of allegiance held him to the Old King, who had appointed him, and they also held him to the Young King, who was his immediate lord. William, in fact, was in the uncomfortable position of having two masters, and feudal law had never solved just what a man should do in such a case. William stuck by the Young King, and old Henry never seemed to harbor a grudge for it. In fact, he may well have been glad that his son still had a level-headed counsellor.

At the beginning of it the Marshal was granted a signal honor. The Young King was old enough to be knighted. When the sword was brought to him, he said, "So God please, the best knight of all time shall gird me with the sword." Though the brother of the French king was present, the Young King turned to the Marshal, saying, "From God and from you, good sir, I wish to have this honor." The biographer cannot refrain from a comment. "This great honor God gave to the Marshal that day. In the presence of counts and barons and men of great name he girded the sword upon the king of England. And he owned not a furrow of land, and had nothing except his own knighthood."

As to what the Marshal did in the war, the biography makes absolutely no mention, and so, we may assume, he did nothing very notable and nothing of which he himself was especially proud.

In fact, it was not a glorious war, and scarcely any fun at

all, for the Young King and his knights. Though not many of them were killed, the Old King began capturing and destroying their castles, and ravaging their lands, until they had, as the biographer puts it, "not enough left to give alms to a beggar." So, in the next year, the Young King made his submission. The Marshal was considered an important enough person to be one of those whose names went on the treaty as witnesses.

The Marshal stood just as well off as he did before the war. This might be called luck. Still, not luck, but a good reputation and a record of good conduct were responsible for the Old King allowing him to continue with his duties.

The treaty concluded, Old King and Young King packed up and were off, bag and baggage and retinues, to England. There the Young King busied himself with tournaments, though England was not the real home of them, and with hunting, which may have been better than it was on the continent. The mention of hunting is of interest, since the Marshal presumably accompanied his master. But he seems not to have been much devoted to hound and hawk. Not a single anecdote of the biography is concerned with his exploits "in wood and by river."

After a year the Young King was all for returning to the continent. His father allowed him to go.

There was a great flourishing of tournaments in the next few years, and the Young King dispensed extravagant sums of money. The Old King grumbled, but he may have thought it cheaper to keep his son thus busy than to have him at leisure to plot with the French.

The Marshal throve at tournaments. He captured many knights, and often was judged to have done the best of any. We may assume that he himself sometimes was captured. But it must have happened rarely, and the biography makes no mention of it. The Marshal operated at a handsome profit.

Yet the biographer assures us that the Marshal did not strive for riches, but for honor. Doubtless this was true in those tournaments in which the Young King took part. In them the Marshal had no chance to go tearing around on his own. The Young King's knights had to fight as an organized squadron, now directed to charge this way and now that way, now to hold back and wait for the proper moment. The Marshal had to give the orders, or at least to advise when to give them. Besides, in the melee, the courageous young Henry was likely to be rash beyond his strength and his skill in arms. To have him captured would be both a disgrace and a financial disaster. So the Marshal had to keep close, and on several occasions he pressed in to the rescue.

By the laws of proper conduct, the Young King should have been filled with gratitude and should have drawn ever closer to the Marshal in friendship. By the ordinary laws of human nature, it would work out in just the other way. One might rather wish to be captured occasionally, on one's own, than always to have to thank that paragon the Marshal. Henry, being twenty-one, would prefer comrades of his own age, and might well begin to be irked at the supervision of an oldster of thirty-two.

In 1177 there was a break in the relationship. The biographer passes the matter over lightly, assigning no special cause. Possibly a coming event was already casting its shadow.

The Marshal merely arranged to go off as a *knight-errant*, entering into a partnership with another of the Young King's men, a Flemish knight, Roger de Gaugi. Now, when a highly responsible man, holding a position of great trust, merely walks out, we can assume that he has ceased either to be essential or to consider himself essential. The Marshal remained the Young King's "man," but he stayed away for two years. France being a roomy place, he may not even have seen his master in that time.

He and de Gaugi did extremely well. In that heyday of chivalry, up and down those duchies and counties that formed the loose-knit kingdom of France, a *knight-errant* could get to a tournament about once in two weeks. In one period of ten months, according to a good contemporary authority, the Marshal and de Gaugi captured 103 knights. As the Marshal himself once stated, the number of knights that he had taken at tournaments reached the total of five hundred.

The Marshal had to support a staff of squires and servants. Still, the income must have been excellent. There was no way to invest money, and merely to hoard it got a man a bad name. Open-handedness was one of the great virtues. Besides, it won and kept retainers and friends, who are worth, in the long run, much more than gold. The biographer carefully records several instances of the Marshal's generosity.

Besides money, success in tournaments won a man fame, though not altogether in the best fashion. The Marshal was something like a professional athlete, and we can be sure that many of the lords, among themselves, sneered at him for a landless man and a mere adventurer.

Years later, the Marshal used to tell stories of those good old days, often with a touch of humor. . . . Once, when he had captured a knight and was leading him in on horseback through a village, the captive caught hold of some overhanging bit of a house and pulled himself out of the saddle; William, unaware, went on, leading the riderless horse, to everyone's great amusement. Again, having won the prize at a tournament, he could not be found; finally, his friends located him at a blacksmith's shop, with his head laid on the anvil, and the smith working to loosen the helmet, which had got jammed from the blows upon it. Another time, some ladies came out before a tournament to see the sport. Along with other knights, William joined with the ladies in dancing on the grass, and a minstrel sang a song with the refrain, "Marshal, give me a good horse." Soon a knight of the opposing party appeared. William mounted and hastened off, captured the newcomer, then, in answer to the words of the song, he presented the horse to the minstrel.

Unfortunately, going to tournaments was a young man's game, not a real career. So, some time in 1179, the Marshal went back to his old duties. The Young King was mustering an extraordinary number of knights for an equally extraordinary tournament at Lagni-sur-Marne. The occasion is supposed to have been the coronation of the new French king, Philip Augustus. The participants, we are told, included three thousand knights, besides nineteen counts, the Duke of Burgundy, and the Young King — quite literally it may have been, as the biographer declares, a tournament "such as one never saw, before or after."

The Marshal, returned to duty, had his hands full rescuing his master on one occasion, and no captures of his own are recorded. In this tournament he served under his new rank, as *knight-banneret*, displaying his own banner, not a mere pennon, and outranking the *knights-bachelors*, who served under him.

During a period of about two years the Marshal remained with the Young King, and then the break was spectacular. Certain knights informed Henry that the Marshal was the lover of the Young Queen, Margaret of France!

To get at the full truth is impossible. The Young King seems to have accepted the story. If the Marshal had ever categorically denied the charge, one would believe him, knowing his reputation for honesty. But, more likely, he merely

kept silent, never having the question put to him directly.
Who would have done so? No knight would have dared to
accuse the Marshal and have to meet him in trial by combat. As for the Young King, the husband is in too embarrassing a situation to ask, "Did you do it?"

The gossip spread fast — people, as was usual in such cases,
being not so much troubled by truth or falsehood as by pub-
licity. Secrecy in such matters was part of the code.

Henry could only look with disfavor on the Marshal, and
both of them were very uncomfortable. In a Renaissance
court a hired killer and a stiletto could have provided the solu-
tion, but the chivalrous code of the twelfth century gave the
Marshal protection.

As to the story itself, there is an almost overwhelming
plausibility. This was the age of Courtly Love. Its priestesses,
Eleanor of Aquitaine and Marie of Champagne, pronounced
that love was incompatible with marriage. Queen Margaret
was Marie's half-sister, and was married to Eleanor's son.
The Marshal, as befitted a courtly lover, was unmarried. He
was in his early thirties, the most notable knight of the court,
or even, one might claim, of Christendom.

The triangle Margaret-Henry-Marshal is startlingly similar
to Guinevere-Arthur-Lancelot, and Isolde-Mark-Tristram. In
each case, for instance, "traitors" brought the word to the
king, who would just as soon not have had to face the issue.
The analogies are so many that one begins to wonder if the
romancers were borrowing details from the real-life story.

Before long, only one action was possible. The Marshal
left the court. Things would never be the same. His young
manhood was over. Those romantically minded may say that
he had loved his great love and had it turn to bitterness.

As he rode off, he must have been (if the romantic interpretation is true) a troubled man. By the laws of Courtly Love

he had, we may suppose, done well. But, by the feudal laws, he had been a traitor to his lord, by thus becoming involved with his lord's wife. This was the tragedy, the conflict of loyalties, that both Lancelot and Tristram faced with bitterness and humiliation. Both of them offered trial by combat.

The Christmas season of 1182 the two Henries kept at Caen, with great festivity and magnificence. There, in the presence of both the kings, entered the Marshal. Addressing the Young King, he offered to fight the best three of his accusers on three successive days. If, in any of the encounters, he should be worsted, let him immediately be hanged as a traitor!

The Young King refused.

The Marshal then offered to allow any finger of his right hand to be cut off, and then to undertake the same conditions.

Finally, he applied to the Old King for safe-conduct to leave the Angevin territories. Such precaution was necessary, since the Marshal, having applied to his lord for feudal justice and been refused, was now a lordless and unprotected man. His request granted, he left the court.

It is an unbelievable and at times almost ludicrous scene, impossible except for that high age of chivalry with its magnificent absurdity of the love code and its splendid anachronism of trial by combat. It is a particularly amazing scene for the Marshal, who everywhere else in his life seems to have shunned histrionics. One imagines him, in later life, being a little sheepish if people talked of the matter. In any case, it opens up another vista into his character.

Still a landless man, and now a lordless man, he went off to see a bit of the world and profit his soul by making a pilgrimage to the shrine of the Three Kings at Cologne. At the word that such a noble knight was detached, offers came pouring in from the Count of Flanders, the Duke of Burgundy, and other lords whose domains lay outside the realm of the two Henrys. Some of them even offered him lands, besides a stated income, and one lord added the promise of his daughter in marriage.

One can scarcely think that the Marshal refused these offers because he was a patriotic Englishman or because he was indissolubly devoted to the House of Anjou. At the moment he was little more than a soldier of fortune; he had spent nearly all his active life in France; French was his native language. Given time, he would probably have accepted an offer. But events moved too fast.

Within two months the Young King, leagued with his brother Geoffrey, Count of Brittany, was embroiled in revolt. A third brother, Richard, Count of Poitou, known as Cœur-de-Lion, was on his father's side. The fourth brother, John, was still too young, though plenty would be heard of him in later years.

Immediately Henry and Geoffrey found themselves outmatched. Needing good advice and a good warrior, they decided to summon (of all men!) the Marshal. The Young King had a change of heart, and decided that the "traitors" had been guilty of slander.

The Marshal started back at the whistle, almost too much like a faithful dog. But he had, we should remember, a big investment in the Young King, who must have been to him like a wayward son. Besides, of all men, in spite of his recent eclipse, the Marshal had the best chance to be mediator and peacemaker. In fact, old Henry gave him a safe-conduct, so that he could join the Young King at this moment.

Riding toward his rendezvous, the Marshal had a strange adventure. He cannot have been very proud of it, and yet he

told the story, and his biographer retold it, with approval.
. . . On the road the Marshal encountered a man and a
woman, richly dressed and riding fine palfreys. This was a
strange sight, considering the disturbed times, and the couple
aroused curiosity, if not suspicion. The Marshal demanded
the man's name, and an altercation arose. The man's cap fell
off, and he showed a tonsure. He then admitted that he was
a runaway monk, and was eloping with the lady. She turned
out to be a sister of one of the Marshal's friends, but refused to leave off her madness and accept his offer to return
her to her home.

Being asked if he had any money, the monk was naïve to
the edge of simple-mindedness. He pulled out the large sum
of forty-eight pounds, and said that he and the lady expected
to live by putting this money at usury.

Now usury was both a crime and a sin, and the Marshal's
attitude shifted sharply, though we may hope that it was not
because of the sight of the purse. He ordered his squire to
take the money, and sent the miserable couple on, saying,
"Since you will not return to virtuous life, let bad deeds
engulf you. Go! And may the Devil be your guide!"

The Marshal (at least, we cannot accuse him of avarice)
shared the money with two knights who accompanied him.
One of these suggested taking the horses and the baggage as
well. But the Marshal, who must have had some qualms,
rejected this idea.

All that we can say of the incident is that it was justifiable
by the standards of the time. Knights were supposed to exercise police-power, and even to execute their own judgments.
Certainly, such a foolish fellow as the monk would have lost
his money, later if not sooner. Besides, the Marshal, even
though he led the good life on the whole, must be granted an
occasional lapse. The amazing thing is that, living in the

twelfth century, he so generally fulfills the standards of conduct which are still acceptable. The biography especially notes him as being merciful.

He was a warrior, living in an age of war. Such conditions breed impetuosity, violence, and callousness, if not cruelty. On one evening the Marshal was eating dinner when word came that someone had made off with his horse. Dashing out, he located the animal in spite of darkness. He then hit the thief such a blow with a club as to knock one eye out. Other knights, coming up, were for hanging the fellow. But the Marshal interceded, saying that the punishment was great enough already. So we must at least grant him a more developed sense of pity and mercy than his fellows possessed.

In such an age, hasty as he could be on some occasions, the Marshal was known far and wide for his prudence and sense of balance. And so it was then, when he rode toward his meeting with the Young King.

He scarcely made it. On June 5, 1183, at a castle far in the South, aged only twenty-eight, Henry Plantagenet, who through history lives in eternal youth as the Young King, died of a fever.

As he had lain dying, he remembered his unfulfilled vow to go as a Crusader. Turning to the man whom he knew to be most trustworthy, he cried out, "Marshal! Marshal!" He then put upon him the task of carrying his cross to the Holy Land.

It was, doubtless, a good death scene. But there was a touch of sordidness afterwards, when the faithful Marshal found himself seized as security for one of the Young King's debts.

The Marshal went to King Henry, who paid the debt, and then ordered him to escort the body to Rouen for burial.

The Marshal had served the Young King, with one brief

interval, for thirteen years, passing from young manhood to middle age. About all that he had to show for it, in a permanent way, was the promotion to *knight-banneret*. He had enhanced his reputation as a winner of tournaments, but he was now, at thirty-nine, at an age when he must expect to yield to younger men. He was landless, except that he may have already accepted an insignificant holding from the Count of Flanders. He had many friends, and also some enemies. He was still unmarried.

But all these shortcomings were as nothing in comparison with one gain. Already the men of keener judgment were realizing that the Marshal was the man among many thousands for steadfastness and honesty. And, among such men of keener judgment, none exceeded the Old King. Before the Marshal left for the Holy Land, Henry arranged for him to return as a member of his household or personal administrative staff.

Then, as in the song, departing for Syria, he stayed there two years. The biographer is able to report nothing about his adventures, taking refuge in the rhetorical flourish that in two years he did more deeds than another man would have done in seven. More likely, since nothing was remembered, the Marshal did very little, presumably having no opportunity. The period was a time of truce between Saracens and "Franks."

From a later reference we learn that he bought two rich and beautiful pieces of silk to wrap his body for burial. As a man of forty he should, by twelfth-century standards, be thinking of death. In any case the cloths both suggest an esthetic quality in their buyer, and show an engaging touch of vanity in a character which sometimes looms oppressively in almost unflawed goodness.

The Marshal left the Holy Land at just the wrong, or right, time. By staying a month or two longer, he would have had plenty of chance for glory, and for death. The truce at an end, Saladin fell upon the Christian armies in May of 1187, crushed them, and took Jerusalem. The Marshal was already with King Henry when the news arrived.

The King, in this year, was fifty-four, getting old, as things were then judged. The rising star was the heir to the throne, Eleanor's favorite son, that Richard who was called Lionheart. Richard, himself a shining light of chivalry, would undoubtedly have liked to have the Marshal in his train, and a man looking into the future might well have preferred to serve the son instead of the father.

Henry, to begin with, seems to have thought the Marshal a useful person, but not of much importance. He bestowed on him a very modest land-holding, the manor of Cartmel on the Lancashire coastal plain. Its possession did not raise the Marshal to the rank of baron, but it made him more eligible, at Henry's pleasure, to marry an heiress.

The regular way for a king to reward a deserving knight and to bind him in loyalty and gratitude was to see that he got lands and the title that went with them. The best lands available were those that had been held by lords who had died without a son. The king then became the guardian of any female heir. *In loco parentis*, he enjoyed the income from the lands, and with this inducement he might, theoretically, keep the daughter unmarried. But custom was strongly against such procedure, and there was even strong objection if the king married a girl to someone of too low rank for her.

No one — not even the daughter — considered an arranged marriage distasteful. The king was merely giving the girl in marriage, as her father himself would have done, if he had lived, or as her brother would have done, if she had had one to succeed to the title. Usually, she got a more distinguished man by the king's choice, because in that case all the lands went with her, not just what her father and brother thought would constitute a dowry. In feudal society, as in most societies except for our modern Western one, marriage was unromantic and business-like.

Such marriages, with neither loving nor liking taken into account, gave ground for the contention of the Courtly Love codifiers that love could not exist in marriage. Actually, by and large, the system may have been as good as the American one of marrying for love, or imagined love, and ending up in divorce. Many of these marriages were excellent ones. You always, so to speak, married "the-girl-next-door." Whether she came from Northumberland or Normandy, she spoke the same language, had the same church, and looked upon life in the same special feudal way that her husband's mother and sisters did.

By the time he joined King Henry, we may conceive, the Marshal at the age of forty-three was a little cynical about marriage. Certainly, he had turned down the offer of a French lord's daughter. Since he had long been an outstanding knight, impecunious fathers must, for years, have been trying to entice him with their most attractive daughters, in hopes that he would take one of them without adequate dowry. He need not have been a man of exceptional shrewdness to have escaped. He was merely well-enough versed in feudal life to know that it was not done in that way. He was not to be trapped into marriage by *beaux yeux*.

What happened, sometime late in 1187, is intriguing enough to call for a direct quotation from the biography, though some of the words lack modern equivalents.

The demoiselle of Lancaster, who had much property, [the King] gave to [the Marshal] along with her holdings. And he maintained her in great honor and kept her from dishonor a long while, as his dear friend, except that he did not marry her.

Some have supposed, especially because of the suggestion in modern French of the words *chère amie*, that the Marshal kept her as his mistress. As a matter of fact, since the heiress's father had died only four years previously, she may still have been a little girl playing with her dolls. There are other overwhelming reasons against the supposition. For instance, the "long while" is misleading; it was a matter of months, not of years. Moreover, to name a former mistress in an official biography would have been an affront to the Marshal's widow. The words "great honor" and "without dishonor" could scarcely be used if the Marshal had taken her to his bed. Moreover, the girl was later married to another of the King's knights, who might not have taken a discarded mistress.

The heiress under question was named Helvis, and she was the daughter of William of Lancaster, Baron of Kendal, one of Henry's minor officers. By marrying her, the Marshal would have gained a small fief and the title of baron.

He was in England for several months in the spring of 1188, and very likely saw Helvis. This would have been a natural time to marry her. But the Marshal chose to play it differently. Again, we must remember, she may have been only a little girl. Even if she had been nubile, he could have put the marriage off for a year or two without embarrassment, although at a longer delay the girl's uncles and cousins might have started making trouble.

But the Marshal was rising rapidly in the royal esteem. By delay he might be awarded a much richer heiress, and, for that matter, a much more attractive one also, for we know nothing about Helvis, one way or the other, and can only suppose her ordinary.

Then, as usual, trouble arose. The Marshal went back to the continent with the King, and for a whole year he had no opportunity for marriage, and little chance to think about it.

The brief sojourn in England, however, had been important in one respect. The Marshal had picked up a new squire, called Jean D'Erlée — in English, John of Earley — who took his last name from a village in Berkshire. John was to follow the Marshal as squire and knight, well and loyally, until the deathbed at Caversham. In fact, his services still continued, since he supplied most of the material for the biography. In many ways John seems to have resembled the Marshal himself.

The occasion of the return of King Henry to the continent was a recurrent one — an outbreak of hostilities with the King of France. We need not get involved in all the shifty politics and warfare. Our concern is the Marshal. A *knight-banneret*, past forty, he served as a kind of staff officer — advising the King, executing orders, and now and then getting a chance to lead a raid on his own.

But Henry was ill, and his fortunes worsened as his body weakened. Richard, the heir, went over and allied himself with Louis, and Henry's whole feudal structure crumbled, as lord after lord assured his own future by joining Richard. Among the few who stayed loyal, his nature being such, was the Marshal.

That spring of 1189 the old and ailing King kept gloomy court at Le Mans — his men few, his enemies pressing in.

Still able to think as a king, he knew that one who was faithful under stress should not go without reward. He gave to the Marshal a great heiress — Isabel de Clare, daughter of Richard de Clare, that Norman conqueror of Ireland, the almost legendary Strongbow.

She was about eighteen years old. The description "good and beautiful" may be only the conventional words of the official biographer, but we know enough of her later life to tend to accept the praise as truth.

But, at least, there was no question about the goodness and beauty of her lands. She brought with herself the earldom of Striguil (Chepstow, it now is) on the boundary of England and Wales. She brought also the earldom of Pembroke in southwestern Wales, and the lordship of Leinster, which included the best of southeastern Ireland — to say nothing of her scattered holdings in England. These lands were reckoned at almost two hundred knights' fees; that is, their lord stood pledged to supply that number of knights to the King's host. At one step the Marshal had attained the first rank among English magnates.

Or had he? The pledge was only the word of a ruined and dying king. A prudent man would still have stolen away some night, to join Richard and get confirmation from him, as the price of treachery.

But Henry had always been a judge of men, and still was, as he lay dying.

The end came swiftly. There was a wild flurry of fighting at Le Mans, as the French horsemen, in overpowering numbers, came splashing through an unguarded ford. There was the confusion of combat, with the Marshal, as if in a tournament again, capturing knights right and left. Then the town was suddenly in flames. The Marshal got smoke from a burning feather bed inside his helmet and was almost overcome. John of Earley and the other squires hastily ripped the helmet off.

But it could be no more than a delaying action. The ailing King made off. The Marshal and a few other knights formed a scanty rearguard.

It is almost a *déjà vu*. That moment — looking down or up, as the case might be — the spirit of that rough baron John the Marshal might have cried, "Well done, boy!" remembering how he himself had once covered the flight of Queen Matilda, who was this Henry's mother.

Hard in pursuit spurred the impetuous Count of Poitou, Lion-heart, the son and heir, Richard. So hotly had he come on that he had not stopped to don armor.

Suddenly he was aware of an unhelmeted knight charging upon him with leveled lance. He recognized the face. Lion-heart, famed warrior himself, knew that death was upon him. He called out, for once in his life, begging mercy.

In that second, as the horse plunged onward, the Marshal made his decision, crying out, "No! The devil kill you! I shall not." Then he dropped the lance point, and pierced, not Richard, but his horse. It fell, pinning Richard to the ground. The Marshal swung around, and was off.

He had created the right diversion. Richard's men swarmed around to aid him, and the pursuit slacked off.

About two weeks later, having been hunted from castle to castle, and humiliated by the harsh terms of a treaty, the once-great Henry lay dead at Chinon. Still in attendance were a few loyal knights, the Marshal among them. The corpse was taken to the abbey church at nearby Fontevrault.

Soon word came that Richard, the heir, was about to arrive. The loyal knights gloomily discussed their prospects, agreeing that the Marshal, who had just humiliated Richard, had the most to fear. The Marshal maintained with dignity that he did not regret his action. But the best he could do for the future was to put his trust in God. Isabel de Clare was now at the disposal of the new king.

Richard arrived, and stood first to gaze intently at the corpse of his father. He then called for the Marshal and another knight, and took them aside.

By this time Richard had taken refuge in a face-saving device, and he spoke accusingly, "The other day you wished to kill me, and you would have, except that I turned your lance with my arm."

Obviously this was a cue for the Marshal to ask for mercy. Instead, he spoke boldly, and with the feeling of a man whose professional competency has been impugned, "Sire, I never wished to kill you, and I never tried. I am still strong enough to place my lance properly, even when in armor, and more so when I am not. I could as easily have killed you as your horse. In killing it, I do not believe that I did wrong, and I have no regrets."

At the brave and dignified defense, Richard suffered one of those shifts of mood for which he was noted: "Marshal, you have pardon, and I shall hold no anger against you!"

The Marshal thus passed his most dramatic crisis. Obviously, however, Richard was not merely swayed by boyish whim. Beneath his knight-errantry lay an Angevin shrewdness. He knew the Marshal's value, that his loyalty to King Henry was an obvious foreshadowing of loyalty to King Richard. On the spot, indeed, he entrusted the Marshal with an important mission to England.

At this point a knight reminded the King that his father had given the Marshal a great heiress to marry. Richard rose to the occasion with full chivalric generosity to a former enemy, "No, by the legs of God! He did not *give* her to him.

31

He only *promised* her. But I shall give her to him freely, her and the land."

The word "freely" did not mean that Richard made the gift without constraint, but probably that the lands were granted without the heavy payment which the King ordinarily exacted in such a case, as a kind of inheritance tax.

The Marshal transacted the King's business in England. Then, in the summer of 1189, he married Isabel de Clare, whom the biographer declares, in this passage, to have been not only beautiful and good, but also wise and well-bred. He even suggests a honeymoon, declaring that the Marshal took his bride to Stoke in Surrey, "a quiet and pleasant place."

But that cannot have been for more than a week or so, and then the new bridegroom was off, probably on the King's business, clear to Northampton in the Midlands.

The brevity of the honeymoon can be taken as significant of the future. The Marshal, now, was not only trusted for his own abilities, but had become one of the great feudal lords. He was of earl's rank and often so called, though not yet officially so created. Inevitably, in the biography, the man tends to get lost beneath the earl.

Shortly he crossed to the continent, following the King, who was now preparing for his crusade. Isabel went too. Probably they landed at the much-used port of Dieppe, and from there a ten-mile ride took them to Longueville in northern Normandy, a pleasant seat in a large fief which had come as part of Isabel's claim to a half-share of the Gifford estate. The Marshal had just paid the King two thousand pounds, to be put into possession. (The King was very busy raising money to go on the crusade.)

As Isabel grew heavy, she probably stayed at Longueville. But William may have been there too, when the son was born, and named William. "Of good tree comes good fruit."

The Marshal was undoubtedly tempted to seek adventure on the crusade. But he had already borne the cross. He was forty-five years old; he was recently married and founding a family; he had not had a chance to organize his new holdings. Besides, somebody had to keep the shop.

When the King went off, the Marshal took his family to England, and stayed there four years. The King had appointed him Associate Justiciar, which meant that he was one of a council of five, ruling England in the King's absence. He was busy enough in that capacity, traveling about to hear cases and generally helping to conduct the government.

Besides, he had local duties, holding Striguil and Pembroke and Leinster as palatinates; that is, exercising regal power there. He thus controlled the south coast of Wales, but in the hill country to the north the wild Welsh were always restless, and there was raiding and counter-raiding.

Medieval lords were highly mobile, largely for economic reasons. Transport was so primitive that it was often easier to go to the food than to bring the food to you. So, in the April showers or in the crisp sunlight of October, we can imagine many a peasant standing to gape at the Pembroke cavalcade going by — a hundred horses, perhaps, counting the pack animals, with sixty or seventy people. Already a harbinger would have gone ahead at a gallop carrying word to the steward of the next manor to get ready for the master's visit.

First might come a squire, displaying the square-cut gold-and-green banner with the red, rampant lion, forked of tail. Then, the earl himself rode a palfrey, and perhaps talked with John of Earley, who would be a knight by now. Then came two or three other knights with squires. Next, we would imagine the Countess herself, side-saddle on an easy-going ambler, looking motherly, as she well might. By this time young

33

William may have been old enough to bestride his own pony. But the little ones — Richard and Matilda — were in panniers or litters, or carried by nurses.

Behind would follow lesser folk — two or three clerks, a page or two, the chaplain, a cook, Isabel's ladies and maids, a minstrel — since the earl loved good singing. Then came a rabble of grooms and servants, and finally the pack horses and the men handling them.

Pembroke manors were scattered all the way across southern England so that the company, by an occasional forced march, could put up at one of them every night on the 150-mile ride from London to Striguil. But there would be no need to make forced marches. Any monastery would be glad to receive the earl — and his largesse on leaving. The monks would have known that he had even founded a priory on his own, endowing it with his manor of Cartmel, far in the north.

Such a family scarcely had a fixed home, or expected to have one. Isabel may have remembered pleasant Longueville. The manor house at Caversham in Oxfordshire, too, was pleasant. Striguil Castle was probably the official seat. Besides, Isabel had lived there before being married. There is no likelihood that they ever went to Ireland in these years.

The public crisis of the King's absence was the revolt of Prince John. That youngest son of King Henry had been the old man's favorite, apparently a spoiled brat. He betrayed his father at the end. Historians claim that he was a good soldier and administrator, but one has difficulty in thinking a man to be either when his ability at making people dislike him amounted almost to genius. John distrusted everybody, and so people could scarcely do anything but distrust him. Already he was looming as a cloud over the Marshal's life.

The chief event of this revolt was the siege of Windsor castle by the King's barons. The Marshal came riding out of the west with a strong force of his own men, and with five hundred "sergeants," whom the historians put down as Welsh mercenaries, now serving with the men whom they generally fought against. The hen houses of the Thames valley must have had a hard time of it with all those Welshmen loose.

As the famous story goes, the Austrian rat who had held the crusading king captive accepted ransom, and King Richard came home. The Marshal contributed heavily (even beyond the call of duty) to the ransom, probably thinking it worth the money to get rid of John by getting Richard back.

During the next five years, from 1194 to 1199, the Marshal was in the first half of his fifties, and was chiefly following the royal banner in Normandy, fighting against King Philip. But he was back in England at least three times in this period, probably on the King's business, though he would also have had plenty of his own business too. Cross-channel service was fairly reliable. In fact, to get from London to Dieppe and thence to Longueville must have been less work than going, over muddy or dusty roads that were no better than horse trails, from London to Striguil. It is not surprising, then, to find that Isabel spent some of this time at Longueville. It was close to the border, but the line of frontier castles gave it some protection against raids. Besides, we can hardly think that Strongbow's daughter was given to being nervous.

In one place or another the amenities of marital life continued. Though the dating is a little shaky, these years presumably saw the separate and prosperous arrivals of young Isabel, of Gilbert, and of Sybile, who bore the grandmother's name. The good tree was bearing good fruit, and plentifully.

Fortunes improved even a little further, with the death of John, William's elder brother. Since he had been childless,

William succeeded to the family lands, which consisted of a number of manors, scattered across the pleasant countryside of southern England.

William's only moment of crisis in his relations with the King occurred soon after the return. The chancellor, in the King's presence, asked the Marshal to swear fealty for his Irish lands. Boldly and indignantly the Marshal refused. He had already, he declared, done homage to Prince John for those lands, and now to swear homage to the king would be a breach of feudal faith. The King, himself sensitive to feudal rights, applauded this decision. The chagrined chancellor then accused the Marshal of "planting vines," that is, of playing a long-range game of currying favor with Prince John, who might at some time become king.

The incident shows that the Marshal was becoming an authority on feudal rights, so that his decisions were likely to be accepted as legal and proper.

In the war the Marshal served as one of the King's chief commanders. He was perhaps not such a skilled professional as Mercadet, who led the mercenaries. In compensation, his reputation for knightly prowess still made him the idol of a feudal army, and as an earl he exercised a prestige far beyond that of any mercenary captain.

At the great battle of Fréteval the King put the Marshal in command of the reserve, with orders not to commit it unless the main army should meet defeat. As it happened, the French suffered a complete rout. The Marshal followed orders, and thus he and his men of the reserve gained neither glory nor booty. But, after the battle, the King was fair enough to offer special commendation.

On another occasion the fifty-three-year-old Marshal seized a chance to show that he could still act like a young *knight-errant*. The King was besieging a small castle, defended by a wall and dry ditch. The French, fighting vigorously, threw down one scaling ladder, and seemed about to do the same with another. The Marshal went into a fighting fury. He leaped into the ditch, scrambled up the other side, and scaled the ladder, sword in hand. At the top he laid about him so furiously that he scattered the defenders. The King was so seized with the contagion that he himself wished to scale the ladder to the Marshal's support, and had to be held back. But others of his men pressed the attack. At this point the commander of the castle rushed up. The Marshal gave him such a blow on the helmet that he dropped senseless. The English and Normans now swarmed over the wall, and the crisis passed. The middle-aged Marshal felt a bit tired and winded. He calmly sat down on the senseless Frenchman, and waited till the fighting was over. Though the King felt it necessary to reprove the Marshal for conduct not suitable to one of his rank, the reproof could not be real, and the Marshal had obviously endeared himself both to the King and to the army.

On April 7, 1199, the Marshal was at Vaudreuil in Normandy. The Archbishop of Canterbury was there too, and a large assemblage of Norman lords. The King, they knew, was off somewhere in the South. A courier came spurring in, with a confidential message for the Marshal and the Archbishop — the King lay dying!

As their orders ran, the two Englishmen hurried off to seize the castle at Rouen, the key of Normandy. Sorrowfully, even in consternation, they discussed the prospects. Richard had not been the best of kings, but he was a strong ruler, and he had been their friend. Now he was dead, leaving no child, and rival claimants for the throne. Should it be Prince John, the fourth brother, or should it be young Arthur, son of the third brother?

The Archbishop was inclined to support Arthur; the Marshal came out firmly for John. He could have had no liking for that thoroughly unlikable prince. He believed, however, that by English law John was the legitimate successor.

The Archbishop yielded, but as a prelate he could not resist putting on the prophet's robes. "Marshal, it shall be as you wish. But I tell you that nothing you have ever done will give you so much cause for repentance." The Marshal, who had no illusions about John, replied, "It may well be! But, in any case, that is my decision."

During seventeen long years King John wore the crown of England. The Marshal aged from fifty-five to seventy-two. They were not his happiest years or those of greatest fulfillment.

Things started well. At the coronation the King formally girded the Marshal with a sword and created him, at last officially, an earl.

After that there was the usual war with the French, and John won a great success, capturing his rival Arthur. But he might have done better not to have done so. Arthur disappeared, and everyone had the natural idea that John had had him done away with. Since feudal society did not look with favor on the murder of children, John lost much of what little good repute he had ever had, and more and more of the Norman barons grew lukewarm in fighting King Philip. The Marshal — or the Earl Marshal or Pembroke, as one might have called him now — functioned for John much as he had for Richard.

One anecdote harks back to those jolly days of knight-errantry when the Young King still lived. . . . On this occasion the Marshal with two other earls rode up to the gates of Rouen at a moment when the French were in full retreat. The unheralded appearance of such a deal of feudal brass inspired the comfortable burghers with the idea of some vast emergency. The mayor — as in any romance, he was named "Matthew the Fat" — anxiously questioned the three. The Marshal, sensing the possibility of a joke and something more, pulled a long face — yes, the French were at hand, and the earls had come to defend the city. Matthew the Fat gratefully ordered up the best dinner that the city could supply, along with the finest wines, and the biographer even specifies the dessert to have been pears, apples, and nuts. (Was the Marshal, perhaps, like Sir Gawain, especially fond of pears?)

His particular duty in these years was the defense of northern Normandy, where his own Longueville was located. Probably the Countess Isabel was there some of the time, though the Marshal was also in England on several occasions, and once, apparently, in Ireland. At least, the succession of children showed no break. Eve, and Walter, and perhaps Jeanne would have arrived during these years. At the other end of the line, young William was old enough to start his training as a squire, and Matilda, entering her teens, was already marriageable, by the prevailing standards.

But in 1203 Normandy was as good as lost. The Marshal once spoke plainly to the King, telling him that if he could not keep his friends he might as well give up. The King, naturally enough, did not take it well, though it was the truth. Before the end of the year Philip was holding nearly all of the duchy, and John was crowded back to England.

He sent the Marshal twice on embassies to the French, but Philip, the game in his hand, was in no negotiating mood. The Marshal's own situation was complicated. Longueville had escaped the ravages of war, and he, in some sense, still held it. But of whom? It was a fine property, and he had no wish to lose it, though it was only a small thing, compared with his English and Welsh and Irish holdings. He got some kind of permission from John, and then took strange measures. He swore fealty to Philip for Longueville, with a curious phrase to the effect of being his man "on this side of the sea."

Such geographically divided fealty was not recognized in feudal custom. The Marshal interpreted it to mean that he could fight against Philip if the French invaded England, but could not fight against Philip if the English invaded France. On these grounds he pleaded off from accompanying John on an expedition to Poitou in 1205.

John was incensed, though the Marshal claimed that he had received special permission to do just what he had done. But in such a dispute between John and William, few men would be found to support John.

In any case, the Marshal was out of favor at court. The matter of the fealty may not even have been the basic cause. John was a small-minded man, always distrustful. Now and then he took strong measures to cut down the power of some lord, as with William de Briouse, who held broad fiefs in southern Wales and was the Marshal's close neighbor. John hounded William out of England, and as for Matilda de Briouse, William's wife, she gabbled too much about what might have happened to young Arthur, and ended up in one of John's prisons — starved to death, they said.

In general, John merely whittled at the power of his stronger nobles, as he did with Ranulf Earl of Chester, in the early years of his reign, irritating rather than weakening him. John had no power, such as his brother Richard had possessed, of attracting men to him and making them follow him.

So his change of face to the Marshal may have been merely in the natural course of events. Before long John was demanding young William as a hostage. The Marshal could remember something of what it was to be a hostage, but he

sent his son. The only other choice was to go into open rebellion.

A rebellion might well have been successful, but that was
not the Marshal's way. He had served the House of Anjou
through many good years and a few bad ones, and he would
so continue.

Besides, we may put it another way. An American can
hate a particular president and despise his policies, and yet
remain loyal to the Constitution as a matter of course. So,
to a feudal lord like the Marshal, the royal family represented
all that there was of continuing stability. Once let every lord
arise and fight on his own, and you had only the anarchy, such
as older men could still remember, of the times of Stephen
and Matilda.

To overthrow John might not be too hard. But where
would you be then? At the same time, the Marshal had some
assurance that John would not push too hard. Harsh injus-
tice to one feudal lord would bring all the others swarming
out in sympathy, and also in fear that it might happen to
them next.

So, like many another good man before and since, the Marshal bowed to the wind. He decided to retire to Ireland.
There he held much of the best part of the island. With the
support of the other lords, who had no great love for English
kings, he could almost fight a war. Besides, in Ireland, he
would be out of sight and might be out of mind as far as the
King was concerned. In addition, his Irish lands needed supervision.

But the King had no desire to allow another great nobleman to entrench himself in Ireland, and he raised objections
to the departure.

Just about this time the Marshal — with the Countess,
doubtless, having her say too — married Matilda to Hugh,

son and heir of Roger Bigot, earl of Norfolk. Matilda was thus destined to be a countess, and a Marshal-Clare-Bigot alliance was set up.

John finally granted permission for the Irish journey, but he demanded the second son, Richard, as an additional hostage. Since such a demand was insult upon injury, the Countess and the barons urged the earl not to comply. But, knowing that he would never do anything to forfeit the hostages, he replied, "I shall be glad to send all my children, if the King wishes."

The next day, minus two sons, the family embarked at Striguil. This was in the summer of 1207.

But even in the far-off island the King stirred up trouble, and he soon summoned the Marshal back to England to explain some of the difficulties that had arisen. Not since he had ridden away from the Young King's court had the Marshal faced such disaster. He would have to return to England almost alone, and he was putting his head into the lion's mouth.

Before leaving, he assembled his knights and barons at Kilkenny. John of Earley urged him to take hostages, but the Marshal refused sharply. Instead, he came before them with the Countess, and spoke simply, "Gentlemen, see here the countess, whom I lead before you by the hand. She is the daughter of the earl who gave to you your fiefs, when he conquered the land. She stays with you, about to bear a child. Until such time as God brings me back, I ask you to guard her faithfully, for she is your lady, and I hold nothing of the land, except by her."

Back in England, at court, the Marshal lived in miserable suspense. During a stormy winter no news could arrive from Ireland, and the situation gave the King, who was not without a vein of devilry, a chance to play a nasty trick. He declared, solemnly but falsely, that he had just received a message — the Countess had been besieged at Kilkenny; in a battle, several of the Marshal's knights had been killed. In circumstantial detail, the King told that John of Earley had been wounded, and had later died of his wounds. The King ended with a mock compliment, "But the honor of the battle rested with your men."

The Marshal replied with dignity and justice, "That is a great loss of knights. They were your men, and so the affair is even more regrettable."

But when news really arrived, it was that the Marshal's men had gained the upper hand.

In the spring of 1208 the Marshal was able to return to Ireland. Of his reunion with the Countess, the biographer only records that she was very glad to see him — a comment that seems sufficiently restrained. There was a new baby to be admired, too. This was probably the boy Anselm, who thus neatly rounded the family out with five girls and five boys.

The Marshal — on the whole, uneventfully — stayed in Ireland for five years. Little is known of his actions, but the Irish peasants, we may think, prospered from the presence of a lord who was strong enough to keep order.

In 1211 he was, as the phrase goes, "restored to favor," and he returned to England and to participation in public affairs. He was then sixty-seven. His brown hair and his heavy mustache may have been flecked with gray, but he remained a man of vigor. And he was still, we may say, a constitutionalist, a king's man. That was, of course, the reason why John turned to him again, and restored his English castles, and sent back the two sons who had been hostages. He needed the Marshal's help. Not only was John in trouble with the Pope, but also the long-restless northern barons were looking to their helmet-laces.

Finally these northerners rose in 1214, and marched on London, where the citizens, who disliked John, received them hospitably. But the barons of the South and West held aloof, and the leadership of the Marshal may have had much to do with it. As a man such as he could still realize, the revolt only offered, in the long run, anarchy. Besides, the situation was now highly complicated, with the Pope, the Welsh princes, and the King of France all involved, besides the royal and anti-royal parties. From London the rebels were intriguing to bring the Dauphin over, and make the country an appendage of France. Among the lords supporting John there even may have been a faint stirring, for the first time since the Conquest, of something that could be called English patriotism. Shakespeare played it up in his *King John*, with those resounding final lines, beginning,

> *This England never did, nor never shall,*
> *Lie at the proud foot of a conqueror.*
> *But when it first did help to wound itself.*

The barons of the South and West, however, though they distrusted the northerners, had no love for John either. As a result there was compromise all around, and out of such unlikely circumstances sprang the great document known as the *Magna Carta*.

The Marshal was with the King, that spring when the road led to Runnymede. Once, in April, he urged John to grant the rebels' demands. After all, the Marshal himself was a baron, and he could not but sympathize with other barons. Finally, John yielded, and the Marshal, once again, as so many times before, rode off as the King's ambassador. To the barons in London he carried the message that "for the sake of peace and the welfare and honor of the realm" (and the words sound rather more like the Marshal than like John) the King would grant the liberties that the barons demanded.

Exactly what part the Marshal played in the whole affair of the *Magna Carta* is not known. In what seems to some people a strange manner, the biography is silent. But, when the biographer was writing, no one considered the signing of the charter to have been of much importance. Like so many "great events" of history, it made little impression upon the people of its own time. Within a few months the Pope had denounced the charter and John had denied it, and the barons were in revolt again, and the French had actually landed. During the Battle of Britain there was much talk about England never having been invaded since 1066. People seemed to forget about 1216, though it is true that the French then landed at the invitation of English rebels, so that it was not a full-fledged invasion.

During the months that followed, things went badly for John. The North was solidly against him, and he lost the eastern counties too, except for a few castles. The Welsh princes were stirring, and they pinned down the forces of the border lords, who were for John, though largely because they had to oppose the Welsh. Of all the earls, only four stood with the King, and among them was the Marshal.

Then, with everything going to pieces, John solved the problem in a curious way, by falling suddenly sick. From his bed he spoke to the few lords who were with him. (The Marshal was not there, being at Striguil, or near it, watching the Welsh.) In his last moments, the King whom no one loved remembered the great earl whom he had wronged but could never force from his loyalty. He asked the attendant lords to entreat forgiveness of the Marshal for the wrongs done him, and then he committed to him the care of his young heir.

Thus, as had happened more than forty years before, an English king entrusted the Marshal with the care and tutelage of his son.

The partisans of the young Henry took him to Gloucester, not far from Striguil, and the Marshal joined them there. The lords decided that the prince must be crowned at once, so great was the emergency. The question arose as to who should gird the sword of knighthood on the new king. By acclamation the honor was granted to the Marshal, everyone remembering that he had thus girded the Young King, so many years before.

The nomination of the Marshal for the regency was equally inevitable. Now past seventy, he pleaded his age, and tried to be relieved of the charge. But the only other possible candidate was the Earl of Chester. When he came out flatly for the Marshal, there was no choice.

Thus the younger son who had ridden away from his father's house sixty years before finally attained the highest honor by becoming Regent of England, and in his old age he thus assumed overwhelming responsibility.

The situation was almost hopeless. Yet the death of John may have been the worst thing that could have happened for the invading French. New hope came with a new king, and men of all factions could rally to the Regent's banner. More and more the sentiment became patriotic, as the word "English" came to mean something new.

One of the Regent's first acts was to re-issue the *Magna Carta*, thus giving that recently discredited document a new and continuing significance.

But, since the battle of Bouvines, the French knights were

known as the best of Europe, and they would not recoil before the waving of a document.

Seven months after the Marshal had assumed the regency, the English opportunity came, when the Dauphin, overconfident, separated his forces by sending a strong detachment north to besiege Lincoln castle.

The Regent was still not too old to wear armor, and lead a column swiftly across the Midlands. His forces were small, and a battle that might decide the fate of England was entrusted to 406 armored horsemen and 317 crossbowmen. (The exact figures, we may suppose, are from John of Earley, who could have acted as adjutant.) The French forces were larger.

As the battle joined at Lincoln, the old Regent charged with all the impetuosity of a young *knight-errant*. A wild melee followed and the battle swayed back and forth, confusedly, in the narrow streets of the town, the Marshal fighting in the front, taking sword-strokes that dinted his helmet, and giving as good himself. In the end the French were utterly defeated, and many of them taken prisoner — though fortunately, because of good armor and a sensible tradition of warfare, only a few were killed.

"Lincoln Fair," as the battle in the streets was nicknamed, proved to be the turning point. Before the end of the year the French had signed a treaty and withdrawn their forces.

The Marshal continued as Regent, healing the wounds of war, re-establishing finances, assuring that there would be no return of that anarchy which he himself could so vividly remember from his boyhood.

In September of 1218, something more than a year after Lincoln Fair, the Regent visited Striguil, chief seat of his own feudal power. He had no special reason to think that this would be his last sight of that great castle. In January of

1219 he stayed a week at Marlborough, and would have had plenty of time to think of a small boy who had lived there many years before, and of John Marshal and the Lady Sybile. Starting back for London by way of Reading, he would have passed through Newbury, and could hardly have failed to be reminded of a great siege-engine swinging, and a kindly king, playing games with a child.

On February 2 he fell suddenly ill at Westminster. On March 7 he mounted horse, and rode in pain to the Tower of London, and lay ill there. But from that grim fortress his thoughts turned to his own manor of Caversham. It was a pleasant place, and well-beloved. Twice in the past year he had taken time from his busy Regent's life to visit there for a few days. So, about the middle of March, his men made ready a boat. Retracing, as it were, the voyage of the Fair Maid of Astolat, they rowed their failing lord up the Thames, and brought him to Caversham.

By that very removal from the seat of power he had symbolically renounced the regency. It now remained only to do so officially and then to prepare to leave the world — in dignity and honor and decorum, as he had always lived, thus also to die.

Riders spurred across England, summoning his children and his chief knights. Early in April the young King, though not the Young King, came there, with a full retinue of lords spiritual and temporal. "Good sweet lord," said the Marshal, "I wish to speak to you before these barons." He then resigned his office.

But a quarrel arose about who should succeed him. The Marshal then performed a final official act, with statesman-like foresight, assigning the royal boy to the care of the Papal Legate, and thus temporarily freeing him from feudal pressure.

Next, if a man should die well, he must put his worldly affairs into order. The Marshal had little to do. He had already given generously to numerous monasteries. The Countess had her own rights in a rich patrimony. William — the Young Marshal, as he was called — would take the titles and the lion's share of the lands, by right of primogeniture. Now twenty-nine years of age, he was an heir of whom to be proud. He had married the daughter of Baldwin of Bethune, Earl of Aumale, a marriage which must have given his father intense pleasure to arrange. Baldwin had been his closest and most loyal friend during all the years, from the time when they had been young men together at the court of the Young King, and the Marshal had been passing through troubled times.

Richard, the second son, had been vested with Longueville, thus eliminating the troublesome question of double homage. Gilbert, the third son, being not so physically vigorous as the others, was entering the church, as the custom was. Walter, the fourth son, was still too young to be a knight, but a portion had been assigned to him. Anselm, who was still a boy, alone remained.

"Gentlemen," said the Marshal from his bed, "one of my sons, Anselm, has no share, and yet he is very dear to me. If he lives to become a knight, even though he has no land, he will find, provided he is worthy, someone who will love him and will give him great honor, more than any of the others will win. May God give him valor and wisdom!" Thus, almost as if it were a game, the man who had won all by his own efforts and merits, wished that his youngest son should go out to do the same.

But John of Earley protested respectfully that Anselm should at least have enough "to pay for shoeing his horses." So the father assigned Anselm a portion.

Like the sons, the daughters also raised little problem. Matilda, Isabel, and Sybile were already or would soon be the countesses of Norfolk, Gloucester, and Ferrars. Eve was the wife of William, of the important De Briouse family. Already grandchildren must have been springing up, since eventually there were five grandsons and twelve granddaughters.

Only Jeanne, the youngest daughter, remained unmarried. Her father therefore endowed her with some land and money, "to aid her in living, until God takes care of her." By feudal customs, the agent of God would be her oldest brother, and so the Marshal could rest quietly, knowing that the worldly welfare of his children raised no question.

He next, as his illness grew worse day by day, made arrangements for his funeral. He inspected the two silken cloths that he had brought from the Holy Land, long ago. He instructed that his body should be wrapped in them, but that after the funeral they should not be destroyed, but given to the monks. He desired to be buried in the church of the Templars in London.

The Young Marshal, John of Earley, and Thomas Basset watched with him through the long nights. Three other knights were with him through the long days. He was in pain. He could not eat or drink.

Time came for the next step. He summoned the Countess and his attendants, and explained that he had long ago undertaken to become one of the Templars, that order of monastic knights. His chaplain then brought out a Templar's robe which the Marshal had had made some time before. To enter the order he must renounce marriage, and he spoke to the Countess, addressing her not by any formal title, as the public nature of the occasion might suggest, but as *belle amie,* words which in English might be rendered literally as "fair friend," but perhaps better as merely "sweetheart."

"Belle aimie," he said, "now you shall kiss me, but it will be for the last time." She stepped to the bed, and kissed him. Both of them wept, and the knights and attendants wept with them.

Day after day he lay waiting, growing feebler. Every week he confessed, and was shriven. Once he saw a beautiful vision of two men clothed in shining white. But he remained the Marshal, clear-headed and even shrewd.

A knight, one day, suggested the problem of restitution — "the priests teach us that no one will be saved unless he returns everything he has ever taken."

But, good Christian though he was and dying, the old Marshal was not to be bullied or frightened. "Henry," he said, "listen to me a moment. The priests are too hard on us. They shave us too close." He had captured, he explained, his five hundred knights and taken their property, and could not possibly return it all at this date, and could do no more than throw himself on God's grace. "Unless the priests really wish my damnation, they should not hound me any more. Either their argument is false, or no one can possibly be saved."

"Sir," spoke staunch John of Earley, "that is the truth!"

On another day, as John was sitting there, the Marshal spoke from his weakness, saying that he had a strong desire to sing. John, thinking that it might furnish some relief, urged him to do so. "Be quiet," spoke the Marshal sharply, as if John were still a squire, "there would be no use of it. People would think I was crazy."

Instead, Matilda came and sang for him, and then little Jeanne. But Jeanne was almost overcome with her emotions and sang badly. Again the sick man spoke sharply, "Don't have such a sheepish air when you sing!" And he showed her how she should act.

51

Arrangements were made for largesse to the poor at the funeral, and for other details. John of Earley, certainly knowing what he did, asked what should be the disposition of all the furred robes that were in the house. (These were regularly distributed to the Marshal's men at Pentecost, which was now only two weeks off, though the Marshal might not live that long.)

At John's words one of the chaplains spoke up eagerly, suggesting that the robes should be given to the church to win forgiveness of the Marshal's sins.

Still again, the great earl spoke sharply. "Be silent, evil man. I have had enough advice from you, and want to hear no more. Soon it will come Pentecost, and my knights have a right to their robes. It will be the last time that I distribute them. And here you are, trying to hoodwink me." He then gave instructions to John.

A few days later, about noon on May 14, the Marshal lay quiet. The Young Marshal sat by the bed. John of Earley entered, trying to make no noise. But the sick man heard.

"Who is there?" he asked.

"I, John of Earley."

"It is you, John?"

"Yes, my lord."

"I cannot sleep."

"How could you sleep, when, in two weeks, you have taken nothing?"

A shock of pain struck the Marshal. Then he spoke again.

"John, hurry and open the doors and windows. Have the countess and the knights come here, for I am dying. I cannot wait, and I wish to take my leave of them."

When they had come, he said a few words. "I am dying. I commend you to God. I am no longer permitted to be with you." Then, for a moment, the knight and warrior of long

ago seemed to speak, as if against a confronting adversary:
"I cannot defend myself against Death."

He did not utter words again, but he remained conscious
a while, and made a few signs. He received absolution,
clasped his hands, and adored the cross. Then, as he had
lived — duties completed, all in good order — he yielded to
that last opponent before whose onset he had finally admitted defeat.

INTER-CHAPTER I

VAGUE THOUGH any definition of the good life must be, few
will be found, I think, to deny that the life of William the
Marshal falls somewhere within that area. Any who would
do so, indeed, must presumably restrict the good life to the
practitioners of religious devotion, or else would reserve the
accolade for those who have committed themselves to humanitarian ideals.

The Marshal, we can agree, was not one of these. Though
a simple and even devout son of the church, he was a layman.
His words on his deathbed show that he considered religion
to be only a part of his life.

Yet we should not neglect his humanitarian services.
Throughout an age which was always close to anarchy and
violence, he stood for justice and order. His re-issuance of
the defunct *Magna Carta* might well be held to make him a
hero in the struggle for civil liberties and the freedom of the
individual.

If there is any other criticism to be made of the Marshal's
case, it must be that of the devil against Job. He was granted,
some might say, too much at the beginning. Though a
younger son, he was still one of the nobility. His inborn
strength and dexterity, more than any strivings of his own,

made him the most redoubtable knight of his time. In the same way, the devil might go on, his excellencies of mind and of character were natural endowments.

His life, for these reasons, may fail to afford as much inspiration to the ordinary person as it otherwise might. "Who am I?" such a one may say. "How may I, with my indifferent endowments of body and mind, aspire to live the good life?"

So, for a second example, we present Heinrich Schliemann.

In pure intellect, indeed, he was much more highly endowed even than the Marshal. But he was no born favorite of the gods. He lacked the graces. Only after years of struggle, and toward the end of his life, would he attain that integration of spirit without which the good life can scarcely be held to exist.

HEINRICH
SCHLIEMANN

A DEVICE which more than one novelist has found useful is
to present the hero, initially, in a state of nudity. The sym-
bolical value is obvious. The hero thus begins with nothing,
stripped naked before the world. He then goes on to attain
what success his fortune has in store for him.

A biographer, lacking information, cannot ordinarily thus
begin. With alacrity, therefore, I seize the present opportunity.

The time was early morning on December 11, 1841. The
place was the island of Texel, off the coast of Holland. During several days a great gale had been blowing from the north,
so that the coast was a lee-shore. The islanders, therefore,
cannot have been surprised to learn that a three-masted ship
had struck on their sands.

Born wreckers as most islanders are, they turned out to see
what could be salvaged. They had little hope that the crew
had survived. But — on a sandbank, mercifully bare at low
tide — they saw a solitary and miserable figure. It was a
young man, naked from the waist down, his shirt and jacket
soaked, his body bruised and cut from having been rolled
ashore by the huge waves.

The hardy Dutchmen launched a boat in the comparatively
quiet water inside the sandbank. The castaway was so weak
and so benumbed with cold that he could not even reach the
boat, and had to be carried to it.

He was soon put to bed and given some hot coffee. He then fell asleep. No doctor was available. His condition was such that there seemed little hope of his survival.

Thus we may present Heinrich Schliemann at the age of nineteen — half-naked, almost dead from exposure, battered and bleeding, in a foreign country, destitute, without support of friends or family. From this point onward, any possible progress had to be upward. . . .

Having thus utilized the novelist's device of presenting the hero, and also having used the epic poet's device of beginning *in medias res*, I now assume the biographer's duty, and tell something about birth and early years.

The baby born in the Schliemann family on January 6, 1822, was soon christened Julius. There were already several children, and one of these was called Heinrich. When this child died during the course of the year, the parents transferred his name to the already-christened baby. Thus — somewhat equivocal even in its origins — we have the name Heinrich Schliemann.

The father was the Lutheran pastor of the village church at Neubukow in Mecklenburg, then a small, semi-independent state in northeastern Germany. He was not a man of great piety, and seems to have been rather cynical-minded. He was something of a scholar, knowing Latin, Greek, and at least a little Hebrew. He was also something of a scamp, and soon after Heinrich's birth he was pursuing, successfully, the kitchen maid.

Of the mother, only a shadowy impression survives. She married at sixteen, and was thirteen years younger than her husband. She lived with him unhappily. She bore him numerous children. Heinrich, who came near the middle of the family, seems to have remembered her somewhat vaguely as a loving parent.

When Heinrich was a year old, his father assumed the duties of the church at Ankershagen, also in Mecklenburg. This village was the setting for Heinrich's childhood — that setting which he interpreted so romantically in his later life.

Because of known inconsistencies in his writings about himself, we must remain somewhat skeptical of the way in which he thus made his life as a child anticipate the excavator of Troy. Still, the incidents themselves may well have happened. Granted, Ankershagen lived in the shadow of medieval legend, as many a German village does. Granted, there were stories of buried treasure, and young Heinrich, like many other boys, dreamed of digging them up. Granted, he saw in a book a picture of burning Troy, believed that such great walls could not vanish without trace, and considered trying to find them. Certainly, he was always a dreamer of dreams, and once as a land-locked child he wrote his name "Heinrich Schliemann, sailor," showing that even then he thought of far horizons.

But, having allowed so much, we cannot go farther. Though he may once have thought of excavating Troy, he did not keep that as his fixed goal throughout all his early years. Perhaps he thought of it occasionally, as an imaginative young man may, but the story of his life shows that he could scarcely have been more than that.

A little different is the story of his early love. Eight years old, at dancing class, he was smitten with Minna Meincke, a village girl. She returned his love, in such fashion as we can use the word for eight-year-olds. They planned romantically.

But we should not merely smile. The effect upon Heinrich, for reasons at which we may guess, was profound. If he did not think of Minna continuously throughout his life, at least he returned to her intermittently.

Piecing together what little we have — as he himself in

later years might reconstruct a city — we get some impression of the boy. He was on the smallish side, quick and light, active, not strong enough to impress other boys and perhaps not even to hold his own among them. He played largely with his brothers and sisters, and was shy. He was, however, able to establish some other friendships. He was phenomenally alert and intelligent.

From the very beginning, the local situation must have quickened his interest in language. Plattdeutsch was the local speech, and Heinrich learned it as a matter of course. Even in later years, a Plattdeutsch word once slips into one of his letters. But the language of educated people was German, and it was probably used, regularly, in the pastor's house. From childhood, therefore, Heinrich was bilingual.

The Ankershagen idyll, if such it was, ended with the death of the mother, self-pitying and still unhappy, in 1831, when Heinrich was nine. As generally happened when a large family was left motherless, the children were sent to different kinsfolk. Henry went to an uncle in nearby Kalkhorst.

There he went to school, and he also enjoyed the company of his pretty cousin Sophie, who even tended to compensate for his lost love. But Minna's image remained — inviolate and always the more ideal, because she was lost somewhere in the abyss of time and space, infinite to a child, and because she remained as part of a vanished fairyland.

Heinrich seems to have looked back on this sojourn at Kalkhorst as pleasant enough. Undoubtedly, however, the death of the mother and the break-up of the family was a serious blow to his sense of security. Besides, the father's affair with the kitchen maid had now become a public scandal. His expulsion from the church was threatened, and his finances were in disorder.

Heinrich was a promising scholar. On both his mother's
and his father's sides there was a tradition of Lutheran ministers, that is, of learning. Heinrich seemed destined for the
university, and then for the church, or a professorship. After
two years at Kalkhorst, he was sent, in the fall of 1833, to the
gymnasium in Neustrelitz. This was progress, but the second
break must have been hard on a boy who was not yet twelve.
To cap it all, he remained in the gymnasium only three
months, and then had to withdraw because of his father's
inability to pay the tuition.

Heinrich then went to the less-select *realschule*, from his
eleventh to his fourteenth year. He must have learned something, and probably at this time he laid the foundation of
his knowledge of French and English that later did so much
for him.

This was a period that not even he, apparently, could ro-
manticize by making it into something either very good or
very bad. His father had now married the kitchen maid, and
was raising a new family. The finances were growing worse,
but the father, apparently, still assumed some responsibility
for the children of the first marriage.

The final blow fell at Easter in 1836. Heinrich was barely
fourteen. His father, however, as good as turned him out.
Probably, indeed, the ousted pastor was himself so badly
pressed that he had no choice. Such thoughts would not
greatly have softened the blow to Heinrich, as all thought of
further education, and the university, thus vanished. He was
apprenticed to a storekeeper in the little village of Fürstenburg. He could work through his apprenticeship in four or
five years, but to a boy of fourteen, such a period is an eter-
nity.

In his later life, Heinrich romanticized Ankershagen with

a roseate glow. He could do nothing, one way or the other, with Kalkhorst and Neustrelitz. But Fürstenburg he could dramatize in deep purples and in black.

He worked, according to his story, an eighteen-hour day, from five in the morning until eleven at night. He waited on customers, he swept out, he ground potatoes for the still to make vodka, he wrestled with casks and boxes and bails. The hard physical work left him neither time nor energy for study, and he even forgot much of what he had already learned.

The single ray of light — this, again, in the romantic version — shone from the incident of the drunken miller. This man had almost finished his course at the gymnasium, but had then taken to drink. He still knew some Greek.

He came reeling into the store one evening, spouting out the hundred lines of Homer that he remembered. Young Heinrich, as middle-aged Heinrich recalled it, was fascinated by the beauty of the language, without understanding a word. He bribed the miller with glasses of vodka to repeat the lines and then to repeat them again. He swore to learn Greek, if he should ever have the chance. (It was a vow, if he made it, that he was very slow in fulfilling, even when the chance came to him.)

The reality at Fürstenburg was probably not so bad. His successive employers were not ogres, and for one of them the reminiscence even permits the adjective "excellent." One may grant an overwhelming sense of futility and hopelessness, especially for a boy, to whom a year is the equivalent of an older man's decade.

Still, he had his fantasies. Like young Joseph himself, young Heinrich was always the dreamer. Again, as when he had written "sailor" after his name, he imagined tall ships and far voyages. Also, through this hopeless time, the ideal of Minna, with no rival to replace her, remained to charm him. He had seen her once, momentarily, when they were both fourteen. She had been as beautiful as ever.

Gradually the years wore away, and at last came a crisis. By then he was nineteen. He began to spit blood. He feared that he was consumptive, but also thought that he might have broken a blood vessel by straining too hard at lifting a cask. In one story of his life that he wrote later (but had the grace not to publish) he said that his employers discharged him as being in broken health and of no more use. Thereupon, the account continues, he walked the thirty miles to Hamburg, taking ten days to make the distance. The reality, as he told it in a contemporary letter to his sisters, was almost wholly different, though the blood-spitting seems to have been real.

By this time Heinrich had presumably served out his apprenticeship. The great German migration to the United States was beginning, and nothing can have been more natural than that he should join it. His arrangements, however, fell through.

Still, he was no longer bound to Fürstenburg. Though he had been able to save no money during his apprenticeship, he was now of an age to receive the tiny sum that he inherited from his mother. It amounted to about 120 *thalers*, and would enable him to live frugally, without working, for several months. He went to the Mecklenburg city of Rostock.

Heinrich expected to live temporarily in his father's house. But that household was tumultuous, with father and stepmother quarreling loudly, even to the disturbance of the neighbors. It was not a place where anyone could study, and so Heinrich took a room in town.

He was through with physical labor. He was not strong enough for it, as his blood-spitting testified. Besides, it got a man nowhere. He would start out in business, and as a beginning he undertook the study of bookkeeping.

The course was supposed to take a year or eighteen months to complete. Henrich worked from early morning to late evening, and did everything in one summer. So he wrote to his sisters, and in such a statement one believes him, implicitly. His intelligence certainly touched the genius level, and achievements which would be miracles to ordinary people were everyday accomplishments to him. But no wonder, as he remarked, that his teacher and fellow pupils were astounded!

During the summer he had been forced to expend nearly three quarters of his scanty inheritance. He took the twenty-nine *thalers* that remained, and set off for the big city, that is, Hamburg.

He did not, we may add, walk. And he did not take ten days to do it. He traveled by various public vehicles, and he took only three days.

During the journey he stopped for a meal with some friends in a town where his pretty cousin Sophie happened to be visiting. At parting he pressed two ardent kisses upon her mouth, seemingly having forgotten about Minna. (But it was only a temporary forgetfulness.)

In Hamburg he gawked about, as any country lad might. He even went to see the bright lights of a dance hall. But he did not fall for sharpers, or lose his money.

On the contrary, on the very first afternoon he went about presenting the few letters of introduction that he had brought with him, and applying for a job. Having received some encouragement, he arose the next morning at five, and prepared fourteen samples of business letters in German, French, and English. He presented these as specimens of his handwriting and of his proficiency at languages.

Unfortunately, the demand for smart young bookkeepers was nil, and in a week or two he was close to being down-and-out, in spite of a temporary job or two. He had to write to an uncle for help, and received ten *thalers* along with an insulting letter. The sharp affront made him realize that he was really cut off from his family. Always sensitive, he vowed that he would starve to death before making another such appeal.

He managed to get some kind of job. But, suddenly, he had electrifying news. There was a chance to go to South America! This opportunity came through the good offices of J. H. Wendt, a ship broker, who had been a schoolmate of Heinrich's mother.

At this sudden chance to attain his dreams of travel and seeking his fortune, Heinrich did not hesitate. He left his job, presented well-written letters in three languages, and collected letters of introduction from Wendt. With difficulty he got together enough money to buy a few clothes and a blanket, and was ready to embark.

The ship sailed on December 1. Then foul weather struck. During ten days the storm grew worse and worse. Propped up in the cabin, Heinrich studied Spanish, though now and then thrown clear off his balance by the pitching of the ship. The discomfort and cold were extreme, and almost no food could be served.

The wind shifted to the north, and made the coast of Holland a lee-shore. About midnight the ship struck the sands.

In shirt and jacket, soaked to the skin, Heinrich clung to the rigging through the long freezing hours of early morning. The wind howled, the ship's bell rang mournfully, hard-blown snow pelted in fine flakes. When the ship broke up, he managed to seize a floating cask. He was one of three men to be washed ashore. . . .

As he lies there in the bed, as he stirs, and gives some evidence of surviving, we may take a kind of inventory of this young man, now approaching his twentieth birthday. What evidence does he supply that he may gain a success in some ordinary sense of that word, or that he may at some time play that even more difficult role, the good life?

Physically, he is much as he was when a boy — small and slight, active but not strong. He is not handsome or attractive-looking, and is even the less so at this moment, having just had two front teeth knocked out.

He is destined, recurrently, to suffer severe illnesses. But there is a vein of toughness in him. Just as he is now to survive the ordeal of the wintry shipwreck, so also he will be cured of his blood-spitting and of his many attacks of fever. He will pay a price, however, by becoming something of a hypochondriac, and a health faddist. Already, in Rostock, he has spent eleven of his scanty *thalers* for a "water-cure." He will remain through life an advocate of cold water and sea-bathing to cure everything short of senile decay.

Mentally, he is blessed (or "cursed," if you will) with an extraordinarily high intelligence. He has, in particular, an almost miraculous facility at learning languages.

He has imagination — possibly, even too much of it. His imagination is riotous, and lacking in discipline. He can never be a novelist, for he lacks that consistency of imagination which is necessary, in a long work of fiction, to produce the touch of reality. In this connection he will live, in some sense, a double life. In business dealings — and later, in scholarship — he keeps his imagination in check, and is reliable. But when it comes to writing about the past, particularly about his own life, he "romanticizes" so freely that one often wants to use a harsher word.

Emotionally, one might consider his dominating quality to be a basic and great insecurity. One can easily suggest how this insecurity grew out of his early experiences.

The very change of his name from Julius to Heinrich suggests that his parents did not quite accept him for himself, but wished him to be the beloved older child that had just died. An intriguing father and a self-pitying mother produced what almost amounted to a broken home. The mother's death meant the loss of what love she had had to offer, and the casting of a child upon the charity of kinsfolk. A little later, from the point of view of the boy, the father deserted him.

Many of the man's unfortunate qualities which he later had to overcome seem to be tied up with his general insecurity. He is touchy and easily offended, and prone to compensate by sudden rages. He has an inordinate love of praise, and of success, titles, and honors. His almost neurotic desire to travel may be similarly connected, for by travel a man finds escape and symbolically leaves his mistakes behind him. He is a man with only a little humor; the insecure man has to be too much on his guard.

Perhaps also his fixation upon the past is tied up with his insecurity. As he escapes, by travel, into space, so he can escape, by digging, into time. The present is changeable and strident, and strikes back. The past is fixed and quiet, and makes no protest. Also a treasuring of the past is his sentimentality. Minna, the red-cheeked eight-year-old, remains constant in his memory, or even improves with age.

Other qualities may, or may not, be tied in with insecurity. As with many highly intelligent people, his sense impressions are apparently not especially vivid. He seems not to have possessed the characteristic German love of music, though once or twice his letters mention opera. Though he himself discovered great works of art, he was more moved by their evocative quality than by their esthetic appeal. Literature, aside from the Homeric poems, does not seem to have meant much to him. A few mentions of a wine cellar suggest a man acquiring status rather than pleasing his palate.

A restricted childhood, particularly the long years of Fürstenburg, probably crushed much out of him. The poor apprentice learns to eat what is eatable, and to make do.

In one respect he remains the child of conscientious Mecklenburg housekeepers. He hates dirt, messiness, and crawling insects.

Religiously he has already sloughed off Lutheranism. Indeed, his father, though a pastor, was probably three-quarters skeptic. During the shipwreck, humanly enough, he calls upon God, and he later professes himself a deist. He may go to church, usually to get practice in whatever is the language of the sermon. (In later years, however, he will tend to return to "the religion of our fathers.")

We might maintain that he is religious without being of any particular religion. He believes rather simply and strongly in something outside of himself, but he calls it, not God, but Fortune or Luck. In much the same way, he believes in dreams and intuitions.

This belief in luck is a rather attractive part of his character, for it takes away from his egotism. After a great success he can quite simply maintain that it was merely his good luck.

In himself, as he lay in the Dutchman's bed, Heinrich was thus not without resources. Materially, he had nothing except an old shirt and jacket. He had no family on whom he could call, and no sure friends.

In this situation only a few things sustained him. He had youth and the wonderful courage that goes with it. He had his sense of luck, and this must have told him that bad luck could not hold forever.

Thus situated, he made a decision that was remarkable for courage and resolution. In spite of everything, he would not slink back to Germany. He would go forward. Since he now had no means by which to reach South America, he would go to Amsterdam. He considered enlistment as a soldier, probably with the idea of being sent to one of the distant Dutch colonies, though whether the Dutch army would have welcomed such a recruit must be held doubtful.

Schliemann arrived in Amsterdam at eight in the morning on December 20. He was, we may say, the prince in disguise, come to win his kingdom. He was wearing wooden shoes, and was clothed in cast-off garments of kind Dutchmen. He was destitute, and still in bad physical shape.

He obtained a little money from the consul, and then spent a few days in the hospital, largely because he could there get free bed and board. At this desperate juncture, his mother's old friend Wendt, who had aided him before, sent him a small amount of money, in reply to a letter. He bought some decent clothes, and rented a little room on the sixth floor. Wendt also sent him letters of recommendation, and Schliemann got a position as a messenger-boy.

Once he was started, nothing could keep him down. But for a while things went slowly. European business was still dominated by family firms, and the era of the self-made man was just commencing. During more than two years Schliemann ran errands and copied letters for the meagerest of salaries. He lived meanly and poorly. But he considered himself lucky to be alive and working. Still a country boy, he delighted in the life and motion of the great city. Every extra penny he spent for books in various languages, and for lessons, but the pennies were few.

Some biographers have looked upon Schliemann's fascination by languages as a vagary of an eccentric and unaccountable genius. The present biographer — who, himself, has sometimes studied languages for the pleasure of it — does not think so at all. Schliemann had an almost superhuman gift for language-learning, and people generally like to do what they can do well, even if it be something no more important than shooting partridges. Besides, he who learns languages, in a sense, travels. And Schliemann was fixated upon the thought of distance. Finally, his languages were living tongues, and important in business.

According to the legend that he later built up for himself, he set to work, and in these two years learned English, French, Spanish, Dutch, Italian, and Portuguese. But a letter of February, 1842, indicates that he already knew English and French, and had some beginning in Spanish. Even so, the achievement is remarkable.

Schliemann has left records of his methods of learning a language, and they seem to have depended upon sheer memory. There is, moreover, no doubt about his mastering the languages. He later conducted correspondence in most of them. At this time he had no interest at all in dead languages, and he never had any interest in structure and linguistic relationships.

Word must have got around the city that one of the local messenger-boys was a prodigy. In addition, some letters of recommendation (the Schliemann family was not without its connections) came from Germany. On March 1, 1844, as Schliemann always remembered the date, the prominent merchant B. H. Schroeder came into the office where Schliemann was working, picked him out, and offered him twice the pay that he was getting.

The Schroeder firm was a leading one. In the chief cities of Europe it maintained branch offices, most of them conducted by members of the family. But the Schroeders recognized talent, and Schliemann was pushed ahead rapidly. After a year or two he was in charge of fifteen clerks. Then someone at the top saw how the firm could make even better use of Schliemann's linguistic prowess.

In those years Russia was a great market, but the language was troublesome. Why not have this remarkable young fellow learn Russian, and then take charge of the branch in St. Petersburg?

Nothing could be better, as far as Schliemann was concerned. So he learned Russian, though he was human enough to admit it a more difficult language than those which he had already mastered.

In January, 1846, Schliemann went to St. Petersburg, as the Schroeder representative for all Russia.

At twenty-two, he had still been a mere messenger-boy. At twenty-four, after a dazzling advance, he was a prominent young businessman. He could even, on an expense account, indulge his passion for traveling. In a little over a year, he went four times to Moscow, visited Odessa, and took a swing across northern Europe clear to London.

It all went to his head a little. He began to receive letters from headquarters in Amsterdam, instructing him firmly to calm down, cut his expense account, and stop committing the firm by too optimistic promises. This Mecklenburg genius was apparently not long going to have a place with such a conservative firm as Schroeder's.

After a year, Schliemann went into business for himself. At the same time, he continued to handle the Schroeder affairs in Russia, and he remained on friendly terms with members of the firm. Schliemann busied himself with what we would call the import-and-export trade. He specialized in indigo, but was ready to make a deal as opportunity offered.

Shortly after this, the sentimental side of this amazing man suddenly took over. If he had been accustomed to indulge himself after the fashion of unmarried businessmen, there is no record of it. By and large, he seems in these years to have been extraordinarily shy, and much of what he did suggests a young man badly adjusted and even sex-starved. Moreover, the memory of his childhood love seems always to have haunted him. During his years of drudgery and poverty, he had not dared to approach Minna, even by letter. Now, at last prosperous, he wrote, proposing marriage. Word came back that she had recently been married to a local landowner.

Deep-engrained romantic though he was, Schliemann was also too much of a realist to spend the rest of his life mourning a lost love. He began to go about socially, with an eye upon young ladies.

By this time the gap in his upper jaw had probably been closed by artificial teeth, but he was still scarcely to be called handsome or attractive. His mustache was smart, but perhaps too suggestive of a captain of hussars. It made the little businessman look falsely fierce. His high hat and fur-trimmed coat were stylish, but they dwarfed the man beneath and inside them, making him look slightly ridiculous. Besides, his temperament created difficulties. He broke off with one lady, when he became jealous of her attentions, or supposed attentions, to an officer. Another lady turned him down.

Even in a materialistic way he was not especially attractive. He was getting along, and making some money. He was granted entrance into the wholesaler's guild. But he was not really rich, and he was a speculator, who might end up in bankruptcy.

Then came the news of the discovery of gold in California, and the world set off to make its fortune by the Sacramento. That Schliemann did not go at once shows that he was already doing well in Russia. But eventually he succumbed.

His brother Ludwig had gone to California in '49, and had done well for himself as a trader. Then word came back that he had died, leaving a fortune.

This was too much. Schliemann left St. Petersburg in December, 1850 — fraternally, to see to his brother's grave; in the interests of the whole family, to collect the fortune; and in his own interest, to make another fortune for himself. On leaving he sent some money to his sisters, with a letter warning them that this might be the last that they would receive from him, since good luck could change to bad luck so easily.

Bad luck did strike, and Schliemann's second attempt to reach the New World proved almost as disastrous as his first. Although he sailed on a fine three-thousand-ton steamer, she met disaster in a mid-Atlantic storm. The ship limped back to Cork, and Schliemann, disdaining a bad omen, tried again. This time he made it, arriving in New York on February 15, 1851, and in San Francisco on April 2.

Going at once to Sacramento, he did his duties by his brother's grave, but found that the fortune had vanished. He liked the Americans, and characterized them with words that might have been self-appraisal — as valuing money above everything, as having boundless energy, and as never being daunted.

Before settling down, Schliemann took a trip into the mining country, but he himself never was a miner. By 1851 the glamor of the Gold Rush had worn off, and miners were little better than day-laborers. He also visited San Francisco again, and happened to be there at the time of the Great Fire on June 4. He contrasted the despair of the Europeans who had lost their property with the nonchalance of the Americans, who laughed and joked, and immediately set out to rebuild.

Having left Russia with some capital, Schliemann set up a bank in Sacramento. He established relationships with the house of Rothschild, and during the latter part of the year a professional card in a local newspaper announced, "Banking House of Henry Schliemann and Co." Located "in the Brick Building, corner of Front and Jay Sts.," the bank offered "exchange on sight" with Rothschild agencies in New York, New Orleans, London, Paris, Hamburg, and Frankfurt.

Business was good, and Schliemann, as always, was indefatigable. He once wrote that he had worked harder for the past week than any slave. He declared that he had been able to eat only once a day, and had to simply forget all the other wants of nature, a statement which we may respectfully take to be an exaggeration, even though he is known to have been chronically constipated. This period was apparently a time of emergency, when he had lost his clerks, and had to stay constantly in the bank to guard it. He declared that he passed every night in feverish horror, with loaded pistols in both hands.

In the Babel that was early California, his ability to talk to almost anyone was a great asset. He daily shifted among eight languages. He even learned to transact business with the numerous Chinese, who brought much gold dust in. But Chinese was one language that he never set himself to learn.

As always, a rigorous insistence on honesty and expedition brought him a good reputation.

Unfortunately, frontier lack of sanitation still prevailed, and Schliemann twice came down with a dangerous fever. He became discouraged, and realized that no place appealed to him so much as did St. Petersburg. Again he liquidated his affairs, and took a steamer.

Back in Europe, he spent a few days of what he considered to be idle and dissolute life in Paris. He then revisited Mecklenburg, and spent some sentimental hours at Ankershagen, where he found the initials H.S. scratched and cut in dozens of places, an interesting evidence of boyish self-love. Joyfully he arrived in St. Petersburg on August 4, 1852.

He had considerably increased his capital in California. He might now be called a man of fortune, and his energy and business skill had been well proved. On the very day after his return he paid his respects to Miss Catherine Lyschin, who had previously been cold to his advances, but now received him with favor, apparently being sensibly (in two meanings of the word) influenced by his augmented fortune.

She was the sister of two of Schliemann's friends in the world of business. Everything seemed suitable, and Schliemann himself was nothing if not impetuous. On October 24 they were married. On the last day of the year he wrote that he was enjoying all the comforts of domestic life, and would never think of leaving St. Petersburg again!

He busied himself with buying, selling, and engaging in speculative ventures. As always, he made money, we may say, by the barrelful.

Busy, successful, married, having gained some social acceptance — what more could he wish? Children, perhaps? And there was every expectation of them. Now, finally, he could settle, we might think, to happiness.

But, even in the first year of marriage, the devil of discontent was gnawing within him. In 1853, at the age of thirty-one, he began to think of retirement.

First he toyed with the idea of buying an estate in Mecklenburg, and living as a country gentleman. A worse idea can hardly be imagined. He would have been bored to death on the second day. Nature has never abhorred a vacuum more than Heinrich Schliemann abhorred an empty hour. He himself came to realize the absurdity of the idea, and abandoned it.

He did not, however, abandon the thought of retirement. In 1853, then, we may say, began a sixteen-year period of transition, during which the businessman slowly shifted into the archeologist.

All this goes counter to the legend that Schliemann himself did so much to create — that the excavation of Troy was a fixation from childhood, and that, once having earned the necessary fortune, he devoted it to realizing his archeological ideal.

On the contrary, from the age of thirty-one to the age of forty-seven, he was making the transition. Biographically speaking, these are the most interesting years of his life. They display a talented but awkward man, struggling to conquer his insecurities and to fulfill himself.

In fact, brilliant money-maker though he was, Schliemann seems to have found little satisfaction in business. To make a fortune, indeed, was pleasant — especially since it killed his basic economic insecurity. He enjoyed money, as much as anyone else did. At times, he enjoyed the excitement of making it, and was happy in the long hours of feverish activity, the pitting of his brains against the uncertainties of world trade, the taking of the gambler's chance — with confidence in his own luck.

But there was the other side. Often he exhausted his not-too-strong body. His kind of business did not breed much security. He was a speculator, chronically overextended, never unconscious of the haunting possibility of bankruptcy.

Besides, buying and selling did not yield much basic satisfaction to a supremely intellectual man. If he had been in production or development, he might have realized himself. Being a mere middle-man was not enough.

The Crimean War, lasting from March, 1854, to February, 1856, sent him into a frenzy of profitable speculation in such military supplies as lead and saltpeter.

Curiously, right in the middle of the war, though he had never been working so hard and making such profits, he found that business did not satisfy him, and he went into a veritable orgy of studying languages. Also curious, though one hesitates to draw conclusions, is that this linguistic frenzy coincided with the pregnancy of his wife.

In April, 1855, he returned to the study of Latin, which he had never fully mastered in school. He also took up modern Greek, and then passed on to the classical language. But he still maintained more interest in living languages, and in this year mastered Polish and Swedish. About the same time he added Slovenian, Danish, and Norwegian to his list.

At this time Schliemann stated that he had learned Polish and Swedish, both, in twenty-four days, and could speak and write fluently in fifteen languages. Such claims, with most people, could be written off as boastful lies. But Schliemann's endowments in this area were so extraordinary that one is inclined to believe what he says.

We can scarcely be surprised, however, to have him declaring that he had overworked himself and that his health had suffered.

In the autumn of 1855 a son was born, and called Serge.

Schliemann, strongly oriented toward family, was delighted.

Unfortunately, the birth of the son actually inaugurated an era, not of happiness, but of strain. His wife's attitude changed sharply, as if she had developed a neurotic antipathy to her husband. She withdrew from him physically. Since this change succeeded to the birth of the son, she may have been suffering from a horror of childbirth. But Schliemann wanted not only his wife but children as well.

As with most marital difficulties, the psychological roots reach too deep for any excavating tools that can be marshaled by a biographer. The marriage bumped and dragged along through the years, as so often happens when divorce is not readily available, or even when it is. There were reconciliations and then new quarrels. Schliemann himself was not an easy-going man. Unfortunately, he had not been able to remove his sense of insecurity by marrying Catherine.

As the years passed, two more children were born. But, as Schliemann once wrote almost brutally, he had had to steal them from her.

By all the rules, this unhappiness should have caused him to concentrate on business. Indeed, at times, he had little choice. The war boom held on until November, 1857, and then everything crashed. During several months, he had to work day and night, in terror of having his whole fortune collapse. He came out with moderate losses, but physically exhausted and emotionally shaken, and with gray hair at the age of thirty-six.

He now had so much money that the secure preservation of his fortune rather than its further increase seemed more reasonable. He began to think in terms of finally liquidating his business, and finding sound investments. Believing too firmly in the likelihood of inflation to be interested in bonds, he turned, as it would be put today, toward a diversified portfolio of common stocks and some urban income-property.

But what was he, a retired man-of-fortune in his mid-thirties, to do with himself throughout the remaining three or four decades of life that he might expect? He had, indeed, an answer, though only a vague one. He would devote himself to *Wissenschaft*. Unfortunately this German word, without a good English equivalent, represents an ideal rather than a discipline. Though sometimes it means "science," it can have meant to Schliemann only something like "knowledge," or "scholarship."

He was, however, coming upon the scene at least a hundred years too late. This was no longer the Renaissance when a man might take all knowledge as his field. It was no longer even the eighteenth century, when the portals opened to the talented and wealthy amateur. It was the middle of the nineteenth century, and the trained scholar and the specialist had taken over. Schliemann, who had missed his chance at going to the university, realized all this fully.

His only immediate project was to travel. This was reasonable enough. He had always suffered from itchy feet, and travel would give him a chance to look around and perhaps to decide what he would do with himself. Among other places that he would visit, as he wrote at this time, was "the homeland of my favorite, Homer." Perhaps the German would be better translated as "my darling, Homer." The difference is not significant, and there is no suggestion that Schliemann intended to do anything more than to travel in Greece. In fact, there is nothing to indicate that Homer held first place in his imagination — rather the contrary, for another letter merely listed Homer second in a series of four classical writers whose works Schliemann was reading with enthusiasm.

He spent the rest of 1858 disentangling himself from his affairs. Catherine was not to accompany him on the extended trip that he was planning. In fact, her fixation on St. Petersburg was one of their standing causes of trouble.

Early in 1859 he was off. He did not hasten to Greece. Instead, he went down through Italy and crossed to Egypt. There, of course, he learned Arabic.

In later years he told his family a story, which, he further said, he could never publish for fear of being killed by a fanatical Mohammedan. Having learned Arabic, he told, he then had himself circumcised, and made the pilgrimage to Mecca. As so often when he told of himself, Schliemann was romancing. Possibly he submitted to the operation with the wild idea of making the journey. He nursed many strange projects in the course of his life.

He actually crossed the desert from Egypt to Palestine by horse and camel, adventurously journeyed to Petra, and went on to Syria. Finally — as if by afterthought — he arrived in Athens. There, as so often happened, he was taken ill. Deciding to return to St. Petersburg, he went by ship to Constantinople. He therefore passed through the Dardanelles, but this may have been at night. He never mentioned having seen the site of Troy at this time.

After a brief rest at home, if it could be called such, he was feverishly off again, for two months in Spain.

In all this traveling he apparently saw and experienced about what any intelligent and vigorous tourist may expect. These months produced no great change in him.

Finally returning to Russia, he found trouble. The man to whom he had sold out was bringing suit against him, and he faced being involved for several years with the slow-moving Russian courts.

Thus tied down, he went back into business, largely out of mere boredom. He made money. That was easy! He declared that he doubled his capital.

He played at being the rich *bourgeois* — horses and carriage, a fine riding horse, exercise in a gymnasium, a skating club. In his letters is no mention of *Wissenschaft*. He collected businessman's honors which are difficult to translate: Commerce Advisor, Honorary Citizen, Judge of the Board of Trade, Hereditary Member of the First Merchant Guild.

To obtain the last, he even prolonged his stay in Russia, thinking that the hereditary feature would benefit his children. He was still interested in them, but the marriage had ceased to be of importance.

In spite of this seeming acceptance of commercial ideals and his intellectual doldrums, he continued to work toward a final retirement.

The suit decided in his favor, his business sold out, his investments made, his will signed and sealed — the best that he could think to do was to set out on his travels again, early in 1864, once more alone.

Economic insecurity — for many people, that greatest of bugaboos — Schliemann had now finally slain. His investments made reasonably certain that he could live in luxury. Yet he was still a man without the security of a wife and home, and he was unfulfilled in love. Moreover, he was wholly without sense of mission, and his tremendous intellect lacked other goals than a vague dedication to *Wissenschaft*, and the parrot-like proliferation of languages.

So he traveled, the eternal tourist, seeing everything, and always from the outside. This time, he did not come back at all. He kept on going, and eventually the curved surface of the earth returned him.

What did the other travelers think of this eager and intense little German with the graying hair? Or was he Russian, perhaps? He spoke all the languages in the book. He was certainly wealthy, but he attributed everything to luck. Did he have a family? Where was he going? Yes, they might ask that last question in two senses. Did they feel anything of genius, or of greatness in him? Probably, not.

He went to Tunis, to Egypt, and still to the east. He took his time. That was something of which, after all these years, he at last had plenty. Still, he abhorred idleness, and one wonders how he passed the days on shipboard. Of course, he kept a diary, as travelers, especially Germans, are likely to do. He was devoted to cold baths. He was conscientious about exercise. He enjoyed talking with his fellow-passengers, and was not snobbish, his mentions of other people being often laudatory.

Reaching India, he spent some time there. He worked at Hindustani, but there is no evidence that he mastered it. At forty-two his eardrums may have been thickening a little (they would give him trouble later), and he would have lost some of his quickness at language.

In April he was in China, and Greek met Greek when Heinrich Schliemann went to call upon the well-known polyglot Robert Thomas. The German, able to claim proficiency in eighteen languages at this time, outscored the Englishman, whom Schliemann's narrative credits with only ten. But Thomas held the edge, locally, by including Japanese and Chinese in his repertoire.

In China, typically, Schliemann decided to do something spectacular. He visited the Chinese Wall. Also, as he was to do at other places, he declared that he had had an active curiosity in the wall ever since his "tenderest infancy." He then spent several weeks in Japan, which had been "opened" by Commodore Perry scarcely a decade earlier. He did well enough to get to Japan at all, and was not able to go farther than the vicinity of Tokyo.

Next he embarked on a small and slow-sailing vessel for San Francisco. On the tedious voyage he rewrote some of his diaries for publication.

The nineteenth century was the heyday of the travel book, and Schliemann must have read numbers of them. They were commonest in English and German, but he chose to write in the language of the home-loving French.

He finally reached San Francisco, continued on by the Nicaragua route, and returned to Europe, early in 1866.

He settled down in Paris. By this time, there was no point in returning to St. Petersburg. The marriage, at last, was dying. But, like many another such, it died hard — at least on Schliemann's part. To Catherine and her advisors he wrote impassioned and sometimes foolish letters. He tried to lure her with promises of luxurious life and platonic marriage. He wanted his children, and he wanted a German education for them.

In return, Catherine let him know that she disliked his mingled extravagance and meanness, resented his tempers, looked with disgust on his passion for traveling, and hated his enthusiasm for languages. She committed the final wifely insult by urging him to take a mistress. Even a husband must have begun to realize that she did not care for him.

Whether Schliemann took a mistress is not in the available public record. One passage in a letter suggests that he had lost his earlier shyness with women, and may not have shunned casual affairs. Either way, it makes the very slightest difference.

He does not seem a man who was looking for sensual gratification or for whom it could have meant much. His whole being cried for the security of a home, and a family. He needed a wife who would give him, hopefully, love. At least, she must give him stability and acceptance.

During the next few years Paris was his base, rather than his home. He lived luxuriously. He still traveled widely, almost madly. Once he started for Persia, having already studied the language. He got as far as the Caspian Sea, but had to return because of illness. Once he went to the United States and Cuba, partly to make investments. He also bought Paris real estate, to such an extent that 270 families lived in the buildings that he owned.

The magic of Paris held him, as it has held so many. Here at last, though still without definite goal, he could approach *Wissenschaft*, and woo the intellectual life of the great city. He went to theaters and visited museums. He assiduously and miscellaneously attended lectures — on literature, on philosophy, and even on hieroglyphics. He read books, and collected a library. Twenty years late, he was trying to catch up on the university education that he had missed.

He was not the kind of man to whom doors flew open because of his charm, and in intellectual circles he had little to offer. He had a fine mind — even, a great brain — but it was running in a vacuum. His gift of tongues might make him a curiosity, like an unusually talented raven. But one imagines the Gallic epigram, "He talks eighteen languages, and has nothing to say in any of them."

But he made some progress. At least, he got to know Ernest Renan, who was one of the intellectual leaders.

Perhaps the publication of *La Chine et le Japon* in 1867 gave him a small reputation. It is not a bad little book, though the accuracy of its observation has been impugned. The best part is that which describes his visit to the Chinese Wall, and any interest that people displayed in this account must have turned his mind toward ancient walls and their rediscovery.

These Parisian years, from early 1866 to mid-1868, were

critical. Unfortunately, no evidence is available as to the steps of his development. He must have learned (he may never have known before) that there was such a thing as archeology.

Actually, it was in a feeble infancy. Still, Pompeii had been partially uncovered; there had been digging in Egypt; Layard had plundered Nineveh; rather advanced work had been done on the stratification of Swiss lake-dwellings.

In the late spring of 1868 Schliemann set out to visit the Homeric lands. The itch for writing had taken hold of him, and he now, after so many years, focused sharply upon the backgrounds of the *Iliad* and the *Odyssey*.

His conception of these poems at this time (he would change somewhat, later) was simple. They were sacred script — not only historical, but true in each and every line. Inconsistencies bothered Schliemann no more than inconsistencies in any holy writ bother the faithful. Even the appearance on earth of the Homeric gods did not seem to concern him especially.

His first stop was the island of Corfu. He accepted the idea, of some respectability among scholars, that Corfu was Scheria, where Odysseus was shipwrecked among the Phaeacians.

If so, there must somewhere still be the stream where Nausicaä had gone with her handmaidens to do the washing. Schliemann went to look, and after some difficulty (would you believe it?) he found the exact spot! Yes, this was the place where the girls had played at ball, and where their excited screams had awakened the great hero as he lay beneath the wild olive tree. Schliemann's account is utterly naïve, and sometimes rather charming.

Next stop, Ithaca! The palace of Odysseus must be around somewhere, and also the stoutly built pigsty of the divine swineherd Eumaeus. Schliemann found the remains on top of a mountain.

And now, for the first time, he hired some workmen, and started digging. He soon discovered what he knew to be (and woe unto those who have little faith!) the palace of Odysseus. He even found the bedroom, as described in the poem.

Schliemann's luck had been running thin for many years. Now it was returning. Even in the rich soil of Greece one cannot expect to recover much in a few hours of casual digging. But Schliemann struck a whole nest of small urns. They contained a powdery substance which he immediately took to be human ashes, though he had never seen human ashes before, and we wonder how he knew. He at once declared these to be the ashes of Odysseus and Penelope, though he added as a scholarly caution, "or their successors."

This identification is, among other things, a good example of Schliemann's uncontrolled and faulty imagination. He should have remembered the prophecy that Odysseus would die far from the sea.

After quick glances at Mycenae and Tiryns, Schliemann went on to the Troad. He accepted the prevailing theory that Homeric Troy had been located on a hill called Bunarbashi. He went there, but immediately asserted his own independence of judgment. It would not do. Why, in one place Homer tells that Achilles pursued Hector three times around the walls of Troy! It could not be done at Bunarbashi. Schliemann went around the hill himself. In one place there was such a steep ridge that it was difficult to climb, and no one could possibly have run there.

Thus spoke the naïve Homerist, but the practical man of business, and the budding archeologist, did something more. He hired some workmen, and dug some holes. Already he had seen at Mycenae that the site of an ancient city is thickly strewn with broken pottery. His workmen uncovered no pottery at all at Bunarbashi. Therefore, "No city!" Therefore, also, "No city, no Troy!"

It was an epoch-making juncture for Schliemann. He had dug to solve a factual problem. It was epoch-making, too, for archeology.

Schliemann then took a quick look at Hissarlik, a largely artificial mound in the plain near the Dardanelles. He decided that Troy must really have been located there, and he began to make plans, at last, to dig it up.

Back in Paris, he quickly prepared a small book: *Ithaka, der Peloponnes und Troja.* He wrote in German, and no one has ever bothered to publish the work in another language. It was, again, a travel book, but this time a little more. By observation and by digging, he attempted to reconstruct the Homeric background.

Unfortunately the worst parts of the book came first. Anyone wading through the nonsense which was presented about Corfu and Ithaca was probably too much out of patience to appreciate the sound, if small, contribution that Schliemann had made in the Troad.

But he need not mind poor reviews. At last he had a goal. He would excavate Troy at Hissarlik!

First, however, he had two bits of unfinished personal business to settle.

He wanted a degree to lend authority to what he wrote. Rostock was the university of Mecklenburg, and some of the Schliemann family had influence. He himself was known as a local boy who had made a great fortune and learned many languages, and was beginning to have some reputation as a traveler. As a thesis, he submitted his second book, translated into classical Greek. He may have stood some kind of examination. Residence was not required. In any case, he thenceforth used the title Doctor. One hesitates to suggest that there is a slight smell about it all, but many a poor and hard-working German scholar, we can be sure, felt some resentment at a degree thus granted to a rich man.

Also, he must get a divorce. The decision to do so at this time suggests that Schliemann, returned from those tiny but decisive excavations on Bunarbashi, had at last resolved to begin a new life. He went to Indianapolis (yes, the one in Indiana!) which was the divorce mill of those days. He settled down luxuriously in a house with two Negro servants, interested himself in the local scene, made some investments, and waited while the legal mills ground on. He wrote many letters — especially to Frank Calvert, an Englishman resident at the Dardanelles, who owned part of the mound of Hissarlik and was eager to cooperate with the excavation.

Also, Schliemann was conducting another correspondence, not altogether heading the adage about being off with the old love. In Russia he had studied Greek with a priest who had now become an archbishop in Athens. Even before leaving Paris, Schliemann had written the archbishop a good straightforward request. He wanted a wife. Diffidently enough, considering the rich man that he was, he told what he would like. She should be poor — no hard requirement in Greece. She should be well educated, and enthusiastic about Homer. It did not matter whether she knew any foreign languages. She should be of a Greek type, and it would be nice if she were beautiful. But the main thing was for her to be good and loving. The poor rich man ended, pathetically, that he was opening his heart as to a father confessor, and that there was no one else in the world to whom he could entrust such secrets.

The archbishop may have been a little surprised, but probably not too much so. The arranged marriage was a part of

Greek life. Here was an opportunity to marry some good Greek girl to a very wealthy husband. Even from Schliemann's point of view there was nothing so very startling about it. The arranged marriage was still common enough in Germany.

The archbishop, focused on his own family as any Greek should be, thought of his cousin's daughters. Sophia might be the one. She was just sixteen, beautiful and clever.

She had no fine clothes. So she wore her sister's clothes for the photograph, and they were too big for her.

But the archbishop played it fair. He did not send only the picture of his cousin's daughter, but those of other girls as well.

The packet of pictures came to Indianapolis, and the gray-haired German, forty-seven years old, looked at them. He was drawn to the portrait of Sophia Engastromanos. He did not say, in his answering letter, that she was the most beautiful, but he said that she looked the most lovable. Perhaps it was only the luck of Heinrich Schliemann. It was probably good judgment too.

Certainly, from photographs of Sophia taken a little later, any man old enough to see something more than mere prettiness would have to declare her a supremely beautiful woman. The face had serenity, combined with all the dignity derived from thirty centuries of Greek civilization. At sixteen, one would think, she looked a young forty; at sixty, a slightly older forty.

Which one of the heroines did Schliemann see in her? Not Helen of Troy, certainly! No maid of tragedy either — not Antigone, or Iphigenia, or bitter Electra. Andromache, perhaps, in the days before Hector wore his helmet. Nausicaä, when she said good-bye to Odysseus.

Conditions of residence satisfied, Schliemann obtained his

divorce. Thereafter, though he remained always the internationalist at heart, some of his American editions identified him as "Citizen of the United States of America."

In August he went to Athens. He had wine and cakes in the modest Greek home, with all the large family standing around. Probably as ill at ease as any other man would be under such circumstances, he asked Sophia some questions, which seemed to be a previously prepared examination. Would you like to go on a long journey? When did the Emperor Hadrian visit Athens? Can you repeat some passages of Homer? Sophia passed.

On the third day, he saw her alone. And, like a man determined to destroy his own happiness (or perhaps he was merely curious, as always), he asked why she wanted to marry him. She was surprised, but she told him the truth, from the shoulder. She wanted to marry him because her parents said that he was rich.

Schliemann was horrified, went off, and wrote her a nasty letter breaking off everything. Was he angered because she had not said that she loved him? Possibly — but that is not what he stated in the letter. She should have said she was marrying him so that they could excavate together, and enjoy Homer.

Of course, it was only one of his quick rages. He did not leave Athens, as he threatened. On September 24, they were married.

Again, Schliemann had hurried into matrimony. This time the luck was with him.

He was old enough, as the saying goes, "to be her father." Did she ever love him? Who knows? And who knows all of what love is and what it is to be a wife? She was a Greek girl, given in marriage by her parents, as Greek girls have been since Homer's time and Agamemnon's. Their marriage bed was made in many places, often on the windswept height of Troy. She bore him two children. When he called, she was there to answer. She was his wife.

Did he love her? Yes — or, at least, he came to do so. He loved her in as far as love could come to a nature such as his, and we cannot demand of any man more than what lies within him. In his letters to her, there is sometimes a strange and moving tenderness. "Little Sophie, best of wives," he addressed her. He found, at last, something firm and enduring.

Only half a year after his marriage, in April, 1870, Schliemann made his first excavations on the mound at Hissarlik. There was trouble with Turkish landowners and officials. (Such troubles were to be chronic.) So the work of that season was slight and only exploratory. But, with Sophia and Troy, he was at last beginning to fulfill himself.

Early in 1871 he spent some time in Constantinople, negotiating for the proper permit to dig. At that time he spent eighteen days studying Turkish, and then wrote to Sophia that he could write and talk fluently, having a vocabulary of 6,000 words. Since this was to be his last language, we now total up his score, granting that both "language" itself, and to "know" a language are difficult terms. He may be credited with Plattdeutsch, German, Latin, French, English, Spanish, Dutch, Italian, Portuguese, Russian, Polish, Swedish, Greek (ancient and modern), Slovenian, Danish, Norwegian, Arabic, Persian, Hindustani, and Turkish. The totals are: two dead languages, and nineteen current languages or dialects, not counting what Chinese he picked up in California.

This year, also, the Germans were besieging Paris. Schliemann, still an internationalist and businessman, had little emotional involvement in a war between his fatherland and one of his adopted countries. But he feared lest the bombardment destroy his houses. With false papers he adventurously went through the German lines, attributing his success to calling every private a major and every lieutenant a general.

He found the houses undamaged, and was back in Athens in May for the birth of his daughter Andromache. They had intended to name the baby Odysseus, but the will of Zeus, as Schliemann probably put it, fulfilled itself in another way.

On October 11, 1871, he commenced serious excavations at Hissarlik, and he continued to work, during the favorable seasons, for three years.

The legend emphasizes the naïveté and ignorance of Schliemann when he began his archeological work. Granted, he was by nature somewhat naïve. Granted, also, he was ignorant as compared with Dörpfeld, Semple, and Blegen, who came after him at Troy. But they stood on his shoulders, and they were ready to acknowledge it, and to pay tribute to him. His was the ignorance, and the greatness, of the pioneer.

But, by the standards of his time, he was not ignorant. Not for nothing had he spent so many months in Paris. He knew the basic facts — that there had been a stone age, that sites might be stratified, that bits of pottery meant much.

He professed a simple ideal, that he had no other object than to find Homer's Troy. That, as the scholar in me now speaks, was thoroughly reprehensible. He should have said, "Here is a mound. I shall dig into it. I shall see what it tells me." As it was, he hurried on from anything non-Homeric, and even destroyed it in his haste to discover the true word. What saved him was the circumstance that he could seldom be sure what was Homeric and what was not.

At Bunarbashi he had merely said, "No city, no Troy!" That was logic. He thought that the situation at Hissarlik would not be much more complicated. He would dig down through the ruins of Graeco-Roman Troy, and there would be the ruins of Homeric Troy. By inference from a passage in the *Iliad* he believed that this Troy had been founded on a site not yet inhabited. So, continuing to dig, he would pierce through the debris left after the sack by the Achaeans, and he would soon come to virgin soil or rock. Simple enough!

Very shortly, all this lovely simplicity vanished. Instead, city lay beneath city in shocking confusion. A lesser man would quietly have thrown the work over, or just gone mad. The pages of Schliemann's report are spattered with "I am surprised," and "I am astounded."

Once several cities were possibilities, how could you decide among them? Homer mentioned palaces, temples, a wall, a gate, a tower. But all the cities had these.

At last he concentrated upon what he called the Burnt City. It was not on the bedrock, and, instead of being directly below the Greek ruins, it was separated by some fifteen feet of deposit. Embarrassing circumstances! But that city had been burned, and a few human bones suggested that bodies might have been left lying in the streets after the sack.

At last, one morning, quite early, he and Sophia were digging at a place in the Burnt City where he had recently found an unusual copper object. Curiously, though Schliemann was a great man for dates, he never recorded this day, though it was, in most ways, the greatest of his life. It was close to the beginning of June, 1873.

Suddenly he saw the gleam of gold. He and Sophia were by themselves, but many workmen were nearby. Also there was an inspector of the Turkish government to see that the excavator, as by contract, rendered up half of all his finds.

Schliemann hurriedly told Sophia to go and call out that there would be a holiday — this, he had remembered, was his birthday, but everyone could have full pay.

Sophia called, and the workmen (as what workmen would not?) quickly dispersed, before the boss could change his mind. The Turkish inspector was off somewhere.

Then the two of them dug out the Great Treasure. As they collected the objects, Sophie wrapped them in her red shawl, and carried them to the little house where she and Heinrich lived. The hoard contained remarkable objects in copper, silver, and electrum, but most intoxicating was the gold — jewelry of various sorts, 8,700 beads, three vessels, two magnificent headdresses — all in clean, yellow gold!

Schliemann believed in luck. Doubtless he would have held the finding of the treasure to be his greatest piece of luck, and most people would agree with it. But, it can be argued, the discovery was the result, chiefly, of good hard work. Also, it may be counted to be partially a misfortune.

In the first place, it led Schliemann into a disgraceful action. He broke his contract with the Turkish government, and smuggled the whole treasure across to Athens. Of course, he justified his own action, but the argument is casuistic. All we can say is that he acted under a kind of compulsion. After all these years, he simply could not surrender the gold that he believed to be King Priam's treasure.

Also, the discovery was a misfortune in that it riveted his attention to the Burnt City, and thus tended to vitiate his judgment.

On the good side, the treasure brought him the fame that he so craved. He was a man who for years had lacked and needed glory, recognition, and even acceptance.

With a touch of genius, which is often close to the ridiculous, he once adorned Sophia with the treasure — headdress, heavy shoulder-reaching pendants, necklaces. Then he had her photographed in all that gleaming gold that he believed, or wished to believe, had once adorned no other than Helen herself. In the picture little Sophia appears just a trifle ill-at-ease. It may be rated her greatest triumph. Any other woman would merely have looked silly.

The Turkish government brought suit, and won the case. But it was a Greek court, where a Turk was not likely to get more than bare justice. Schliemann had to pay a moderate fine. He added a large amount of his own free will, as con-science-money or a bribe. And so he was able to get further permission to excavate in Turkey.

When Schliemann left Troy in 1873, he considered that his work there had been completed. He was wrong. The Achaeans besieged Troy for ten years; Schliemann, for twenty-two years. Agamemnon, in the end, captured Troy; Troy, we may say, captured Schliemann. He amassed great spoil at Troy and won high fame, but Troy took him as an active man of forty-six, and cast him out as a dying man of sixty-eight.

There is even a certain irony. Schliemann did not like His-sarlik. It had many scorpions and little brown vipers, and swarms of insects, all of which he despised. The mound was windswept ("windy Troy," indeed!), and it was, in fact, much like Hesiod's Ascra, which (as every schoolboy knows) was bad in winter and sultry in summer and good at no time.

Still, as he wrote once, in character, "Amid all the fatigues and troubles of the excavations there is this, among other pleasures, that time never hangs heavy on one's hands."

The last twenty-two years of his life belong to the history of archeology. Schliemann went to look for Homer's Troy, and found two millennia of the development of mankind. As to all that he uncovered, is it not recorded in his own books and in many later ones? We cannot consider it all; it is too much. We are not excavating those superimposed cities; we are only trying to excavate a man.

He dug at Motye in Sicily, briefly, in 1875. The next year, having made his peace with the Turks, he was at Troy for a short while, and then at Tiryns. But the great dig of 1876 was at Mycenae, where he found gold and treasure of art equal to what he had found at Hissarlik. In 1878 and 1879 he did major excavation at Troy. At the end of 1880, running over into the next year, he dug at Orchomenos, which Homer called "rich in gold," but there was no treasure. In 1882, he did a little work at Marathon and major work at Tiryns.

One should not think that Schliemann continued to dig in an amateur way. Largely because of the stimulation that he himself had given, the methods and techniques of archeology were developing rapidly. Young, newly trained men were coming along, such as Wilhelm Dörpfeld, who was Schliemann's assistant and then his successor. But he himself remained the old master.

Was it luck or was it shrewd judgment that had led him to enter a field where energy, money, and native intelligence counted the most, and where there was as yet no special requirement of training and education? And Schliemann had the power of developing as he went along, even though he grew older. Carl Blegen, his great successor in the fourth generation at Troy, has paid him the tribute that he learned from his own mistakes, was very quick at learning. Moreover, Blegen declared, Schliemann made himself into an excavator, "who could hold his own with anyone." J. L. Myres, one of the great British scholars, has written that Schliemann's method and outlook marked "a turning point in the history of archeology," that is, that he shifted the emphasis from the attempt to find *objets d'art* to the study of the human record.

Besides developing in his excavations, he developed strikingly in his writing. *Troy and Its Remains* (1874-1875) still suggests the travel book. It might be called *My Seasons at Troy*, or *How I Dug Up the Treasure*. He himself described it as a "sort of diary," and he exercised the diarist's prerogative of changing his mind as he went along. But even in this one book we can notice the ideas maturing.

The large volume *Mycenae* (1878) shows further advance. The focus is upon the ancient city itself, not upon the way in which the digging was done.

Then came *Ilios* (1880-1881). Schliemann, when he worked on this book, was in his late fifties, at the height of his powers. He really presented the Trojan problem. The book runs to 900 pages of closely reasoned and well-documented scholarship. It is not recommended for light reading, but it *is* recommended for the inspection of anyone who thinks that Schliemann was only an amateur. In this volume he throws the authorities at you with all the abandon of a long-time professor. An object excavated at Troy will be compared with another one described from a report of a site in Hungary or Switzerland.

This volume remains Schliemann's masterpiece. *Orchomenos* (1881) is slight, and *Troja* (1884) is only a kind of progress report. *Tiryns* (1885-1886) maintains as high a standard as *Ilios*, but much less than half of it is Schliemann's, the rest being the work of collaborators.

The amount of energy expended by Schliemann upon the preparation of these reports, entirely aside from the digging, was tremendous. *Ilios* alone would have kept an ordinary scholar busy for half his career.

During these years Schliemann's great mind was employed up to its full capacity. When he was not studying the daily results of excavations, he was in Athens working on the books and their translations, or else he was developing the general background of his scholarship by wide reading, by visiting museums throughout Europe, by talking with other scholars, and by attending conferences. These activities, fortunately, allowed him to satisfy his need for travel.

In Athens he lived graciously — at last. He also lived busily, and fruitfully, and full of honors. He built a spacious and beautiful house, a little way down the street from the royal palace, and it still stands there, almost as much a landmark as the palace itself. He called it *Iliou Melathron*, meaning House of Ilium, and he had the name put on the front of the house in prominent letters, so that he who runs may read.

He was arriving at the time of life when a bit of eccentricity rather lends charm. He gave classical names to all the servants. He began to swear, "By Pallas Athene!"

Still, he retained his American citizenship, and evinced little interest in modern Greece. He thus remained a businessman and an internationalist, devoted to his own ends. If it is a weakness, it is one that grew out of his early life, when he lived for so long as a non-citizen, necessarily without political involvement. In Russia he accepted the rule of the czar, and as a *bourgeois* he seems not to have been concerned by serfdom. The Crimean War and the American Civil War involved him chiefly for their effects on business. Though he showed some concern for the bombarded Parisians of 1871, his chief fixation was upon his own property. Curiously, the only political struggle with which he expressed deep sympathy was Italian nationalism, which may have appealed to his romanticism.

When labor was involved, he was an employer of his time.

Once, at Hissarlik, he observed that cigarette smoking caused loss of time, and forbade it. Seventy men quit working, and angrily threw stones at the men who remained on the job. Schliemann recruited more workers, broke the "mutiny," as he called it, and then added an hour to the working day. But we might also remember that he expended, for the first excavations at Hissarlik alone, the equivalent of $50,000, a stupendous sum at that time. Most of this went as cash for wages, to bolster up a depressed economy.

Slavery he judged in its economic, not its humanitarian, aspects. Nevertheless, he was without race prejudice. Having heard Negro orators in Mississippi and Louisiana in 1867, he regretted that he was not a Negro, wishing to be able to speak as they did.

Late in life he swung back, sentimentally, to his country of birth. He finally gave the Great Treasure to Germany, and was given in return the high distinction of Honorary Citizenship of Berlin. (He always appreciated *quid pro quo.*) Even though they did not get the treasure, the British showered rewards upon him. He was Honorary D.C.L. of Oxford, Honorary Fellow of Queens College, and a gold medalist of the Royal Institute of British Architects.

On his numerous trips to "Europe," as the Greeks say, he sometimes took the family along, and sometimes went alone. But he always came back to Athens and Iliou Melathron and Sophia and the children. The boy, born at the time of the Mycenae excavation, was named Agamemnon, when Schliemann thought he might really have discovered the veritable bones of Agamemnon, King of Men, the face covered by a gold mask.

Schliemann appreciated his children. He carried on a correspondence with his Russian son, who was a grown man by now.

In these years, for the first time in his life, he was one of a group. He corresponded on equal terms with Gladstone, Müller, Schöne, Burnouf, and the other great scholars whose fields touched his. The remarkable Rudolf Virchow — pathologist, anthropologist, and statesman — became his particular friend. Dörpfeld, at first a hired assistant, became colleague, friend, and advisor.

Even in these years Schliemann could be thin-skinned, touchy, and quick to anger. Once, at some imagined insult, he broke off relations with Virchow, and several months passed before a reconciliation was effected.

Always, just as he looked back into the past of Troy and Mycenae, Schliemann looked back, romantically, into his own past. As he advanced into late middle age, a glow illuminated the years at Ankershagen. He not only sent money to support his own family, but also as Lord Bountiful, to other people in the old village, one of whom had even mistreated him when he was a child. In 1879, he started a correspondence with Minna, who had been married, now, for more than thirty years.

You may, if you will, imagine her as a buxom and solid Mecklenburg *hausfrau* with faded blond hair, approaching sixty. But, for Schliemann, she was still his apple-cheeked sweetheart whom, at the age of eight, he had loved at dancing class. He even went to visit in Mecklenburg, taking Sophia and the children. He saw Minna. Even so, the vision lingered.

One wonders what Sophia thought about it. As a Greek wife, she might have expected to have her rich husband keep a smart and expensive mistress. But this idealization of Minna must have been a bit embarrassing. It was as if Heinrich had gone off to the nursery, and started playing with tin soldiers. Let us not forget that this was the age of Romanticism, and that the Germans, when they grow sentimental, go the whole way.

In keeping with his general backward-looking nature, he turned to autobiography — preparing a brief account of his own life, as a foreword to *Ilios*.

It is nothing if not mythopoetic. It has also been so successful that the accepted image of Schliemann is just that which he projected. His contemporary letters show that much of this account is highly distorted.

Here we have another strange view of this remarkable man, and must even venture a repetition. Everything that he wrote about himself is likely to be inaccurate, and must be carefully checked. But in his archeological work he seems to have maintained the highest standards of honesty and accuracy. Even the Great Treasure, though found under hugger-mugger circumstances, has been accepted by subsequent archeologists.

Schliemann was always remarkable for energy and drive, and the ability to accomplish much in a short time. This quality had worked both for and against him in his archeology. Without it he could never have accomplished what he did, but he was always inclined to rush his work, and to appraise progress, as a businessman might, in terms of 120, 158, or 160 men at work, or the total of cubic yards of earth moved. He also, perhaps, rushed the preparation of his reports. Prompt publication is rated as a virtue among archeologists, but this is only because most of them are likely to be dilatory.

The excavations at Tiryns in the summer of 1884 mark a kind of penultimate point. Schliemann was sixty-two, old enough to become confirmed in his habit of autobiographical writing. So he devoted some of the first pages of the report to himself, with vivid and charming results.

First, he and Dörpfeld lived in a deserted farmhouse, but the accumulated dirt was too much for Schliemann. With a confirmed repugnance at being overcharged, he refused to pay the rent asked for the only good house available. He moved to a hotel at Nauplia, a few miles off.

From this point, let him tell his own story.

My habit was to rise at 3:45 A.M., swallow 4 grains of quinine as a preservative against fever, and then take a sea bath; a boatman, for 1 fr. daily, awaited me punctually at 4 o'clock, and took me from the quay to the open sea, where I swam for 5 or 10 minutes. I was obliged to climb into the boat again by the oar, but long practice had made this somewhat difficult operation easy and safe. After bathing, I drank in the coffee-house Agamemnon, *which was always open at that hour, a cup of black coffee without sugar, still to be had for the old sum of 10 Lepta (a penny) though everything had risen enormously in price. A good cob (at 6 frs. daily) stood ready, and took me easily in twenty-five minutes to Tiryns, where I always arrived before sunrise, and at once sent back the horse for Dr. Dörpfeld. Our breakfast was taken regularly at 8 A.M., during the first rest of the workmen, on the floor of the old palace at Tiryns. It consisted of Chicago corned beef, of which a plentiful supply was sent me by my honoured friends Messrs. J. H. Schröder & Co., from London, bread, fresh sheep-cheese, oranges, and white resined wine (rezinato), which, on account of its bitter [taste], agrees with quinine, and is more wholesome during heat and hard work than the stronger red wines. During the workmen's second rest, beginning at 12 and lasting at first an hour, in greater heat one hour and three-quarters,*

*we also rested, and two stones of the threshing-floor at the
south end of the Acropolis, where we afterwards found the
Byzantine Church, served us for pillows. One never rests so
well as when thoroughly tired with hard work, and I can assure
the reader, that we never enjoyed more refreshing sleep than
during this midday hour in the Acropolis of Tiryns, in spite
of the hard bed, and the scorching sun, against which we had
no other protection than our Indian hats laid flat upon our
faces.*

*Our third and last meal was at our return home in the
evening, in the restaurant of the hotel. As my London friends
had also supplied me with Liebig's Extract of Meat, we had
always excellent soup; this, with fish or mutton, fried in olive
oil, cheese, oranges, and resined wine, completed our menu.*

In this passage, the sexagenarian may protest a little too
much as to his own vigor, and in preparing the report on
Tiryns he worked as if he must get it done before something
happened. At Athens, he had the first part of the book ready
for the printer, and Dörpfeld, at Tiryns, was still moving dirt.
Excavations that were made in the middle of June were reported in a large, authoritative, and well-illustrated volume
which was published early in November. This probably sets
some kind of record.

But with that year something seems to go out of Schliemann. He had never been robust, and he had driven himself
as few men ever have. He had often been ill with malaria,
and with other unidentified fevers. A certain quite untypical
indecision began to affect him. He wanted to excavate at
Knossos in Crete, but could not get the arrangements made.
On one occasion he complained to Dörpfeld in a letter that
he could not possibly take up a certain piece of work, because

it was too much for him. But it was the sort of thing that he would have solved between luncheon and dinner a few years previously. In other words, he was suffering from a common complaint — the aging process.

He took to traveling again. Once more he went to the United States and Cuba. Twice he made an extensive voyage up the Nile, going in style, with his own chartered boat. Virchow went with him on one of these trips, and the boat, which carried a military guard, became involved in a local brawl. For a few minutes there was a lively discharge of rifles and a whistling of bullets. The two savants seem to have taken the matter calmly.

In 1887 he was definitely in ill health, though he dug a little on the island of Cythera. He made 1888 into what he called a vacation year, though he traveled around Greece to some extent, looking at possible places which would be worth excavating.

Archeological work had increased tremendously. He was the old-timer now.

But his long Trojan War was not quite over yet. Symbolically, it was right that he should return there, in these times when he was fading, year by year.

Something was not just right about the Trojan excavations. Some of the pieces of the puzzle had not yet fitted together. Literally, they were certain pieces of pottery.

Ever since the first excavations they had been turning up — unmistakable, different from anything else. There had never been, curiously, any city at Hissarlik to which they could be surely assigned. Yet there they were, not to be ignored!

They were from one of the upper strata, close below the Roman ruins. And was not that where the ruins of Priam's

Troy should lie? But Schliemann had placed it far below, in the Burnt City, where he had found the Great Treasure. And he had assigned these troublesome bits of pottery to a vague Lydian settlement.

But it had never been a situation about which one could be altogether comfortable. In a sense, also, Schliemann had refuted himself. Digging at Mycenae, he had found more of this unmistakable pottery. It had turned up in other places also, where he and others had excavated sites of what was coming to be known as the Mycenaean civilization.

This pottery had now even been given a name — Gray Minyan ware. What did it all mean? Why, if Agamemnon and his contemporaries used this ware, then the stratum containing it at Hissarlik must be the Troy that Agamemnon and his contemporaries had destroyed!

Dörpfeld and others could see the plain writing on the wall. Schliemann could hardly be expected to accept the conclusion until it was really forced upon him. To do so would be to cast down his own Great Treasure from its high place. No longer could those be the headdresses that had once framed the beauty of Helen of Troy. They would only be, as Emil Ludwig put it, "a gift from some nameless barbarian to his women."

There was another matter turning Schliemann's attention back to Troy. A certain nobody, Captain Ernst Bötticher, had never even been at Hissarlik, but was impudently declaring that Schliemann had found no cities there at all. No, it was all a fire-necropolis — whatever that may be! Bötticher was of the lunatic fringe. A secure scholar would have ignored him. But Schliemann was thin-skinned, and the attack worried him. So he decided to summon an international conference at Hissarlik with the attacker present. Thus everyone, including Bötticher, would see what was really there, and the upstart would be annihilated.

This was a good deal like ordering out the Imperial Guard to apprehend a pickpocket. But a conference of eight internationally known scholars at Hissarlik was not in itself a bad idea. Of course, Bötticher was annihilated, but he had never been anything in the beginning.

Then, in 1890, Schliemann and Dörpfeld started the digging again. They found what they knew already must be there — the ruins of the city that went with the Gray Minyan ware. The trouble had been that the Romans, when they built their own city, had scraped off these upper layers from most of the site. The Troy of Mycenaean times was left only around part of the edge.

Schliemann prepared scarcely more than a pamphlet on the excavations of 1890. It was in the nature of an interim report, and he could postpone definitive conclusions until the digging was finished. But he must have known. He could no longer hold to what was probably the most cherished of all his beliefs.

It was a time for reappraisal, a time to grow old, a time, as the poem goes, "to take in sail." The brave buccaneering days of twenty years past had gone forever. The specialists had taken over.

So they were not the adornments of Helen of Troy? Yes, but now, because of what he had dug up, the world was becoming convinced that Homer had written of a real siege. Few people, any longer, talked the nonsense of mythology, about the forces of darkness storming the battlements of light.

On another occasion he spoke, or in words to that effect, "Well, so it was not Agamemnon whose bones we found there at Mycenae! So it was somebody else." Then, and it must have been with a twinkle of the eye, he said, "Let us say that it was somebody named Schultze!" So, after that, when they talked of Mycenae, they referred to Schultze.

They stopped excavations in August. Back in Athens, Schliemann had trouble with his ears, which had been paining him for some time. In the fall he set out for Germany, to see other doctors. He went alone, as he generally did, though at his age and in his state of ill health, he might well have taken someone along to help with the mechanics of travel.

The romantic interpretation would be that Schliemann, the greatest illusion of his life now destroyed, had nowhere to go, and must escape before he finally faced the reality. This would be nonsense. By this time, Schliemann was a devoted scholar, and he knew that a scholar must face the truth, unpleasant though it be. He had already had to renounce many a cherished theory.

On November 13 he had an operation at Halle. It seemed to be successful. But after three weeks, his ears still pained him, and his doctor advised against traveling. Keeping up a good front, Schliemann wrote a letter, "To the wisest of all women, little Sophie." (In the Greek there would even be a tender little play on words, since Sophia means "wisdom.")

Early in December he felt better, and was off. It was his usual kind of mad traveling — to Leipzig, to Berlin, to Paris.

Then, perhaps, he felt some forewarning, and he had always been a man to rely on intuition. He started for Athens, to be home for Christmas. Still traveling by himself, he got to Naples. There he felt so ill that he dared not go aboard the ship, and be without a doctor. He wired to Athens to postpone the festivities. Probably he hoped to be home for his sixty-ninth birthday, January 6.

On Christmas day, walking to his doctor's office, he collapsed, unable to speak. But, even at the end, luck did not desert Heinrich Schliemann. That morning, he had been mentally alert and still possessed of some physical vigor. The very next day, he was dead. Praised be Pallas Athene!

INTER-CHAPTER II

THE INDIVIDUAL cannot, generally speaking, affect his own environment to a significant degree. Even if he attempts to escape from it, he merely escapes into some other one. Therefore, any life — good, bad, or indifferent — must be seen and judged against the background of environment.

William the Marshal does not exist without feudalism. To accept him we must also accept — at least, temporarily and dramatically — feudalism as a whole, including social inequality and a monolithic orthodoxy of religion.

Schliemann's integration was effected under the conditions of nineteenth-century capitalism. It surrounded him as water surrounds the trout, and he assumed it as the trout assumes buoyancy and dissolved oxygen.

The subject of the next sketch must be presented against the background of an environment differing from ours even more than do those of the Marshal and of Schliemann. To understand Joab, son of Zeruiah, we must enter imaginatively into the life of a primitive and aggressively warlike tribe. We must consider manslaughter as an everyday matter. We must accept the idea of the blood-feud.

So, when Joab killed the killer of his brother, he struck — to adapt Brutus's words — as a sacrificer, not as a butcher. Against such a background we are forced to consider the possibility of his having lived the good life.

But not only because of difference in environment does the telling of Joab's life history present a challenge. Though he lived in a literate age, he lived three thousand years ago, and little has been preserved about him. We know only a small number of incidents included in those highly condensed records, the books of *Samuel*, *Kings*, and *Chronicles*, together with one mention in *Psalms*.

Moreover, with Joab, his enemies wrote the story. At least once, we can even maintain, his very name has been dropped from the text, and fails to stand where we have every reason to think that it formerly did.

Fossilly speaking, all we have left of Joab is a broken shinbone and half a jaw. At least, there is a challenge in trying to reconstruct the whole from the fragments. There is a pleasure, also, in trying to pierce through the propaganda. Finally, there is always a satisfaction in trying to set the crooked straight, and to do justice to a slandered man.

JOAB
BEN-ZERUIAH

WHEN A SMALL BOY called David was growing up at Bethlehem-of-Judah, there was a still smaller boy called Joab. This Joab's mother was Zeruiah, a daughter of Jesse, and Jesse himself, as the accounts in *Samuel* make clear, was an important person in Bethlehem.

Joab had two brothers whose names are known, and there may have been others less notable whose names have gone unrecorded — to say nothing of sisters. Of the three, Abishai was apparently the oldest, with Joab next, and Asahel the youngest. They were a lion's brood!

What is curious, even lending a touch of mystery, is that they are regularly named as "the sons of Zeruiah." In a strongly patriarchal society, they thus are identified by the maternal line. In this, they seem to be unique in Israelitic history. Hundreds are identified as sons of a father, but only these three as sons of a mother, without even mention of the father's name.

It touches the imagination. Was Zeruiah a woman of such exceptional qualities that her sons thus were known? If so, we could expect to be told something about her, and we never are. Did the sons thus try to claim kinship with the royal family? But in the comparable instance of Amasa, the father's name is given. Did Zeruiah consort with many men, so that the father of a particular child was uncertain? But the close resemblance of the three brothers suggests a single father. Besides, for Asahel, the father is mentioned, even if not named. Moreover, he was a man of respectability, and a Bethlehemite, for he had a family tomb there.

We may, at least, assume that the father died young. The Philistine wars and the recurrent pestilences would see to that. If the three brothers were reared by a widowed mother, they might the more easily have been identified by her name. In the end, we can only say that we are sure of nothing, except the fact itself.

As for the name, Joab tells us nothing. It means "Jah is father," and Jah was the tribal god, known as Jehovah in the King James Bible. But Joab was a common name, and probably no one was much concerned with its literal meaning, any more than we today think about the literal meanings of William or Charles.

This sketch began with reference to a small boy, David. As a rule, one should name one's chief character first. But the present case admits exception. David is almost as important in the life of Joab as is Joab himself. Without David there would have been no Joab, but we may also say, "Without Joab, there would have been no David." Traditionally the association is David and Jonathan, but that friendship — of whatever kind it may have been — ceased when David was still an unimportant and young man. The association with Joab, however, continued throughout David's days of greatness until his death. To describe it, one has to search for a biological word, such as commensalism or symbiosis.

David was a son of Jesse, and he therefore was Zeruiah's brother and Joab's uncle. We think of an uncle as being a generation older than his nephew, but it need not be so. The patriarchal Jesse had fathered many children over a considerable period of years, and Zeruiah may have been fifteen or even twenty years older than David, who was her youngest brother.

As to the relative ages of David and Joab we have only general probability, with their life stories as evidence. If we think of David as being the senior by five years, we have a situation that is reasonable in the light of all that is known about the two men.

Even with so small an age gap, they would not have been intimate as boys. But, as boys of the same village and members of the same family, they must have known each other. If one were writing a historical novel, one would declare that David was the recipient of the younger lad's hero-worship. In fact, the likelihood is so great that one is almost ready to make the statement in a work of non-fiction. For, throughout all his youthful years, David inspired hero-worship as naturally as he breathed. His charisma was like a shining light. As few men have, he possessed "the power," that strange force that makes men turn and follow.

Even one theory of the name David is that it means "darling." It is borne by no other person in the Bible, and it may, in fact, be a descriptive by-name rather than a true name. If so, it describes fully — the universal darling. Ruddy of countenance (whatever that may mean), beautiful to look upon, the singer, the dancer, the player on the harp, the poet, skilled at arms, courageous, the anointed (they said) of the Lord! So people were drawn toward him. But more than all, he swayed them by that ineffable and probably unconscious charm, so that even a chance-uttered wish sent strong men to risk their lives for the gratification of his whim.

Now Joab, whatever he may have been, was nothing of this. Good qualities he had, and some of these outlasted the more brilliant ones of David. But he was not a man of "the power."

And no one said, or ever would have said, that he was the Lord's anointed. . . .

Bethlehem, when the two boys were growing up, was what can be described as a large village of the early Iron Age. Archeology helps to reconstruct its life, and *Samuel* helps even more. The Bethlehemites were of the tribe of Judah. In a vaguer way they considered themselves to be Israelites, because Judah was one of the twelve tribes of Israel, which formed a loose alliance and did not always avoid inter-tribal wars.

The Bethlehemites lived, chiefly of themselves and by themselves, on the products of their fields and hill pastures. In the fields, they raised wheat and barley, along with beans, lentils, and a few other minor crops. On the nearer hill slopes they tended olive trees for oil, and vines for grapes and for making wine and raisins. They raised some figs and pomegranates.

Equally as important in the economy were the flocks. They ranged on the hills, and over the stubble fields, after the grain harvest. The sheep supplied meat and wool, and the ewes could be milked. Goats, however, supplied most of the milk, and cheese was an important foodstuff.

The villagers kept a few cattle, and used them for plowing and for hauling. An occasional "fatted calf" served for food at a banquet.

The only dogs were pariahs and scavengers. Apparently, they were not even trained to help with the sheep. They may have been useful, by their barking, to warn against marauders by night, but their chief value seems to have been to supply base comparisons: "Is thy servant a dog?" or "As a dog returneth to his vomit."

There were no horses, and the Israelites had not, as yet, learned the use of war chariots. The men of Bethlehem knew about camels, but had no special need of them. The useful and long-domesticated ass served as a beast of burden, and was even ridden, though chiefly by old men and by women.

Swine were taboo. Besides, the dry hillsides of Judah were not a country for pigs. Cats had not yet been brought from Egypt, or hens from India.

The land had been long settled, and wild game had ceased to be abundant. The villagers, probably not yet tied strictly to the Mosaic Law, may have enjoyed an occasional hare or rabbit. Now and then someone might have the luck to put an arrow into a roebuck or wild goat. But, as with the dog, the game seems to have been chiefly useful in the service of language — to live "on the rocks of the wild goats," to be "as light of foot as a wild roe," to pursue "as when one doth hunt a partridge in the mountains."

The villagers wore clothing made from the wool of their own sheep. They may have raised a little flax, or may have depended upon trading to get "fine linen" garments. They lived, comfortably enough and with little thought of sanitation, in mud houses.

It sounds like idyllic primitivism. So, indeed, the later Hebrew writers pictured their ancestors in *Judges*, as living peaceably and peacefully until disturbed by cruel and wicked invaders — Midianites, Amalekites, Moabites, Ammonites, Edomites, or Philistines. In truth, the Israelites were invaders themselves and just as warlike as anyone else. They were hill people, and the testimony of history is that hill people are troublesome neighbors, and raid the lowlands at every opportunity. After a while, the cities of the lowlands send out a punitive expedition, and so it goes.

Like hill people generally, the Israelites must have relied upon quickness of movement — upon the ambush and the sudden rush to bring them to close quarters, and then upon individual prowess with spear and sword.

They knew the bow, but were not, as a people, proficient archers. They preferred the sling, a much less effective weapon in pitched battles, but a cheaper one, being made of a few leather thongs, and using for missiles the pebbles that could be picked up in any stream bed. Arrows required iron arrowheads, and iron was a problem.

The Israelites as yet had no smiths, and so iron weapons had to be bought from the outside. Much of the surplus of the flocks and herds had to go for these purchases. Of course, any well-conducted raid might yield its spoil.

Another great help in the warfare was the tribal god, Jah, or Jahweh, or however the name should be rendered. This god — or, at least, the priests' teaching of him — encouraged the men of Judah to go out and smite their enemies in good conscience. But the men of Judah also worshipped other gods occasionally, probably feeling that it was a good idea to have a foot in more than one camp.

A boy in Bethlehem, once he had reached seven or eight and begun to escape from the womenfolk, was sent out to herd sheep — at first, small flocks close to the village, and then larger flocks and farther away. He soon learned to use the sling.

Actually, there must have been little occasion for defense. If robbers or Philistines came, the best the boy could do was to run to the village with the alarm. Folk tales of lions and bears floated about, and of the shepherd-boy who had valiantly killed such beasts. But by the time of David and Joab only an occasional lion can have wandered in from the wilderness, and Judah would never have been much of a land for bears. Indeed, the chief use of the sling would have been to throw a stone on the far side of a wandering sheep, and thus urge it back to the flock.

Only five miles north of the village stood Jerusalem, the impregnable hold of the Jebusites, set upon its hill. The pasture lands of Jerusalem and Bethlehem must have impinged. There was no particular quarrel between Jebusites and Judahites. The men of Bethlehem would sometimes have gone to Jerusalem for trade or negotiation.

All during their boyhood David and Joab would have heard "Philistine!" as a name of execration and terror. The Philistines lived in the plains country off to the west. They are an unfortunate people, in that they are known only from the records of their enemies. If we had the histories of the Philistines we should find that they, a peaceful folk, were constantly raided and driven to distraction by the fierce warriors of Israel, who descended from the hills. Then the Philistines were forced to retaliate. Such retaliation, politically, is always a tricky matter. Pressure from the outside may force the hill tribes to forget their local animosities and their blood-feuds, and so to unite.

This is what happened. A war-leader named Saul arose in the tribe of Benjamin, and other tribes united behind his leadership. Saul began to use the title king.

All that Saul could do was to drive the Philistines back. Their war chariots still dominated the plains, and their walled cities remained safe. During a dozen years the fighting ebbed and flowed, with raid and counter-raid. These were the years when Joab was still a boy, and David was becoming a man.

That David ever went off to the army and killed Goliath with a sling-stone is now doubted by most scholars. But it is exactly the right kind of story to be told about him. In any case, when he was about eighteen, David went to join Saul, and, we may say, to make his fortune. But this is not David's story.

Joab remained in Bethlehem with his mother Zeruiah and his brothers Abishai and Asahel. The three were all growing up, and they must already have been making something of a name for themselves in the village for their courage and prowess. Though they watched sheep and worked in the fields like other village boys, anybody would have predicted that they were going to become good warriors. Abishai, one would guess, was the biggest and strongest, but perhaps a little slow-witted. Joab was strong and skillful also, and had a vein of shrewdness and a strong sense of responsibility. Asahel was famous as a fast runner.

Word kept coming back about David, the village boy who was doing so well. He had become such a great warrior that people had made a song about him. He was a favorite of the king, and ate at the king's own table. He had become the bosom friend of Saul's son Jonathan, himself a great warrior. Finally, word even came that David had married one of the king's daughters.

Now and then, since the land was small, David must have come back to Bethlehem. The successful village boy likes to show himself off at home. And there he was, with all his charm! He was gracious, we can be sure. He called old friends by name, and reminded them of bygone incidents. The three sons of Zeruiah must have worshipped.

But, at last, word came that David was out of favor, and to be out of favor at the court of such a king as Saul means that life is at hazard.

Then, one day, David was in Bethlehem again, a few men with him. He was an outlaw, flying for his life. He was off to find refuge in the southern hills.

In Bethlehem he had quick work to do. He could not

leave the members of his family to be held as hostages, or merely to be killed to satisfy Saul's anger. So he sent his old father and mother to Moab. Most likely, also, David's brothers and sisters and their families fled with him into the hills.

At this time Abishai and Joab were in their late teens — active, courageous, skilled with their weapons, perhaps already seasoned by a raid or two against the Philistines. They would have been natural recruits for David's following.

David drew to himself a hard-bitten band of exiles, and they made their haunt in the rugged cave-shotten southern hills, "upon the rocks of the wild goats." And Saul, forgetting the Philistines, went to hunt David, "as when one doth hunt a partridge in the mountains."

In later times the village storytellers had their repertoire of tall tales about David's exploits as an outlaw in the wilderness. But some of them must be true. No one attains David's reputation as a result of pure fiction.

One of these tales might be called "David spares Saul," and it exists in two versions. In one of these, Abishai says a key speech. In the other, it is said by "the men of David" collectively. There is a possibility that Joab originally said the words, and that his name was later deleted purposively. At least, the words are suitable to Joab.

At that time Saul, with an overwhelming force of three thousand men, was hunting David. Saul came to the entrance of a cave, and being, it would seem, a modest man, he went in "to cover his feet." Now this phrase is a euphemism, meaning (by another euphemism) "to ease oneself."

Then, we may think, Saul took his cloak off, as a man generally does at such a time, and laid it upon a nearby rock. He then assumed that position in which (as even our modern manner of speech suggests) a man is most easily taken by surprise. It happened also that David and his men were actually hidden in the deeper recesses of the cave. They crept stealthily forward, and saw Saul thus helpless and exposed to attack.

And the men of David [or Joab, it might well have been]
said unto him, "Behold the day of which the Lord said unto
thee, 'Behold, I will deliver thine enemy into thine hand, that
thou mayest do to him as it shall seem good unto thee.'"

That was certainly, throughout his life, the way in which Joab approached a problem.

But David had the true touch. Instead of killing Saul, he quietly cut off a piece of the cloak, and stole out of the cave (perhaps by another exit), leaving the king to concentrate upon his present problem. David thus, piously, refused to raise his hand against "the Lord's anointed," and he also, prudently, kept free of a blood-feud with Saul's sons.

Then, once out of the cave, he called to Saul. The king (we are to imagine him as still squatting) turned around. Then David showed him the bit of cloth, and protested his loyalty — and everything was very magnificent and David-like.

At that gesture, Joab and those other simple outlaws, who had been all for the swift spear-thrust, knew David's greatness, and worshipped him the more — and so there was a folk tale of it, and there were many others of David.

During these half dozen years, Abishai receives one mention in the narrative; Joab, none at all. This need not surprise us, knowing that there was, in later years, a kind of conspiracy of silence against him. In fact, Joab is not even included in either of the lists of the *gibborim*, David's "mighty men."

As the story goes, David collected a band of six hundred men in the wilderness. Of these, thirty-three attained special rank. Of these thirty-three, three were set off as chief of all.

A list of the *gibborim* is given in *Samuel*, and a considerably differing list in *Chronicles*. Abishai was included in both, as one of the highest ranking of the thirty, but not one of the three. Joab is not mentioned. This omission might suggest that Joab was notable as a general rather than as a warrior. Surely, however, no such distinction could well have been made at that time. Moreover, Joab's armor-bearer is included in both lists, though he himself is not. In the *Chronicles* list another curious feature is that only two names are given under the heading of the first three. The obvious implication is that the name of Joab was at some time deleted from the list which came down to the writer of *Chronicles*. In the list in *Samuel*, the name of an otherwise unknown Shammah stands where Joab's name might be expected.

During several years when David was an outlaw chief, Joab was still young. He may only have come to the front gradually. But, from the high position that he holds shortly afterward, we may assume that he gained experience in the wilderness and in the year and four months that David spent among the Philistines. Presumably Joab shared in the smiting of the Amalekites, and he is not likely to have been one of the two hundred who "were so faint that they could not go over the brook Besor."

Then King Saul rashly met the Philistines in a pitched battle, and the chariots broke the host of Israel. In the rout that followed, Saul and three of his sons were killed.

This disaster shattered the newly formed kingdom of the Israelites, and almost destroyed the freedom of the people. The Philistines, however, had little sense of establishing an empire. They withdrew to their cities, content to collect tribute.

Having spent some years as an outlaw chieftain, having been forced to sell his sword to the Philistines, David had, at last, his opportunity. In the confusion following the great defeat, he moved quickly, and established himself as king of his own tribe of Judah, fixing his seat of government at He-bron. He was then thirty years old. At Hebron he established a court, of sorts. He also established a harem, running the total of his wives up to at least six.

Probably David was paying tribute to the Philistines, for there are no stories of Philistine battles. The outlaw band, always given as numbering six hundred, remained as the nu-cleus of an army, or as a king's guard. Joab, about twenty-five years of age, was one of its captains — possibly, the chief captain. Then came the affair at Gibeon.

Exactly what happened is obscured by epic legend and faulty text. But the important facts are clear enough.

Abner, who under Saul had been Captain of the Host, had rallied the Israelites after the disaster, and had gathered some remnants together, with Ish-bosheth, a younger son of Saul, as a puppet king, living in the far-off lands of the trans-Jordan at the city of Mahanaim. The Northern tribes acknowledged Ish-bosheth's rule (or Abner's rule), but they were flat on their faces before the Philistines. There was thus a northern kingdom, ruled from Mahanaim, and a Southern kingdom, ruled from Hebron — and both of them, more or less, under Philistine domination. Under the circumstances, we must consider it a tribute to the native vigor of the Israelites that they still could fight with each other.

The ancient and holy city of Gibeon was a border town, lying a few miles inside the Northern kingdom. Not long after David had settled at Hebron, Joab led a detachment of the army north to Gibeon. Though the men were fully armed, the mission was ostensibly a peaceful one. They perhaps went to sacrifice at the ancient shrine, or to enter into some negotiations. Abner himself came to meet them there, also with an armed detachment. The meeting was peaceful, but one might as well have thrown tow into the fire and have expected not to start a conflagration as to have hoped for peace that day. These were men of war. They had been idle lately, and they were spoiling for a fight.

There was a pool of water at Gibeon, and the men of Judah sat down on one side of it, and on the other side sat the men of Ephraim and Benjamin and the other Northern tribes. Being soldiers, it is to be assumed, they surreptitiously and against orders made insulting gestures. The Northerners implied that the Southerners were sons of dogs and sheep-stealers. The Southerners replied that the Northerners were sons of dogs and had run away at the last battle.

Then Abner himself, perhaps to relieve the tension, proposed an exhibition. Twelve men should be chosen from each side and they should give a display of swordsmanship.

As might have been expected (and it perhaps *was* expected) the twenty-four champions turned this into a real and bloody contest. Then everyone on both sides charged into the fray, "And there was very sore battle that day; and Abner was beaten, and the men of Israel, before the servants of David."

The general rule of such a battle is that, as long as you keep your front, you suffer few casualties, but that you suffer bloodily, once you have broken. The men of Judah pursued the Northerners, slaughtering as they went. The three sons of Zeruiah were all there pursuing with the others. Young Asahel, "light of foot as a wild roe," pressed upon Abner himself.

Then Abner looked behind him, and said, "Art thou Asahel?" And he answered, "I am." And Abner said to him, "Turn thee aside to thy right hand, or to thy left, and lay thee hold on one of the young men, and take thee his armor."

But Asahel would not turn, and Abner again warned him, "Turn thee aside from following me: wherefore should I smite thee to the ground? How then should I hold up my face to Joab thy brother?"

Now, Abner was a veteran warrior and was not afraid of the youth who was pressing him. What he did not want was a blood-feud, with the redoubtable Joab.

But Asahel gave him no chance. Then, suddenly and craftily, Abner struck backwards, driving the spike of his spear-butt clear through Asahel's body.

Joab and Abishai pushed the pursuit until sunset, and then called their men back. "And they took up Asahel and buried him in the sepulchre of his father, which was in Bethlehem."

After this outbreak there was "long war" between South and North. The Philistines watched complacently. And, as half a dozen years passed, Joab and Abishai remembered the death of their brother, and cherished a blood-feud. They could no other. It was a matter of honor and conscience.

The idea of the blood revenge is not only ancient among us but comes closer to most of us than we commonly remember. It lingered in the Scottish highlands until the clans were finally broken at Culloden. Backwoods and western Americans acted upon it clear down into the nineteenth century.

But to find an opportunity against the general of the opposing forces is not easy. In those years, Joab and Abishai must have felt the unspoken reproach that they were men who had not kept their honor unsmirched.

"But David waxed stronger and stronger, and the house of Saul waxed weaker and weaker." At last Abner came to Hebron to negotiate, offering allegiance to David. Joab, and probably Abishai with him, were away on an expedition. Doubtless David and Abner had planned it in that way, to avoid trouble.

Abner started back north, and Joab returned, almost immediately. He was hot with anger when he learned of Abner, and he stormed in before the face of the king himself. It shows how little the name of king meant, then, in Judah, that a captain could thus speak, "What hast thou done? Behold, Abner came unto thee; why is it that thou hast sent him away, and he is quite gone?"

Joab then accused Abner of treachery. More likely, Abner had come in good faith, but the question was not to be an important one.

Unknown to David, Joab sent messengers to Abner, to return. In his evil hour, Abner did so. Then Joab "smote him there, under the fifth rib, that he died, for the blood of Asahel."

Later redactors, always unfavorable to Joab, emphasized his treachery and deceit in the matter. It makes, perhaps, little difference. Once Abner had returned, and found himself in the power of Joab and Abishai, he would have known that his head was in the trap, and that he was a dead man.

David, the good politician, with an eye toward Northern sentiment, disowned the murder, gave Abner an honorable burial, and fasted. He also is reported as saying, "I am this day weak, though anointed king: and these men the sons of Zeruiah be too hard for me."

Personally, I do not believe that he said any such thing — at least, not at that time. The words sound like those of the querulous old man, such as David came to be, some thirty years later. But the words do not sound like the strong young king of Hebron. If we accept them, we must suppose that David was already a *roi fainéant,* and that Joab and Abishai were the real founders of the kingdom of Israel. But this seems too much to suppose, even if we assume a concentrated attempt under Solomon to exalt David and degrade Joab.

Such an attempt could hardly have succeeded unless David had been already established as a folk hero. So it seems more reasonable to assume that this particular passage was at some time invented, or perhaps shifted from a later to an earlier date. Though the general thesis of this account is that Joab has been decried, this does not mean that we should attempt to reverse all history.

In any case, that night after killing Abner, Joab must have slept the peaceful sleep of a man who has at last been able to do the right thing, even though he has risked the king's displeasure in doing it.

We should not underestimate King David at this time in his career, even though he was beginning to pay rather too much attention to that harem. His policy of waiting it out was a shrewd one. With Abner gone, the Northern tribes had only a puppet king, and before long, he was murdered.

The assassins brought the head to David at Hebron. He, with infallible instinct, acted in just the proper way, having the murderers executed, and the head given burial. So the Northern tribes, having nowhere else to go, and recognizing David's greatness, came in with their homage. After seven and a half years as king of Judah, David was now king of all Israel. The Philistines must have begun to view the situation with alarm.

Immediately, showing once more his political genius, David moved against Jerusalem.

The continuing existence of this Jebusite stronghold in the very heart of Israelite country was an anomaly. (According to one tradition, the men of Judah had captured Jerusalem once, a couple of centuries before. If so, they had later lost it.) The Jebusites, one of the old Canaanitish tribes, held what seemed to be an impregnable fortress on a ridge. The ravines fell away steeply on all sides except the north. The city could have been starved out, but the disunited Israelites, with all their quarreling among themselves, were not capable of such a long-continuing blockade. The Jebusites had insured their water supply by tunneling into their hill from the spring that lay at its base. The water then flowed inward, until it came to a pool at the bottom of a fifty-foot shaft. From the top of this shaft, inside their walls, the Jebusite women drew up the water. Similar tunnels existed in other cities. This tunnel and shaft represented a tremendous amount of labor, but it was a good investment, and it paid off by insuring the city against capture for many years. (Modern archeologists have explored and plotted this water system.)

The Jebusites had become confident, or overconfident. They boasted that even the blind and the lame could defend their fortress. Overconfidence has delivered many a city to the spoiler.

David wanted Jerusalem, because it would give him a capital, on the border of North and South, captured from the enemy, and therefore neutral. Besides, the capture would be a great exploit, and it would be a joint exploit of Northern and Southern tribesmen.

Possibly from the beginning he had his plan of operations. Both he and Joab had grown up at Bethlehem, only a few miles away. As reckless boys, they may have done a little exploring, or they may merely have picked up the gossip about the tunnel and the shaft that pierced the rock. As to discovering exactly what happened, we are plagued by brevity of text, and by its corruption — and, probably, by prejudice. The account in *Samuel*, as might be expected, gives no credit to Joab, but mentions the "gutter," or "water course," as figuring in the capture. The account in *Chronicles* is reduced to epic simplicity: "And David said, Whosoever smiteth the

Jebusites first shall be chief and captain. So Joab, the son of Zeruiah, went up first and was chief."

Judgments differ as to just what happened. I myself choose the most spectacular of the possibilities, for the simple reason that an impregnable fortress is not captured except by a spectacular exploit.

The hills were brown in late summer, the dry season. The time had been selected carefully. Usually the water stood so high in one part of the tunnel that no one could pass through, and the Jebusites thus considered that the tunnel offered no threat. Besides, the vertical shaft at its end was fifty feet deep.

It is all hypotheses. So now let us drop "probably" and "possibly," and tell a story.

One evening at dusk, maintaining secrecy until the last moment, Joab gathered a dozen of the *gibborim*, including his ever-staunch brother Abishai. The men left their shields and spears, and heavy armor. They kept daggers and short swords. Joab himself carried a fifty-foot rope.

The spring and the entrance to the tunnel were outside the walls, at the base of a steep natural slope. Under cover of darkness, Joab led his men, stealthily, up the hill, and entered the tunnel. He followed its sinuous course, in utter darkness, foot by foot, feeling his way. The spring-cold water was waist-deep, deeper in places, so that a man could scarcely get his head out far enough to breathe.

Still in black darkness, Joab came to the opposing wall, and knew that he had reached the shaft. The men behind him blundered to a halt, keeping their heads above water. Joab listened a moment, to see whether any sentry above had taken the alarm. He felt around for a dangling rope, for there was the chance that some woman might have let a vessel down and not withdrawn it.

The shaft was roughly cut, with projecting knobs of rock on either side, narrow enough for a man to reach across it, and for a bold and active man to ascend.

Feeling his way, Joab began the climb. Fragments of dislodged rock fell into the water below, with alarming noises, but by now there seemed no possibility that a sentry was stationed above.

Joab reached the top, exhausted and panting. But he wasted no time. In the darkness he attached one end of his rope and dropped the other into the shaft. One by one, his men ascended.

Meanwhile David had mustered the remaining *gibborim*, and silently stationed them as close as possible to the north gate.

When his men had assembled, Joab led them, still quietly, along the easy upper passageway. They came out into the city, where the starlight, by comparison with the tunnels, seemed almost like the brightness of day.

Still silently, trying to seem merely some Jebusite patrol, they made their way a short distance to the north gate, fell upon the sleeping guards, slaughtered them, and threw the gate open to David's men, now rushing up from the outside. Too late, the roar of the alarm roused the sleeping Jebusites.

The custom was that the man who captured a city bestowed his name upon it, and so the Jebusite section of Jerusalem was known as the City of David. There must have been some that said that it should have been the City of Joab. But David had been the commander, and so one cannot take great exception.

Joab had already, probably, been the Captain of the Host for the Kingdom of Judah, while David was in Hebron. He now held the same high post for the whole kingdom of Israel. As such he was the chief field-commander of the army, and was commander-in-chief on the occasions, which became more numerous, when David himself remained in Jerusalem.

The next great concern was that of the old enemy, the Philistines, who now went to war. Doubtless the Israelites, in their new-felt strength, refused tribute. David — or, we might say, David and Joab — once and for all broke the Philistine power, in two great battles.

Perhaps the victories were the result of unity, patriotic enthusiasm, and good leadership. But there may also have been some shift in the method of warfare, some tactics to counter the devastating charge of the war chariots. One passage in *Samuel*, though the text is disputed, is generally taken to mean that David emphasized the use of the bow. By abandoning the inefficient sling, and massing the archers, the Israelites could have stopped the war chariots as effectively as the English longbowmen stopped the French knights at Crécy.

After the great victories there seems to have been some military reorganization. A royal bodyguard of Philistine mercenaries was enlisted, and the command of it was given to Benaiah, one of the thirty, a Judahite, who had probably been with David during the outlaw years. Since Benaiah was responsible to the king only, Joab had no command over the guard. The situation was common enough, but it cannot have worked for good feeling between Joab and Benaiah.

The old six hundred, including the *gibborim*, probably remained as the nucleus of a new army, particularly of the tribe of Judah. They thus were under Joab's command, and this body may have been meant when the term "Joab's men" is used on one occasion.

Most of the army consisted merely of the tribal militia. Every man was still a warrior. When the rains ceased in May and the time came "when kings go forth to battle," the boys and the graybeards were left to keep the sheep, and the men of the twelve tribes mustered under Joab. In their new strength the turbulent Israelites struck out in one direction after another.

To the southeast lay Moab. Relations with the Moabites had often been good, and David had sent his mother and father there for shelter, when he was escaping from Saul. But now the Moabites were conquered and put to tribute. If the text is to be trusted, David was by no means the gentle psalmist in dealing with Moab, but commanded two men out of three to be put to death.

To the north David warred with the Syrians, though tradition may somewhat exaggerate his conquests there. Still farther to the south, beyond Moab, David put garrisons in Edom, "and all they of Edom became David's servants."

David, as became a king, commanded his own army in these wars. Joab acted as a chief-of-staff or executive officer. These wars filled about ten years after the capture of Jerusalem, and at the end of that time, David was scarcely longer to be called young. He was approaching fifty. Moreover, he was growing soft with good living, during the winters, in his fine new palace in Jerusalem, and he was appreciating the comforts of his ever-growing harem. Who can find heart to blame him greatly? He had started young, and he now had behind him thirty years of living among the rocks like a wild goat, and being hunted in the mountains like a partridge, and of going forth to battle at the time when a king should.

Joab was a little younger, and a great deal tougher. Moreover, he was a unified man. It would not, however, be right to call him merely a soldier. On several occasions, he acted as a statesman. He is a man who seems to grow.

The record indicates that he was married; in fact, as Captain of the Host, his dignity would have required him to have more than one wife, and perhaps a concubine or two besides. Since a curse leveled against him includes his family as well, he probably had children. But we are not given a name for Joab's wife, or wives, or for any of his children.

Things being as they were, we are not surprised to find David, after a while, staying home, and letting Joab take the army into the field. The next foemen were the Ammonites, who lived to the east.

The *casus belli*, as *Samuel* records it, was that the Ammonites had wantonly insulted some of David's ambassadors. The Ammonites themselves would have told a different story, but that is to be expected. War was the rule of the day. Generally speaking, one needed a *casus pacis* rather than the other way around. From Dan to Beersheba, the men of twelve tribes mustered again, this time under Joab. He led them across the Jordan, and toward Rabbah, the chief city of Ammon.

The Ammonites had brought some Syrians in for their allies, and they threatened attack from two directions. Not daunted, Joab split his army. He gave Abishai part of it, and sent him to hold the Ammonites off. He himself attacked the Syrians, and routed them. Then the Ammonites fled into the city.

The Syrians were back in the next year, and David himself marched out against them this time. He won a great victory, and the Syrians sued for peace, leaving the Ammonites isolated. (It was David's last active campaign.)

In the third year, David sent Joab again. He drove the Ammonites inside their city, and laid siege to it.

As far as the events of this summer are involved, *Samuel* is chiefly concerned, not with the siege, but with David and the beautiful Bathsheba, and her husband, the conscientious Uriah.

From Joab's point of view the story is this. . . . One day, while the siege was continuing, Joab received a message from the king. One of Joab's captains was a certain Uriah, called "the Hittite," though he had married an Israelite woman, and had adopted the Israelite religion, which he followed with all the scrupulosity that may be expected of a convert. The king's message was an order to send Uriah to Jerusalem. A reason may or may not have been given. Kings do not have to give reasons.

Joab obeyed the order, sent Uriah, and continued besieging the Ammonites.

After a short time Uriah returned, bearing a sealed letter to Joab from the king. (The context implies that both David and Joab could read and write, but they may actually have been using confidential scribes.)

The letter gave succinct orders: to put Uriah in the front of the hottest battle, and then to retire from him, "that he may be smitten, and die."

Joab can only have comprehended the orders with a sense of profound shock. He was being forced into a thoroughly unsoldierly action. He was required, as a general, to sacrifice a trusted and conscientious officer. To do so would mean other needless casualties. If rumor of such doings ever got around, the whole morale of the army would be shaken.

Still, the orders were direct from the king. Joab could only assume that Uriah was mixed up in some treasonable plot, and (for some inexplicable reason) had to be quietly removed. Did Joab even know that Uriah had a seductive and unfaithful and ambitious wife?

The matter was arranged.

Later in the summer Rabbah was about to fall, and Joab sent hasty word to the king. He should come and be present at the fall of the city, so that the Captain of the Host should not have the triumph — "Lest I take the city, and it be called after my name." Thus wrote the loyal subject, and the general who did not want to get involved in civil affairs.

So David came, and the city fell, and what was done to the children of Ammon by David's orders does not make for pleasant reading.

The wars were over. One might say that they had burned themselves out. Except for the Phoenician cities on the northwest (and they were closely allied and largely Israelite themselves), every neighboring tribe and city and nation had felt the heavy hand of the newly united kingdom. The only thing left to do would be to mount a major expedition against farther Syria, or against Egypt. But such a campaign was rather beyond the resources available. Besides, King David was no longer looking for worlds to conquer. He was a man upon whom middle age sat heavily, though he still knew what the grand manner was, and even when he sinned (as in the Bathsheba-Uriah incident) he sinned magnificently. But he cherished no dream of world-conquest.

Why should he, at that age? Was not life pleasant enough as it was? Had he not united his people, delivered them from their oppressors, and enabled them to do a little oppressing on their own part? Surely we may allow him to relax now, and to enjoy his wives, and to look fondly, even dotingly, on his handsome sons, who have grown up around him — Amnon, Absalom, Adonijah, and the others. Besides, his new and favorite wife, Bathsheba, is heavy for the second time, and the baby is going to be named Solomon.

With Joab, the situation was somewhat different. At forty-five he was, as far as we can tell, still as active as ever, hardened by constant warfare. Would he not have welcomed a command to march to the Euphrates or the Nile?

At this time, we may guess, the situations of the two men

began to shift. David is still anointed king, and the charm is still there. Joab, whom no priest would ever think of anointing, is still David's man, and his loyalty does not waver.

But does David still have "the power"? Can he still perform those magnificent gestures — beyond all call of duty or use — that suddenly bind men to him? Now the one who looks to the future and seems to think of the good of the kingdom is the nephew Joab — no longer merely the *gibbor*, now becoming something more even than Captain of the Host.

During the years of the wars, the excitement of campaigning and the satisfactions of loot had silenced dissenting voices throughout the tribes. With peace came the natural divergence of opinion. On the one side were the Strong-Kingdom men. They wanted centralization of government — in the name, of course, of national security. They wanted a Jerusalem adorned with palaces and a temple. Probably they wanted a standing army, with a considerable expansion of the Philistine guard under Benaiah's command. To attain all this, the Strong-Kingdom men wanted taxes (to be paid in kind), and levies of workmen to be sent in from the villages to labor in the capital. The Strong-Kingdom men were powerful at court and in Jerusalem.

But up to this time the Israelites had been essentially free men, conducting their own affairs by villages and tribes, with a fair amount of what we may call democratic action. So, as against the Strong-Kingdom men, we may set others and call them the Tribal men. Comprising, one would suppose, the great majority of the people, these Tribal men were essentially conservative. Among them would have been many priests, and one of them was Abiathar, the chief priest.

It was the recurrent struggle, not yet abated: collective security versus freedom of the individual, the state versus the citizen.

The king, almost inevitably, was a Strong-Kingdom man. But a king who was politically in touch would realize that the situation should not be pushed. Joab, whether by nature or by being closer to the tribesmen, saw the dangers.

A crisis arose with the decision to take a census. The king commanded Joab, as Captain of the Host, to superintend the work. In reply, Joab entered what we may call a formal protest, and it so well expressed the point of view of the Tribal men that it has been preserved, although so much about Joab was suppressed.

Now the Lord thy God add unto the people, how many soever they be, a hundredfold, and that the eyes of my lord the king may see it: But why doth my lord the king delight in this thing?

Joab may have feared real trouble. The situation has curious and almost humorous modern analogies. Some second-sighted seventh son of a seventh son in the wilderness of Judah or the hill country of Zebulon might well have had a vision far into the future, and seen income tax, universal fingerprinting, and punch cards.

So Joab took the census, as he had performed other unpleasant duties. There was no actual revolt, but unrest may have been stored up for future use.

As *Samuel* tells the story, the Lord Himself was angry, and rebuked the king through the Prophet Gad. He also, with His sometimes curious sense of justice, to punish the king, set a pestilence upon the people!

David, who could still be a great-hearted man, prayed that the punishment should not be upon the people but upon him. So, in the end, as we might say, it all blew over, and David and the Lord were reconciled. But there may still have been murmuring in the villages of Issachar and Reuben.

At a certain point something heroic seems to go out of the story, and it becomes one of palace intrigue, and scheming priests, and querulous women. But this, we must repeat, is not David's story, but Joab's.

He, we may suppose, was not so much at court in the next few years. He was not a Strong-Kingdom man, such as went with the new regime. Flattery, too, was much in use, and Joab was a man who had spoken his mind to the king plainly, on more than one occasion. There was also a suggestion, now and then, that the king did not really like his nephew. It may be merely the way in which the story was written later, but kings, it is true, are not given to liking those who have done a great deal for them, and have talked plainly.

Besides, Joab's place was with the army, not at court. In spite of the peace, some kind of permanent organization would have been maintained. The tributary kingdoms must be watched and garrisons retained, and there must be an occasional show of force or punitive expedition.

Psalm 60, in its preface, records a tradition of such an occasion, "When Joab returned and smote of Edom in the Valley of Salt twelve thousand." Just when this expedition occurred is uncertain, but the first line of that psalm runs, "Who will bring me into the strong city? Who will lead me into Edom?" In the psalm, the answer is that God will do so. But one wonders whether this might originally have been a song in praise of Joab — his capture of the strong city of Jerusalem, and his victory over Edom.

Peace dragged along for several years, and Joab, like many a military man, was likely to make mistakes in time of peace.

Absalom, the king's favorite son, was angry at Amnon, the king's oldest son and presumptive heir. Absalom had plenty of reason, but that story has been told often enough. So Absalom had his servants kill Amnon. Absalom then fled to his grandfather, who ruled at Geshur in the north, one of the tributary or allied kingdoms.

But, after all, having your half-brother murdered because he has raped your sister may be more or less justifiable under the code of the blood-feud. Joab understood about such things. So did the king, and he was particularly fond of his handsome son Absalom.

After three years Joab decided that Absalom ought to be brought back. Probably Joab feared the Strong-Kingdom party, which was developing at court, around the clever Bathsheba and her bright little son Solomon, with the backing of Zadok, one of the important priests, and Benaiah, Captain of the Guard.

Joab contrived the device, which (if it was his own invention) shows a good deal of imagination. He got "a wise woman" to present a case to the king, as judge. The case was a parable, of two sons, and of one of them killing the other. By giving a decision, the king trapped himself; having done so, he immediately realized that this must be a device of Joab's.

The king, however, was complacent at the way things had happened, and he ordered Joab to go and bring Absalom to Jerusalem.

Nevertheless, after that, we may suppose that Bathsheba got some work in. When Absalom returned, he remained in disgrace, and the king would not see him. Solomon's star continued ascendant.

Things went on thus for two years more, Joab having decided that he had done as much as he should in the matter, or as much as he could. Perhaps he did not like the way Absalom was developing. Joab refused two requests from Absalom to come and talk the matter over.

So Absalom, who seems to have had efficient servants and some genius for direct action, sent his servants out and had them burn a barley field that belonged to Joab. The servants even did not do it secretly.

Joab took the hint. He must have known what it was all about. He came to Absalom, and asked him why his servants had burned the field. The upshot was that Joab, probably against his better judgment now, interfered again and persuaded David to restore Absalom to favor.

David had passed sixty by this time. There was beginning to be the suggestion of a doddering old man about him. He might not live long, and the question of the succession was becoming important. Adonijah, the oldest surviving son, seemed to be an able and worthy prince. Young Solomon, now entering his teens, had a strong party behind him, and Bathsheba was still the favorite wife. Absalom, who had now lost Joab's support, was out of the running. Such a situation was as good as a death sentence, for the new king, whoever he might be, would have to get rid of such a threat to the throne as Absalom. We cannot much blame a man for trying to save his head.

So Absalom, that handsome young prince with the magnificent hair, spent four years riding around in his chariot and impressing people with his regal manners, and ingratiating himself with all and sundry. And he was a very able ingratiator.

He picked his time. If there was any man to be feared, it was Joab. So Absalom acted when Joab was not in Jerusalem, but was apparently off somewhere east of the Jordan.

Then, one morning, a messenger came panting in with the

shocking news that Absalom had raised revolt in Judah and was marching on the city.

The king seems to have gone into a panic. He had some good soldiers with him, Benaiah and Abishai, with the Philistine guard. But perhaps the city was not provisioned for a siege. As the men of Judah came streaming up from the south, the old king, flustered and weeping, went out at the gate on the other side of the city, and headed for the Jordan. With him were all his women and children (except ten concubines), Abishai and Benaiah, the Philistine guard, and a higgledy-piggledy crowd of scribes and priests and courtiers.

The king paused occasionally to weep and lament, and to be magnanimous toward someone who came out to curse him. This last was almost too much for Abishai, who was all for taking off the head of the man who was doing the cursing.

The king certainly did not behave in any way calculated to inspire confidence or to encourage doubters. One imagines that some deserters slipped away, and went back to make their peace with the new regime.

Absalom occupied the city. Then, in the opinion of most people, he missed his chance by not pursuing immediately, and capturing or killing the king before he crossed the Jordan. That is as it may be, but predictions after the event are always cheap and easy. Absalom contented himself with going in to the ten concubines, and thus symbolically establishing himself in his father's place.

Once across the Jordan, the king had a breathing-spell. It was a big river, with few fords, and a small number of determined troops could hold them for a while. Off in the backcountry somewhere was Joab.

Of course, at first, the king could not be sure but that Joab was for Absalom. If so, everything was lost. But soon word came that Joab was loyal, and, on his record, it could scarcely have been otherwise.

Then David went for shelter to Mahanaim. History was repeating itself, for in Mahanaim, thirty and more years before, Abner had set up what was left of the kingdom after the great disaster.

Before long, Absalom crossed the Jordan in pursuit. He had with him, goes the story, all the men of Israel. This must mean that he had a scattering of the men of all twelve tribes, but surely they did not turn out in full force. That would have made an overwhelming army. Most men would have preferred to wait a little, to see how things shaped up. Both out of prudence and out of loyalty, Joab's veterans would not have quickly taken arms against him, and David's was still a great name.

Absalom appointed a certain Amasa to be Captain of the Host. This man was another grandson of Jesse, and therefore a cousin both of Absalom and Joab.

On the other side, the king had Benaiah's palace guard. They were mercenaries and well-armed, but palace guardsmen have a habit of going soft. Joab must have been able to muster detachments from the frontier garrisons, and he probably had the old six hundred, or what was left of them. Besides, from every village in the North, and particularly from east of the Jordan, hard-bitten veterans must have slipped away, to draw the bow again under their old commander, and in defense of the king who had so often led them to glorious victory.

As Absalom marched north toward Mahanaim, a last flicker of the old vigor and courage stirred within the aged king. He split the army into the conventional three divisions, giving commands to Joab, Abishai, and Ittai, one of the Philistine mercenaries. David himself prepared to take personal command of the whole battle.

There was, however, general protest against his thus exposing himself, and finally the king went no farther than the gate, where he stood and showed himself to the men as they marched out.

Also, in the presence of the whole army, he gave final and most urgent instructions to the three commanders. Did he tell them to bear themselves well? Did he tell them to have hope of quick victory and few casualties? No — he told them, "Deal gently for my sake with the young man, even with Absalom."

The army must have heard such words with a strange coldness, as if the king were asking them to fight with one arm tied behind the back.

Still, they proved to be more than a match for Absalom's men, and soon his army was shattered and flying in rout. Then occurred that famous and strange incident.

The battle had been fought in wooded country. Absalom, on mule-back, galloped away in the rout, apparently having lost his attendants. The mule rushed beneath an oak tree, and Absalom's head caught in the branches. The excited mule rushed on, and the prince was left hanging. (He was caught by the head, and not by the hair, as the story has often been told.)

An active man should have had little difficulty in disentangling himself. But Absalom may have been wounded already, or he may have been stunned by the impact. He hung there, dangling and helpless.

A pursuing soldier saw and recognized the prince. The man rushed off to tell his commander, being himself afraid to act, because of the king's warning.

As luck would have it, and that was the way Joab's luck usually ran, the message came, not to Abishai or to Ittai but to Joab himself. As always, his reaction was quick and sure, to do the work that must be done. He rebuked the soldier for not doing the obvious.

Then Joab himself took three throwing-spears in his hand, though why he needed that number was never declared. He went to where that beloved son and irresponsible traitor was hanging in the tree, and there did the work that had to be done for the safety of the kingdom.

At least, this is the story that is usually told, putting Joab in the worst possible light. But the next words declare that ten young men killed Absalom. This may well have been the actuality and the original version, and the other may have been only part of a systematic campaign to blacken Joab's character, after death. The situation is similar to that surrounding the killing of Abner, when the longer story presents Joab in the worst possible light, and the summation presents a different account.

Also, we might look a little more deeply. By firmly and surely removing the cause of the whole war, so that not even a doting father could give a pardon, Joab — personally, or by means of his "young men" — had removed all necessity for further killing. Immediately he had the trumpets blow the recall, "And the people returned from pursuing after Israel, for Joab held back the people." He thus saved the lives of hundreds of poor tribesmen, who had been lured by the blandishments of a handsome prince.

Then comes that famous scene, when the old king sat at the gate, waiting for news of the battle. Finally two runners appeared in the distance, "And the watchmen said, 'Methinketh the running of the foremost is like the running of Ahimaaz the son of Zadok.' And the king said, 'He is a good man, and cometh with good tidings.' " (That is to say, "He is a brave man, and would not have been the first to run in case of a defeat.")

So Ahimaaz told of the victory, but to a question about Absalom, he evasively said, "I saw a great tumult, but I knew not what it was."

Then came the second runner, who was called Cushi, but that more likely means that he was a Cushite, that is, a Negro, who had wandered north from the Sudan. He told all.

"And the King was much moved, and went up to the chamber over the gate, and wept: and as he went, thus he said, 'O my son Absalom, my son, my son Absalom! Would God I had died for thee, O Absalom, my son, my son!' "

Through hundreds of years, people have focused upon the story of the old king, and have sympathized with the mourning father. But consider the men who, that day, had risked their lives, and seen their comrades die. "And the victory that day was turned into mourning unto all the people. . . . And the people got them by stealth that day into the city, as people being ashamed steal away when they flee in battle."

That night, as men nursed their wounds, there was murmuring around the campfires. Why should we fight and suffer for an ungrateful and maundering king. Every man to his tent! (This last was the old rallying cry of the tribesmen, when they were ready for action.)

Only one man, then, as we might guess, had the knowledge and the courage and the foresight and the sense of responsibility to speak out. And that is perilous work, to speak the truth to a king.

Joab, son of Zeruiah, went to David, and spoke the longest speech that is recorded to him, and spoke it honestly and forthrightly.

Thou hast shamed this day the faces of all thy servants, which this day have saved thy life, and the lives of thy sons and of thy daughters, and the lives of thy wives, and the lives of thy concubines.

In that thou lovest thine enemies, and hatest thy friends. For thou hast declared this day that thou regardest neither princes nor servants: for this day I perceive, that if Absalom had lived, and we had all died this day, then it had pleased thee well.

Now therefore arise, go forth, and speak comfortably unto thy servants: for I swear by the Lord, if thou go not forth, there will not tarry one with thee this night: and that will be worse unto thee than all the evil that befell thee from thy youth until now.

So the king went, and sat again in the gate, and the army came and were reconciled to him. But in the now scarcely rational mind of the almost senile king there must have lingered deep resentment against Joab — not only that he had killed Absalom, but that he had spoken the unpleasant truth.

With the death of Absalom, nearly all the tribes acknowledged David as king, though apparently without much enthusiasm. The anomaly was that Judah, David's own tribe, held aloof, organized under Amasa, who had been Absalom's Captain of the Host.

To reconcile Judah, the king made a deal, which can only be described as being as ungrateful as it was unwise. He appointed Amasa, who had been a traitor, to be Captain of the Host, in the place of Joab, who had been loyal and the leader in victory.

One hopes, though without much expectation of being right, that the matter was done decently and with some attempt at face-saving. Joab was gray-haired now, and had turned sixty. Perhaps there was a retirement banquet where laudatory speeches were made, and platitudes were breathed, and Joab was declared Captain of the Host Emeritus.

But Joab had not yielded to time, as David had. Sixty he might be, but a vigorous sixty. In scarcely any time at all, the king, and the kingdom, felt the necessity of Joab in command.

Things had not settled down. As would be expected, Absalom's open revolt had strained the fragile ties between the Northern and the Southern tribes. Judah had accepted the king again, and a man of Judah was Captain of the Host. This was enough to breed discontent in all the Northern tribesmen, and a certain Sheba, of Benjamin, "blew a trumpet," that is to say, initiated a revolt. "Every man to his tents, O Israel!" ran his pronunciamento, that is, "Back to tribal rule! No more monarchy!"

Revolt flared, and only Judah, under Amasa, remained surely loyal. The king sent Amasa to raise troops in Judah, and then bring the North back to its allegiance. To Amasa it must have seemed as if the frog had been sent out to swallow the ox.

Amasa shilly-shallied, until the king saw that something else must be done. Probably there were doubts about Amasa's loyalty. (The text is fragmentary and corrupt.) Then David, it would seem, committed his last reserve, and he entrusted the command to Abishai. To him he gave the Philistine guard, the *gibborim*, and "Joab's men." These last may have been the old six hundred, with recent recruitings, still under Joab's command. In any case, he went along, in some capacity.

The two brothers found Amasa at Gibeon, the border city between North and South, where there had been the encounter with Abner, as much as thirty-five years earlier.

By the time they had arrived there, Joab had already taken over the command from his faithful and courageous but not very enterprising brother. There, at Gibeon, the gray-haired Joab settled matters again. He struck down the much younger Amasa, and killed him. The account, as usual, makes it an act of duplicity, and that may or may not be true. The tale, as told, of the killing of Amasa, in fact, is rather suspiciously like that of the killing of Abner. At least, the deed was done, and of the three killings attributed to Joab, this one seems to have the least excuse. But it may have been necessary, and Amasa may have been dealing in treachery.

From this point on, Joab superseded Abishai, and was again *de facto* Captain of the Host. He summoned everyone who stood for David, and Amasa's men came over to him. Satisfied at last, the vacillating Northern tribesmen made no more trouble. Apparently they stood by Joab more than by David. Perhaps they trusted Joab to respect their tribal freedoms, knowing him to be no Strong-Kingdom man.

Joab now set out to run down the troublesome but ineffective Sheba, and that rash and unfortunate rebel had no recourse but to flee rapidly northward. His only hope, and that a forlorn one, was to get into some walled city, and try to stand off a siege. Finally he managed to get possession of the far Northern Beth-maacah, though its inhabitants had little sympathy with him.

Joab began a vigorous siege, setting up battering-rams against the wall, and raising a mound, so that eventually his men could advance against the defenders of the wall on even terms. Beth-maacah was not a place of great strength.

Since the sack of the city would follow its capture, the local inhabitants viewed the battering-rams and the mound with considerable distaste. They secretly opened negotiations with Joab, and soon threw Sheba's head out among the besiegers. At this plain evidence that the people of the city had attended to the matter, Joab broke off the siege. He took no vengeance upon Sheba's followers, "and they retired, from the city, every man to his tent."

Though Joab has generally been portrayed as an accomplished master of slaughter and vengeance, we should note that he called off the pursuit after the defeat of Absalom, and that he exacted no toll of death after the revolt of Sheba.

At this time then, "Joab returned to Jerusalem unto the king." If anything was said about his killing of Amasa and his assumption of power, nothing stands in the present record. The next sentence, however, may be considered significant. It reads, "Now Joab was over all the host of Israel."

If Sheba's revolt had used up another year, we may consider that David had failed still further. There were no foreign wars. Under Joab's firm hand, the tribes were quiet. But it was a time of nervous waiting.

The king was infirm and doddering. He held on from day to day, not altogether gone. Now and then he was even capable of a decision. But, obviously, he might die at any time, or fall into extreme senility. He had become a mere symbol, and that symbol might almost be called a cipher.

Joab, Captain of the Host, was a great power in the kingdom. His orders could raise troops from Dan to Beersheba. In every village were the veterans who had followed him. He would scarcely need to revolt. If he wished, he could merely take over.

But Joab was not a rebellious man. Though he has been accused of treacherously killing Abner and Amasa, he remained steadfastly loyal to David, and also, we may say, to the ideal of a united Israel.

One may question why Joab remained loyal to David, since

David seems to have had no great love for Joab, and by replacing him did him a severe wrong and humiliated him. Probably the matter is simple enough. In his youth David had been the inspired and almost miraculous leader, the man with "the power." Joab had given him his allegiance then, and the son of Zeruiah was one of those whose allegiance does not shift.

The king failed still, and they brought for him the beautiful virgin Abishag, who shared his bed at night to keep him warm, "but the king knew her not."

Around the court all minds turned to the question of the succession. There were two candidates and two camps.

Amnon, David's first-born, was dead, and so was Absalom, the third-born. Chileab, or Daniel, the second-born, was probably dead; at least, nothing is heard of him. The fourth-born and oldest surviving son, Adonijah, was a natural successor.

Adonijah was a man of about forty, vigorous, laudably ambitious to be king. Of his capacities or abilities, we know nothing. What can be said for him is that he attracted to his support both Joab and Abiathar, the long-experienced chief priest.

Adonijah's rival was Solomon, conceived in wedlock after David had married Bathsheba, the widow of Uriah. Solomon, aged about eighteen, was far down in the list of sons, and so had absolutely no claim of primogeniture. His youth also was against him, though he doubtless was already displaying some of the acumen that marked him in later life. He had the support of Benaiah, who was more or less Joab's counterpart, and of Zadok, an important priest, who could be set against Abiathar. Probably, however, Solomon's chief strength came from his ambitious and clever mother.

The supporters on both sides must have known that they

The Marshal. The effigy on the tomb in the Temple Church, London, was prepared after his death, perhaps a number of years later, and so is only an idealized portrait. It shows the shield-bearing knight in chain mail, but without helmet. *Photograph by Ministry of Public Building and Works, used by permission.*

Schliemann, about the time of his first excavations at Troy. *An un-dated photograph in the Bettmann Archives, Inc.*

Tresguerras, probably about 1810, from *El Museo Mexicano*, 1843.
Reproduced by courtesy of the Bancroft Library.

The Carmen Church, Celaya, August 1955. *Photograph by George R. Stewart.*

Tresguerras's bridge over the Rio Laja, August 1955, a time of moderately low water. *Photograph by George R. Stewart.*

Detail from a painting of St. Vincent surrounded by various persons, by Nuño Gonçalves, ca. 1450, in *Museu National de Arte Antigua, Lisbon.* The face here shown is generally believed to be that of Prince Henry in middle age. Since he is in an attitude of adoration, his religious nature is emphasized.

Sagres Point. From the beach, the observer sees to the west the southern tip of Europe, with a passing freighter. If Prince Henry looked off to the south, he should have stood at the tip of that point above the high cliffs. *Photograph by George R. Stewart.*

The Bidwells. A picture taken in September 1894, when he was seventy-five, apparently in the grounds of the Mansion. Note the scar from the steamboat explosion. *Reproduced by courtesy of the Bancroft Library.*

were playing a dangerous game. Those who lost might well expect also to lose their heads, as the new king removed all threats to his throne.

Under such circumstances, one may wonder why a man such as Joab, old and full of honors, let himself join a faction. Quite possibly both his emotions and his convictions were involved. He could have believed strongly that Adonijah would make a good king, and he may have hated Bathsheba and Solomon, when he remembered that ugly affair about Uriah. Besides, Solomon stood pre-eminently for Strong Kingdom, and Joab may have feared that any threat to the tribal liberties would only bring new revolts and final disaster.

At last Adonijah decided, with the help of Joab, to consummate a *coup d'état,* and proclaim himself king. Such a movement would be anti-Solomon rather than anti-David, and so Joab could join it. At least, this is the story as told later by the pro-Solomon historian, and it became the official version. It may be true — but then it may not be true. Perhaps Adonijah was merely holding an innocent feast, having invited Joab and Abiathar and many other notable guests. Such an occasion — equally as well as a real *coup d'état* — could have given the opportunity for Solomon and his party to consummate *their* plot. (Our own age has known similar political maneuvers.)

Whichever it was, Bathsheba seized the opportunity to hurry off to the senile king with a scarehead story and with a reminder that he had already promised the throne to Solomon — as, indeed, Bathsheba may well have persuaded him to do.

With a final flare of his old-time vigor, David rose to the occasion, ordered Solomon's anointing, and a proclamation to the people. Benaiah's guardsmen were there to insure the cause of Solomon in Jerusalem. Joab's men were scattered throughout the twelve tribes.

While the old king lived, Solomon did not push matters. Adonijah and his supporters remained alive and at large.

Then David came to the point of death, and his famous final charge to Solomon is preserved in the second chapter of *First Kings*. One of the chief items in the charge concerned Joab, son of Zeruiah, who had grown gray during his years of faithful service. As the text reads, the king told his son, "Do therefore according to thy wisdom, and let not his hoar head go down to the grave in peace."

There have been several schools of thought about David's charge. It may be merely the propaganda of a pro-Solomon historian, trying to shift the onus from Solomon to David, whose heroic reputation was already secure. There is much to support this view. In the first place, since David spoke the words to Solomon privately, and then died, the only possible authority for them is Solomon himself. Besides, David makes an unusually long and coherent speech for a dying man who has been suffering from senility for some years.

But others have thought the charge to be genuine. Among these was the notable Ernest Renan, who declared of David, "he showed the perfidious blackness of his hypocrite's spirit as regarded Joab." There is something to be said for such a judgment. During the last years of the reign, Joab had overshadowed and perhaps overawed the king. The throne is not likely to love the power behind the throne, and the charge may be a final welling-up of suppressed hatred, in forgetfulness of a lifetime of service and loyalty.

At last, as the good phrase went, "David slept with his fathers."

Solomon reigned. The establishment of the throne by the execution or assassination of possible rivals and their supporters was an Oriental custom. Before long, Solomon found a pretext against Adonijah. The holiness of the priesthood protected Abiathar, but he was exiled from court. Joab took the warning, and hurried to the tabernacle for refuge. He had faced death many times, and was probably not afraid, but an old soldier is one to hold on to life.

Solomon gave the work over to Benaiah, who had already accomplished the "execution" of Adonijah.

Benaiah had commanded the guard for many years. He was one of the thirty. He and Joab must have been old comrades, but they may also have been old rivals.

Benaiah, presumably, went with a strong detachment of his guardsmen. He would not have risked the fate of Abner or Amasa.

Joab refused to leave sanctuary, and Benaiah went back for further instructions.

Solomon told him to pay no attention to the sanctuary. The Strong Kingdom was already overruling the ancient tribal custom.

Joab, white-haired at sixty-five, grasped the horns of the altar. "So Benaiah, the son of Jehoiada went up, and fell upon him, and slew him; and he was buried in his own house in the wilderness."

INTER-CHAPTER III

THE MANNER of man that was Joab, we cannot see altogether clearly. Yet, somewhere, we sense one who lived simply by his code of life, and fulfilled himself. He did the work that must be done. He was staunch in his loyalty. And, for the culture in which he was reared, the shedding of blood was only in the way of life.

He pledged his allegiance to David, and maintained it. If David, in his later life, became unworthy of allegiance, that was not Joab's fault.

Second only to David, Joab threw back the Philistines and established the united Israel. He maintained David on the throne, after David himself had become too weak to hold it.

Here and there phrases haunt us. Where was his house in the wilderness, and was he buried there (not in the tomb of his father) as a sign of disgrace? "Joab's men," who were they? Why, again, was he known as the son of his mother? Who were those children, the ones that by implication are included in David's curse? What became of Abishai, the faithful brother?

In spite of it all, we may claim that he lived the life of fulfillment, according to his own lights. Yet we must take something on faith.

That he met failure at the very end need not be counted. By then, he had already lived. Holding fast to the horns of the altar, as he faced Benaiah's sword, he could have died with contentment at the life that he had lived.

As for the one to whom we come next, he was a gentler spirit, though he was ready enough to spring to his own defense, if necessity called. As all men must, he lived how and as he could, held back and weighed down by unusually heavy chains of time and place. Within these limitations he had moderate fortune of birth. He lived in an environment, by most standards, culturally poverty-stricken and hopelessly provincial. By the urging of his own spirit he made something — much, we might think — out of the small opportunity that was offered.

FRANCISCO EDUARDO
TRESGUERRAS

A COUNTRYSIDE bountiful of corn, but not lush; austere and spacious, but never to be called pretty; rimmed by cleanly profiled mountains that are nowhere high enough to dominate — it is a land, one might think, to produce talent and balance, but hardly greatness.

That is the Bajío, a broad valley of the central Mexican plateau. At its eastern end stands the little city of Celaya.

The tourist, driving along Highway No. 45, a hundred miles northwest of Mexico City, sees the domes of Celaya from a distance, and may even note a special one of them, faintly Oriental in outline, yellow, almost luminous in the sun. But the guide book does not encourage stopping. The city manufactures candy; its noteworthy monument is the Carmen church, dating from 1807, the work of a local architect named Tresguerras. All that you can do in the evening, one guide book notes, is to sit in the plaza and watch the townsfolk promenade. So the tourist drives on. If he is knowledgeable in architecture, he considers 1807 a poor date. And who has ever heard of Francisco Eduardo Tresguerras? . . .

At some time when the eighteenth century was getting on toward its halfway mark, a certain Pedro Fernández Tresguerras left his native town of Santillana in the north of Spain, and made his way, by means and route not on the record, to Celaya. He was, it would appear, one of those alert and industrious individuals who are held to be character-

istic of the Basque provinces. He prospered, in the moderate
way which was all that could be expected of the time and
place.

After a while he married, though not brilliantly. His wife
can have brought him no status or family connections of importance, since she was of illegitimate birth, being the
daughter of a priest. In New Spain of that time such a birth
was no cause for scandal, but neither did it mean a large
dowry and acceptance by any family. Her name was Maria
Francisca Martínez de Ibarra. The last name in the series is
of interest, since it is that of the great Ibarra family, who had
long been lords of the northern frontier. She may have had
some connection, even though a left-handed one, with that
powerful clan. Thus could have arisen the later story, of her
son, that he was of one of the most prominent families of
the region.

Of this marriage sprang two sons who grew to maturity,
and perhaps other children. One of these sons was born on
October 13, 1759, and two days later was christened Francisco José Eduardo. He himself, however, did not use his
second name.

Francisco is too common to call for explanation, though
we may note that it was, in its feminine form, the mother's
name. As for Eduardo, that undoubtedly was chosen from
the circumstance that the child was born on the day of St.
Edward the Confessor.

Celaya, during the years when the boy was young, is
better known than might be expected, partly because the boy
himself, grown older, left a description of it, largely in catalogue form. He was even sensitive to historical origins, writing, metaphorically, "My beloved birthplace, the city of Celaya, was a certain poor Mexican woman, pretty and sprightly,
who married with a Basque, at once warrior and farmer." He

thus referred to the founding in 1570, when the viceroy planted a small military colony of Basques to guard the road to the silver mines against attacks from the wild Chichimecas of the northern desert. When the boy was only eleven years old, therefore, his city was passing its two-hundredth anniversary.

As the frontier had advanced northward, the military importance of the city had disappeared, but the agricultural productiveness remained. As the catalogue declares, "Its crops . . . wheat, chile, corn, plentiful and of excellent quality, but its olives finest of all. Its fruits . . . figs, grapes, and melons, watermelons, and pomegranates." But, we must remember, all this picture of abundance was painted by one who was of the more prosperous class of citizenry.

In those years Celaya had about ten thousand inhabitants, and was static in population. Various controls saw to that — high infant mortality, endemic diseases, recurrent epidemics, and even an occasional crop failure with resulting food shortage.

The city was socially stratified, as was all of New Spain. At the bottom were the Indians, perhaps a quarter of the population in Celaya itself, but approaching 100 per cent in the villages round about. They were poor, illiterate, oppressed by peonage, devoted to their priests. Above them came the mestizos, of varying mixed blood, about half of the population, second-class citizens, not only in social rank, but before the law. At the top was the remaining quarter, people who were of pure European blood. Most of these were Creoles, that is, individuals born in America. A few were immigrants from Spain, known as *Gachupines,* who held the power and the government appointments, were of highest social rank, and were correspondingly hated by everybody else.

The theory was that even the accident of birth to the west of salt water created a kind of subtle decadence. Thus, the elder Tresguerras was a *Gachupin*; the son, a Creole. The father might have said to him in anger, as such fathers were said sometimes to do, "No wonder you don't amount to much! You are a Creole."

The Creoles were essentially a propertied class — a few of them, wealthy; most of them, living frugally. Since they were thus supported, they did not work much, and were notoriously idle and pleasure-loving. In this respect the younger Tresguerras was destined to be a most untypical Creole.

Since the boy was to follow, in the very broadest sense, the life of the artist, we may ask, "What early artistic influence could he have felt?" There can have been very little, and nearly all of it would have been tied up with religion. In church he would have heard his most sophisticated music. On the church walls he would have seen paintings. Few except churchmen were literate, and so they, especially the friars, were the masters of literature and learning. Most of all, the church monopolized architecture.

"Its houses . . . small, most of them of adobe." Out of this drab one-story mass — magnificent and overwhelming to a small boy's eyes — rose several great stone churches. There was one of San Francisco, and another, called of the Third Order. There was the church of San Agustín with an unfinished tower. Ancient among them, dating from 1597, was that of the Carmelite friars, known as the Carmen church, which Tresguerras himself, in more sophisticated years, described as "dark, mixed in style, and dominated by the streets."

Boyhood may have been happy enough in this little city — provincial to the point of being isolated, socially stratified, static, largely church-dominated. The family was prosperous and comfortably high in the stratification, even if not at the top. Though things were not booming, they were hardly to be called decadent. The worst of it was, probably, a great weight of conservatism. No one had reason to hope for anything much, or to be forward-looking.

There must have been plenty of games and playmates for a boy. He could see coaches going along on the King's Road, and sometimes mule trains with bars of silver from the mines. There were fiestas and cockfights, and bullfights, country style.

Just a mile or so to the east was the River Laja, and there has always been an affinity between boys and rivers. Probably he learned to swim, and he would have gone out in time of the summer rains, when the stream was coming down high, and you could watch the exciting business of travelers being taken across, rather carelessly, in a basket strung on a cable. And people would be saying, "We ought to have a bridge!"

He went to school — and this was by no means a matter to be taken for granted. But his father was a prosperous *Gachupin*, and his maternal grandfather (though on the wrong side of the blanket) was a canon of a cathedral. Besides, he was the sort of boy who takes well to education.

Probably his teachers were the Franciscans, who had their own school in Celaya. He became a tolerable Latinist, and read Ovid, or someone else, attentively enough to be able in later life to bandy mythological references about, rather glibly. He read *Don Quixote* and some of the Spanish poets, though such reading was probably outside of school. Presumably he absorbed some basic mathematics and some theology. His handwriting must have been a joy and a delight to his masters, unless it was an envy. He was a natural calligrapher. But, most of all, he drew. Like Browning's Fra Lippo Lippi he might have said,

I drew men's faces, on my copybooks,
Scrawled them within the antiphonary's marge.

We can easily imagine that he sometimes got into trouble,
like his Florentine counterpart, for defacing valuable books.
But, as he later put it, "My inclination was always fixed toward drawing; it was born with me; with me it is native." . . .

There came a punctuation point. At the age of fifteen,
he completed his studies in the local school, and made a decision to enter the church and become a friar. It was natural
enough. In all of New Spain the church offered the most to
an intellectual youth. He seems to have been naturally pious,
and to have accepted the doctrines implicitly. In fact, he can
scarcely even have known that anybody doubted them. And
a churchman could live pleasantly, with the sustaining sense
of doing good. The boy's own mother was present proof
that a churchman need not entirely cut himself off from the
pleasures of the world.

As for the friars, they were glad to have him. He was the
kind of lad of whom they could make use — pious and intelligent, and with budding artistic abilities that might be put
to work for the church.

But something intervened — "God," as the man himself
piously wrote later. But God worked "through a trip that
I made to Mexico," and also of importance were, in words
that may be literally translated, "forces of my inclination."

He went to Mexico (what the North Americans call Mexico City) some time in 1774. His object was to continue
his studies in "letters," by which he must have meant his work
in Latin, as training for a career in the church. The great city,
that brilliant capital, must have struck the boy as overwhelm-
ingly as London and Paris have affected many a country lad.

There were, he learned, other things to do with one's life than
to construe Latin, become a friar, and sing masses. As he put
it simply, "I abandoned letters, and devoted myself to drawing."

He does not tell us how he accomplished this revolution
in his life. Were there arguments and sharp words between
him and the friars, and did his father write letters in high
dudgeon? Could he continue at school, merely shirking his
studies, and spending all his time at drawing? He was still
only fifteen, rather too young for a full-fledged revolt. Possibly an indulgent parent still sent him money. Little as we
know about it, the episode seems to fit the man. Not a revolt against, but an inclination toward — that was what
swayed him.

The Royal Academy had not yet been founded. People have supposed that the boy studied drawing under this
or that artist, but there is no certainty that he had any in-
structor at all, other than books, collections of art, and nature. All he wrote of it was, "I remained for about a year,
absorbed in such pleasant study."

Then, being still only sixteen, he returned to Celaya —
probably because his father so told him. Though he had
proved to have a mind of his own, he was not one to press a
revolt very far. In his attitudes toward the church he showed
the same quality.

He had drifted away from his idea of becoming a friar, but
he had not absorbed any free-thinking and anti-clerical ideas
in the capital. Instead, he remained a devout and pious Cath-
olic. He even did not altogether renounce the possibility of
taking orders. Though his best efforts were going into his
drawing, he probably continued his other studies, and the
friars did not altogether give up their hopes in him. After all,

he could practice his drawing in the church, better than out of it. Such decisions are difficult for a young man, and Tresguerras would hardly have been human if he had not displayed some oscillation during the course of a few years. A very human weakness, if it may be called such, finally settled the matter — he fell in love.

Her name was María Guadalupe Ramírez, and she was, in this Year of Our Lord 1781, just fifteen years old. The affair might have been written off as calf-love, except that Tresguerras himself was now twenty-two.

We know little about her. There is a portrait that her husband painted, a few years later. From it, we can see that at fifteen she must have been a delightful slip of a girl. She was black-haired, black-eyed, with heavy eyebrows, as one would expect from her Spanish ancestry. She had a high-bridged nose, and a rather long one, it must be confessed. Still, there is enough suggestion of piquancy to account for her accomplishing the not-too-difficult task of turning the head of a young man. Besides, she was picturesque and paintable, and artists are attracted by that in a wife.

The banns were published. Then the friars made their last attempt. Once married, he was cut off from the church. So they tried, at this final hour, to dissuade him from marriage. But the young man knew his own mind. In the end he put the blame upon himself, not upon the friars, writing, "They believed that there was a virtue in me, though it was in reality only bigotry and ignorance of the world."

So he took the irrevocable step on January 16, 1782. The bride, young as she was, proved herself ready for matrimony. Promptly, but long enough afterwards to escape any hint of scandal, she bore her first child, on December 3. The daughter was christened María Luisa Francisca Javiera. . . .

So, at twenty-three, he had a wife and the beginning of a

family, and he had not much else — except a lot of copy-books full of drawings.

He had shown talent, certainly. But had he the drive and the originality that would lead him to success, especially since he must remain essentially self-taught and since he was tied to this remote province?

The basic problem of economics, at least, seems never to have been acute. By this time we hear no more of the father; and the young man may have come into the family property. There was a farm outside of the city, and there is a mention of small houses, rental property, in the city itself. It meant wheat-bread rather than tortillas, but it did not mean a voyage to Europe. It could have financed an occasional trip to Mexico, but the capital was never to mean much in his life. Already he was beginning to realize, we must think, that the free artist is to himself and of himself, that he does not spring from academies and schools and masters.

Yet neither was he one to retire to the ivory tower. The very environment protected him from that, because he lived always among his own people. There was no "artists' colony" in which he could insulate himself. By normal instinct, moreover, he wanted acceptance and praise. He needed even some of that "success" without which the artist, all too often, turns toward bitterness and frustration.

The first years following his marriage were also years of rapid maturing. Materials on Tresguerras are so scanty that biographers have relied heavily, for this period of his life, upon what is called his *Autobiographical Letter*. The trouble is that this document was written years later, after 1807, and perhaps as late as 1817. It is therefore more an evidence as to the man at that later date than as to what he was at the time of which he wrote. This is not to say that there is any reason to doubt the truth of the actual incidents. But when a period of years is telescoped into a few hundred words, excessive oversimplification results. In one passage he seems to sum up his career in the decade following 1782:

Upon my marriage, I dedicated myself to the noble art of painting, that lovely and most sweet painting. But alas! Nothing throve with my highly ambitious and charming attempts in this enchanting art. I displayed to the public a certain study — of rare conception, of masterful execution, of fascinating style. [Here, as often, there is a bit of tongue-in-cheek.] This picture, done by the rules and in every respect of proper merit, was viewed with indifference. Much as I desired it, I could not find a connoisseur.

Then, still the middle-aged man who looks back at his struggling youth, he continued, obviously maintaining a touch of irony:

Next I daubed a coach with green and red, and its carvings blazed with gilt, and it was smeared with lacquer and varnish and other inanities of that kind — then, my friend, admiration and eulogy rained down, and I had to shove into a corner my studies and projects, and was forced, bowing to such great ignorance, to sacrifice sense and good taste, in deference to so great and almost universal stupidity.

Compressing into one long sentence what must have been the furious activity of several years, he told in summary how he then essayed one art after another, always attaining some competency and then restlessly passing on to something else.

He tried music first. Then, he wrote, "I was engraver for one while, carpenter and woodcarver for another, land-surveyor several times, and, always shifting, got a toe-hold on architecture."

Again, we must remember, all this was written years later by a mature man, humorously and with a certain self-depreciation, summarizing the years of a tumultuous youth. In addition, his very paucity of words creates a faulty impression of the time involved. Reading, one would think of a year or even of some months. Actually, the period from his marriage until the time when he seriously began to practice architecture amounted to ten years. Finally, his summary allows both omission and self-derogation. He does not even record that he wrote both prose and poetry, and at times was putting much of his best energy into such work. Similarly speeding along, he omits any reference to his work as a sculptor.

As for self-derogation, his mention of himself as a "carpenter" may have been literally meant, and we should indeed imagine that honest work with wood must have appealed to him greatly. But, just as likely, he here refers to work in what we might term building and stage-designing.

Also he is self-deprecatory in the suggestion that he thus took up one art after another, failed to attain mastery, and then passed on to something else. With music this was most nearly true, although we do not know what he attempted, whether composing or performance. Still, he attained some facility on the flute, and continued to play on it happily throughout the rest of his life. But in the other arts, even if he did not attain the greatest heights, he not only gained, but also maintained through the years, at least a professional status, and the results were thus cumulative.

During this decade there are few certain dates and fixed events. Sons were born in 1784, and 1786, and a second daughter in 1788. The first son died in infancy. But, in that time and place, bringing three out of four children to maturity was an achievement.

In 1786 he published a small volume entitled, *Verses, secular and moral, by F. T.* In 1787 he painted in oil the still-surviving portrait of his wife.

These few data, added to the evidence of the letter, present us with the very sketchy picture of a young man, establishing a family, of extraordinary activity, of manifold but unschooled creative urges. He was probably supporting his family by the modest income from the farm and other small properties. Now and then, for extra money, he decorated a coach or worked as a surveyor. His interest was in the arts, and his special peculiarity was that he practiced all of them, without settling down to specialization.

Such an appraisal, however, may result in an underestimate. The painting dated 1787 shows him as a competent artist. From this time on, at least, he could have been receiving commissions for portraits and for religious paintings. He seems first to have become known as a painter.

During much of this time he was associated with the city of Querétaro, and may even have been living there with his family. It lay only twenty miles to the east of Celaya, had about thirty thousand people, and thus offered more opportunities for a painter. In these years he may have executed the paintings that are still pointed out as his in the various churches of that city. Unfortunately no canon of his work has as yet been established, and one must remain a little doubtful even about *The Closed Garden,* often cited as his masterpiece.

In 1789 he attained a note in the public records of Querétaro, for having executed the paintings for a monument in commemoration of the new king, Carlos IV.

Similar ceremonies in 1791 brought him his first public recognition in his own city of Celaya. His being thus entrusted shows that he must by this time have gained some reputation. The plans called for the construction of a large stage or platform, adorned with rich hangings and displaying portraits of the reigning king and queen. There was also to be a triumphal arch, with ten portraits of former monarchs, painted in oil and of life size. As a permanent monument, a thirty-foot stone column was to be erected to uphold a statue of the king.

Tresguerras planned the work, supervised the construction, and executed much of the decoration with his own hands — including, probably, the more important paintings. Everything was judged excellent, and he received a substantial fee from the city.

The column remained standing. Indeed, the column still standing in Celaya is believed to be that one, though shifted in location, and considerably altered for political reasons.

These works enabled Tresguerras, at the age of thirty-two, to demonstrate before his fellow townsmen his virtuosity, in sculpture and painting, and at least on the edge of architecture. The ceremonies must have included music and perhaps the recitation of poetry. Even the planning of the hangings and the general stage-decoration were probably his responsibility.

Whether or not this success at Celaya had anything to do with it, he began to move toward architecture.

Again, a vivid and much-quoted passage in the *Autobiographical Letter* is not to be taken literally, for it tells in sarcasm how some of his "rivals" went about becoming architects. It certainly does not present his own ideas or ideals about the profession. But it displays something of the man himself, and even in translation some of the vivid quality of the prose survives.

He took up architecture, the passage begins, because he was thus moved by seeing that the only requirement was to want to be one, though such English cannot equal the deft Spanish, *"que cualquiera lo es con sólo quererlo ser."* He continued:

All that one needs is to learn a flock of prescriptions, like those the physicians use, to babble about whatever architectural writer you have handy — especially the proportions of Vignola — to talk pompously a lot of gibberish about angles, areas, tangents, curves, segments, keystones, apophages, etc. — but cautiously, and always in the presence of women, businessmen, and others who know nothing about it. Then, between giving weight to some works and decrying others, speaking ill of people, waiving a thousand rules, and giving magisterial decisions — there you are, a made architect, and all proper!

In this passage, as an additional humorous touch, he did not use the proper word *arquitecto*, but wrote *arquitete*. He may have been imitating a local pronunciation, perhaps that used in affectation by one of the men whom he was satirizing. So also, instead of *Señor Arquitecto*, he parodied the polite form of address by writing *Seor Arquitete*.

However these others might set about qualifying for the profession, Tresguerras himself proceeded seriously. His two municipal employments had given him experience, as well as reputation. Presumably he then received some private commissions, probably acting as both architect and builder. His energy being so great and his artistic ambitions so all-embracing, he also studied whatever books were available in architecture and its allied arts. His own writings, scanty as they are, show that he at least knew such names as Vitruvius, Vignola, Serlio, Palomino, Mengs, Branca, Muratori, Pons, and Carducci. Some of these he cited in Spanish form — for instance, Viñola instead of Vignola. Probably, therefore, he was familiar with them only in Spanish translations, though he might have been able to handle Vitruvius in the Latin. There is also a lack of more recent writers, as would only be expected. New books did not find their way rapidly to Querétaro and Celaya.

The upshot, however, is that he should not be classed too much as a child of nature. If a "primitive" is to be defined as a self-taught artist, Tresguerras was largely that. Still, consciously and by study, he allied himself with the tradition.

Scholarly name-dropping, of course, is one of the most prevalent and cheap of academic vices. Tresguerras may not have read nearly as many authors as he mentions, and may have been familiar with their ideas only at secondhand, in manuals. But his work is at least a partial refutation of such an idea. He could not have worked in a tradition without knowing that there was a tradition, and something about what it was.

By this time the Royal Academy of San Carlos had been established. Making a second journey to the capital (and, as far as is known, his last one) Tresguerras appeared before the Council of the Academy in 1794, presented an architectural design, and petitioned for professional recognition.

Petition granted, he received what amounted to a license to practice architecture in all its forms. He also began to use the vague title, Professor of the Three Fine Arts, that is, sculpture, painting, and architecture.

Shortly afterwards, in the same year, Tresguerras painted a self-portrait. In an oval border around his head and bust, he inscribed his own name, and stated that he was the painter, being thirty-five years of age. He also added, with a fine touch of local pride, that he was a native of Celaya. With equal pride, he included his new title as Professor of the Three Fine Arts. Curiously also, he described himself as *grabador*, that is "engraver." Since this is not an art for which he is especially notable, we may think that it was his latest addition to the repertoire, and that he was correspondingly proud of it, at the moment.

The portrait suggests that he was of middle stature, slight, endowed with a certain grace of body. His hair, just beginning to recede, was brown, showing his north-Spanish ancestry. His eyes were dark, and thoughtful. His face sloped rather sharply from cheekbones to a pointed chin. The expression showed the sensitivity of the artist, with a strong suggestion of intelligence and determination.

Though the recognition granted by the academy was a source of satisfaction and of practical utility, Tresguerras returned to his own region, and probably did about what he would have done in any case. Two or three years later he was able to write that he had executed architectural works in Celaya, Querétaro, Guanajuato, San Miguel, and Valladolid (Morelia). All these are cities of central Mexico, and they lie with Celaya at the center. In fact, a hard day's ride on horseback should have got the architect to even the farthest of them.

Just what work he did in these cities cannot be specified, in the present state of our knowledge. Much has been attributed to him, and some of these attributions can be proved unfounded. Positive proof is more difficult.

At this time he may have completed the tower of San Agustín in Celaya. This would have been a matter of satisfaction to him, because he must often have looked at it when he was a boy, and thought that it should be finished. As it stands, now, it is a curious structure. The first story, as the tower rises above the church, has round arches. The second story has pointed arches, a rarity in Mexico. The third story has flat lintels. Only this last can be the work of Tresguerras, along with certain embellishments.

At this time, also, he may have done the tower of the

church of San Francisco at San Miguel. It has the free-standing columns, which he favored. There was also a certain roughness about it, which suggests early work.

Certainly, in 1796, he planned and built the fountain of Neptune in Querétaro. Such a comparatively small structure, however, is much like his work in Celaya of 1791, that is, on the boundary between architecture and sculpture.

As the comparative poverty of such works would indicate, the time and place were not propitious for architects. The public buildings, including the churches, had been built in previous generations, and remained adequate. About all that could be done was to finish off a tower, or to attach a new portico in the severe classical style, as preferred by the new academy.

But, at least, the citizens of these little cities of central Mexico possessed a Spanish pride in their own municipalities, and had a magnificent two-century tradition of architecture behind them. Walking those unpaved streets were a surprising number of local architects and artists, provincial and unschooled, but correspondingly touchy, proud of their art, and conscious of the tradition behind them. Tresguerras was not alone. (Artistically, the situation was far advanced over anything that the newly independent states in the north could display.)

So, in 1796, came the tempest-in-a-teapot that such a situation may be expected to breed. One of the local architects in Querétaro was Felipe Suasnávar y Aguirre. He came forth with a satire against Tresguerras, probably circulated in manuscript. Although its text is not preserved, it apparently attacked Tresguerras as an interloper from Celaya, as a bungling architect, and as a dubious person. The eighteenth century was the age of such personal satire.

Instead of preserving the dignified silence that might have

served him better, Tresguerras replied in kind. Probably we should not blame him. That was the way in which the game was then played. Besides, life had a tendency to be dull, and a vigorous interchange of epithets could be generally appreciated by the literate citizenry.

Tresguerras had already been keeping a kind of notebook in which he had inscribed a brief translation from Catullus and an original poem of his own — both written in his beautiful lettering. He now used this volume to continue, in manuscript, what he called his *Ocios*, that is, *Diversions*.

Though thus written, with little expectation of ever being in print, the *Ocios* are addressed to a public, having both a prologue and a section headed "Notices to the Reader." The former is of especial interest for its picture of the writer himself.

"Reader," he began with the usual self-deprecatory manner, "I do not offer these trifles with the pretension of being a poet." After a few lines he was still writing moderately, "I practice modestly the sweet, difficult, and most noble art of painting." But, before long, his naïve and disarming egotism had taken over, and he was stating that he combined in his own work "pleasing music, careful painting, majestic architecture, vigorous sculpture, exact engraving, and most sweet poetry." But then he added, "In nothing, I repeat, am I a master."

Finally he signed the prologue, repeating a word which he had already used, "El aficionado: Francisco Tresguerras."

In this context *aficionado* can probably best be translated as "amateur." In using such a term he was actually over-modest, for he had already done professional work in "the three fine arts." But the passage is of great interest in showing his appraisal of himself, or, at least, the image of himself which he wanted to suggest. Here was a man, at thirty-seven,

who wished to practice all the arts. He could shape a son-
net as he could shape a statue, and could run cadenzas on
his flute as he might design the pinnacle of a tower.

Here was a man whose creative impulses flowed out
abundantly from every tingling fingertip. He is at the opposite
end of the spectrum from those individuals (true artists
though they may be!) who sit all day chewing the end of a
pencil to bring forth one proper word, or devote all their lives
to perfecting themselves in one small segment of one art. As
to which kind may be remembered by posterity, that is another question. But we can scarcely doubt which one, in his
own days, lived the better.

As for the satire that Tresguerras discharged against the
architect who had begun the attack, that need not concern us
greatly. Tresguerras lampooned Suasnávar, under various
misspelled adaptations of his name, and sometimes as Fi-
landro, perhaps with an implication about private habits.
The *Ocios* show Tresguerras to be a man ready to defend himself, with vigor and perhaps even with pleasure, in the street
and the market place, and, some might say, in the gutter.

In addition to being a literary work, the volume is a minor
artistic masterpiece. It might be compared, on a modest
scale, with the work that the contemporary William Blake
was doing in England. The text is all in the writer's beautiful
calligraphy. Sometimes it approaches type in exactitude, but
always it displays the variety, and touch of personality, which
type fails to attain by its very nature. In fact, as one looks
at the page, each example of the same letter seems to be a
little different from the ones that precede and follow, being
shaped to its position in the word or otherwise varied. Each
page, moreover, is conceived as an artistic unit. The prologue, for instance, seems to be cut off, not merely because
the writer had come to the end of what he had to say, but

because he had come to the proper place on the page. The writing was done without any guidance for lines, so that many of them show a slight curving, such as might result from the natural motion of the writer's hand, as it pivoted from the wrist and elbow. Finally, the work is embellished with many designs and some spirited miniature sketches.

One of these is generally taken to be a tiny self-portrait, showing the artist fallen asleep at his desk, leaning upon one elbow. Desk and chair are simple, as we would expect them to be. Manuscripts and books lie strewn on the desk, and two pens stand in a penholder. The artist, if it really is he, is clothed in conventional eighteenth-century style, with hose and tight breeches. One side of the room is symbolically torn away, by the rending of a curtain, and the figures of a dream appear there.

But "Jack of all arts" may not be enough. That way, too, may lie frustration. The end-point of versatility and virtuosity may be, not so much "amateur," as "trifler." The question must be raised whether the expression of a creative impulse in itself brings full satisfaction, or whether that expression must be linked with an environment and with other people. Can the artist live his full life without appreciation, even if that appreciation merely takes such a crude form as money?

Tresguerras was in some such situation, in those years when the century was drawing to its close. He had trained himself in all the arts, and could practice them all fairly well, most of them at the professional level. Undoubtedly he had some kind of reputation as a local prodigy. But he had not as yet shown himself, in any one art, good enough to break through on his own. A dull and provincial environment enveloped him. The citizenry could admire a coach in red and green, but could not give the stimulation which might lead a versatile "amateur" to break through into some kind of fulfillment.

There may be times in a man's life when he needs luck, granted that luck is an altogether unscientific and illogical conception. But luck, if there is such a thing, can take manifold forms. There is even an old proverb beginning, "It's an ill wind — "

The Carmen church had stood in Celaya for two centuries. Its great day of the year was July 16, the celebration of the Virgin of the Carmen.

On this day in 1802, about five in the afternoon, the celebration was at its height, and the images were being carried through the streets in a great procession, comprising most of the inhabitants.

There was a sudden shriek of "Fire!" In horror, the people saw smoke and flame pouring from the windows of the church. The women fell to prayer; the men, to carrying water. Neither activity succeeded. The old church burned like a furnace for five hours, and was left a total wreck.

The building had been the property of the Carmelite friars, who maintained a convent in connection with it. The provincial of that order, as it happened, arrived in Celaya just five days after the fire, on a general tour. The rebuilding of the Carmen church would have been beyond the means of Celaya, as it would also, indeed, have been beyond the city's needs. Even without that one there were plenty of churches. But the Carmelites had money in the treasury, and their prestige — in the face of the Franciscans, who already had a large establishment in Celaya — demanded that the church be reconstructed at once. In fact, the provincial may have looked upon the fire as an opportunity rather than as a disaster, especially since the images had been saved. The money would come from the treasury of the order, though local gifts were to be encouraged. In the end, 90 per cent of the total came from the general funds.

Thus paying the piper, the provincial must also have called the tune. To protect the expenditure of more than 200,000 pesos, he would certainly have been justified in appointing an architect of established reputation in the capital, someone connected with the academy. Instead, the choice fell upon Tresguerras.

The selection, on the face of it, is inexplicable. That was no work for an "amateur" — to design and build a large church with a dome of heavy stonework, more than a hundred feet in the air. All we can think is that Tresguerras was not as much of an "amateur" as he pretended himself to be. He must have had behind him some work as architect and builder of which we are in ignorance.

What seems likely is that the provincial saw him in Celaya at the time, was impressed by his personality, ideas and record, and by reports of him by others. Tresguerras, always a fast worker, may have drawn some preliminary sketches, almost off-hand. He would have been dreaming of such an opportunity for years, and would already have been carrying ideas in his head.

In any case, he was selected, and there must have been shakings of heads in Querétaro among those rival architects — those, at least, who considered themselves as being on the plane of rivals. Even in the capital there must have been some disgruntled members of the academy, for in those days, getting a chance to plan a whole new edifice was something that did not happen every year.

There followed the building of the Carmen church, a work that is probably without parallel in history.

The mere sequence of dates is illustrative. . . . The provincial had arrived in Celaya on July 21. Granted that he may have immediately made the decision to rebuild, some time must have been consumed in deciding upon the architect. After that, Tresguerras would have had to draw the working plans, and there had to be a considerable labor of demolition and clearing of the site from the ruins of the old stone work. With all this preliminary work completed, the first stone was laid on November 4, in less than four months.

At the same time, one must remember that the church, though not of cathedral size, was to be neither small nor simple. The plan called for an overall exterior length of 283 feet. Since the architect was working for space and a sense of a lightness, there could be no dependence upon mere mass. The speed of the work must be attributed partly to the Carmelite authorities, who must have been quick to approve plans. Obviously, however, the chief responsibility rested upon Tresguerras himself. Only an artist, and a man in full harmony with himself, could have worked at such speed. We can think, as Ben Jonson told of Shakespeare, that he never scratched out a line. Partly it was that he was working in a long tradition of architecture. Partly it was that he was working in his own country, in the home of his childhood. Most of all, it must have been personal, a great outpouring of creative energy, abundant and yet disciplined, arising in response to the great opportunity that had finally arrived for one who was already forty-three years of age.

Moreover, we should think it to have sprung from the very simplicity of the man himself, none the less real because it sometimes showed itself as a naïve egotism. No other kind of man could have written, of the building of this church, "to put it briefly, I had guidance from the love of the arts, from the fatherland, and from divine religion."

But he was to be much more than an architect, as he must

have known from the beginning. He was to be the builder, directing and supervising the workmen, checking the results. He was also to be the engineer. When he planned his unusually wide nave for effects of space and light, rising to the height of almost seventy feet, he also — and he only — must design the buttresses that would safely carry such a weight of stone, and convey to the ground its thrust of tonnage.

This was already, in Europe, the age of iron. French architects were insuring the safety of their domes by tying the bases with iron cables. But in Mexico it was still honest masonry.

Architect, builder, engineer — yet he must be even more. The little city of ten thousand inhabitants where no great stone structure had been built in more than a generation — how was it to supply skilled workmen? Nor was he able to import them from other cities. The fire of local patriotism burned too fiercely. They would rebuild their own church! And why should men from Querétaro and Guanajuato — suspicious characters of dubious habits — be allowed to carry wages off to their cities? As he wrote of it, "I taught a lot of serape-makers, confectioners, carpenters, and what-you-wish to be stone-cutters."

Once begun, the work proceeded rapidly. With the single directing intelligence using all these workmen as if projections of his own hands and fingers, the bright and clean walls of new stone rose swiftly above the level of the one-storied adobe houses. Six feet was the standard thickness of the walls, with buttresses beside; eight feet, where the towers were to rise.

Naturally there were difficulties. Trust Spanish bureaucracy to put its nose in somewhere. "I waged war," he wrote, "with sixty officials." And, in spite of his devotion to the arts, he was no man to turn away from a fight. In fact, throughout his life, he seems to have waged war rather well and happily.

So the walls reached their appointed height, and it was time for the more difficult and critical work. Now, with the serape-makers and confectioners and carpenters grown somewhat more skillful, he must cover the high and broad nave with the great vaults. He must continue to build the tower upward. Most dangerous of all, he must raise the drum above the crossing, and top that with a dome thirty-six feet in diameter.

At this juncture — or so it would seem logically, and at least it was in June of the year 1804 — another coincidental event set Tresguerras's now full life to humming even more busily. At this time, no less a person than the viceroy himself, Don José de Iturrigaray, came through the country on a kind of tour of inspection, on his way to the rich silver mines at Guanajuato. It was a very unusual occasion indeed, for viceroys were not given to leaving the capital and visiting the provinces.

Now, to reach Celaya, he had to cross the Laja River. There was no bridge, and in June the stream would have been running high. Rivers are notoriously lacking in respect, and do not even recede for viceroys. Though one flinches from imagining such a breech of etiquette, Don José de Iturrigaray, Viceroy of New Spain, may even, at that crossing, have got his trousers wet.

However it was, the viceroy decided that a bridge should be built. He paused in Celaya long enough to decree a bullfight, the proceeds of which could be devoted to that said project. But, certainly, one does not build a bridge from the proceeds of one bullfight, and presumably most of the financing came from vice-regal funds. Tresguerras, as if he did not have enough on his hands already, was appointed to the work.

There are two possibilities. First, the viceroy gave the bridge a higher priority than the church. Second, by the time plans for the bridge had been completed, most of the general stone work on the church had been completed, so that the gangs could be shifted. Moreover, there was a seasonal element about building the bridge. Its piers would have to be set and brought well up during the dry season. So we can be certain that during the end of the rainy season, in July and August and September, Tresguerras had plans busily in hand again, and was going out frequently to look at the river itself, to consider just where the bridge should be placed, and to eye, dubiously, the swirling brown current. The bridge presented, in most ways, a more difficult problem than did the church — and, therefore, to any good architect, a more interesting problem. The church offered some defiance to gravity, but in a traditional and well-regulated kind of way. There were churches in Celaya, and dozens of them in the cities and villages round about. You had models to follow.

There was no model, nearby, for a large bridge. Even architectural manuals are more concerned with ecclesiastical than with pontifical problems. Besides, the bridge must defy not only gravity, but also the power of running water, and the insidious treachery of a shifting bottom. A designer could not take refuge in mere massiveness. The heavier the piers, the more obstruction they placed in the path of the water, and the more dangerously they pressed upon the bottom. Yet the masonry could not be too light, either.

So he designed four stout piers, each about ten feet broad, pointed upstream and downstream, to split the force of the water. Between these, flattened arches rose to such a height that, to reach the roadway, the river would have to overflow the surrounding country. With its footings on either bank, the whole length of the bridge was about two hundred feet. Tresguerras drew the design, primarily, for a practical piece of highway, topping it off with a broad roadway and a sufficient stone parapet. But the fine proportions of the arches, as they stood out on the drawing board, showed the man whose touch was always that of the artist.

He permitted himself, also, one element of decoration — though it might be called a little more than that, for it served to set the bridge off as a thing by itself, and to make it a welcome landmark to the far-off traveler, coming toward it across the plain. At either end of the bridge, one on each side of the road, he designed high stone forms, with curling lines. Baroque in feeling, they are not after any of the common designs. Neither are they out of nature. They suggest a toppling wave, but Tresguerras had never seen a wave. Viewed from a distance, they suggest majestically resting lionesses, with their feet stretched out in front.

As he progressed with the plans of the bridge, work on the church continued, and at this time the renowned traveler Alexander von Humboldt arrived in Celaya and spent a day there. He wrote approvingly that the Church of the Carmelites was of beautiful design, embellished with Corinthian and Ionic columns. His words, taken literally, would indicate that the church had already been completed, but he was probably projecting himself into the future to the time of publication of his book.

Throughout all of 1805 Tresguerras continued to expend himself freely and fully, directing the work both upon the church and upon the bridge. His family life, too, brought him satisfactions. His son, José de la María de la Cruz, had followed the path that his father had forsaken, by studying for the priesthood. In the course of this same year he celebrated his first mass, in the parish church of Celaya.

Even though Tresguerras continued to supervise both church and bridge, his abundant and easily functioning creative powers enabled him to embark upon even more projects. He served in Guanajuato, at least as a consultant, in planning a road. He built two large private houses, probably in Celaya, though these he mentioned merely as "trifles."

In June of 1806 it was again the rainy season, and the two coaches, bearing the Marqués de San Juan de Rayas and his family, would probably not have attempted the fording of the Laja at such a time. This year, however, they took the road confidently, and on June 12 theirs were the first coaches to cross the new bridge. Undoubtedly, workmen were still busy at finishing off the parapet and completing other details, but the dangerous river at last was spanned.

Still the church continued to rise toward its final pinnacles. . . . The portico, with Doric columns, rose up to the line of the vaults, and then, above the nave, the tower lifted a story supported by Ionic columns. Above that soared another story with Corinthian columns. Corinthian above Ionic above Doric — that was as the rule books had it. But *tower* instead of *towers!* In Mexico, for two centuries and more, a dome and two towers had been the complement for a church, just as a head and two arms are for a human being. If a church showed one tower, or none at all, that was merely because it had not been completed. But Tresguerras planned his church from the beginning with one tower, rising from a portico, set in the east front.

In other ways also he showed originality. Though he owed much to the great baroque tradition and may even be said to have followed it, he broke away from it in many details, using, for instance, free-standing columns whenever possible, instead of pilasters. He has even, with justification, been called neo-classical. But he did not stand with the academy.

From the capital itself dictates went out for a sterile reproduction of Greek forms. But no one could ever accuse the Carmen church for masquerading as a Greek temple.

Finally — by now, 1807 may have been coming in — the tower rose up to its final story and its graceful pinnacle above, almost wholly baroque in feeling. The dome also was shining in yellow tile with a chevron patterning in soft green. At its top it ended in a kind of lantern, surrounded by a balustrade, and surmounted by a light metal cross. The church had taken its final outward form.

Inside, the workmen were still busy. By this time craftsmen had probably been imported, by necessity, from other cities — such specialists as gilders. Tresguerras wrote of twenty-five of them to be directed.

Finally, on October 13, 1807, the church was dedicated with all due ceremony. No one can suppose a coincidence in that this was Tresguerras's birthday, his forty-eighth. On this same day the city council named him Director-in-Chief of Public Works. This, indeed, may be reckoned no dazzling office, but it was, at least, the best that they had to offer. He was not without honor in his own city.

Indeed, few lives can have attained a more perfect culmination. "Better be first, in a little Iberian village, than second in Rome." That, almost literally, was the situation of Tresguerras. Farther east along the road than Querétaro and further west than Guanajuato, no one had heard of him. But in Celaya he had raised a monument — not more enduring, perhaps, than bronze, but at least, after more than a century and a half, still lifting its luminous dome and single tower, clean-cut, against the sky. There is, moreover, no comparable building in the world so much the product of a single teeming brain.

One looks at the elaborate altars, and they are his work.

One sees the murals, and he painted them. One admires the graceful carvings on the wooden doors of the atrium, and knows that he designed them, and may even in part have carved them.

The smallest details must be his. On the buttresses of the nave there is an unusual fret-like ornamentation. It does not hold a horizontal-perpendicular line, but dips inward a little, as if giving visual support to the work that the buttress is doing. This unusual detail must be his, not forgotten or neglected even in that flood-time of months, when so much was happenings.

Whether one likes or admires this style of architecture and this church is not the question here. We view it not as architecture, but as biography.

Certainly, "The work is the man" — and, we might add, "the manner of doing the work." First of all, we may note, Tresguerras had worked with unleashed exuberance, but also with restrained control of resources, both artistic and material. For instance, the church filled the ground that was available, but did not crowd it. At the east front he even saved a little plot for open space so that the wall would not rise directly from the street. At the present time this space is partly filled with a poinsettia bush, in the winter months lighting the front of the church with its flaming red. One wonders whether the first of these bushes may not have been planned, and even planted, by the architect himself.

Not only of space but also of money was the control strict. There was no planning of something vast and beyond present hope of completion. There were no towers left to be completed at some indefinite time in the future. Some may even think this a limitation, that his reach did not exceed his grasp. Limitation or not, it is the man.

Tresguerras himself, writing in the *Diario de México* at the time of the dedication, offered a minute description of the church and some appraisal of his own intentions. His unit of measurement was the vara (slightly shorter than the yard). Again, the simplicity and directness of the man shows in the fact that he worked without fractions. Thus the width of the church was 15 varas, and he noted "exactly." He allowed only one exception, and this was in the width of the small atrium or anteroom, which was permitted to be 13 1/2. He was especially pleased that the church was well lighted and that an uncluttered interior permitted nave, crossing, and choir to impress the observer as a single grand unity. Perhaps he summed it up best in his own words, "all is clean, finished, and well-ordered."

Naturally there were attacks from architects, his would-be rivals. One said that Tresguerras had got hold of the plans of a church in Rome, and used them. Another said that the church was copied from Sainte Genevieve in Paris, now the Pantheon.

The only interest of such accusations is in the replies that they elicited. As when he wrote the *Ocios*, Tresguerras showed himself quite able to take his own part. That the plan came from Rome, he declared was "an outstanding lie." Anyone who said that the model was Parisian "lied in his teeth" — or, if that is too blatant English, let us put it, "lied magnificently." Certainly, the suggestion could only have sprung from sheer ignorance. The Carmen church shows scarcely any resemblance to the Pantheon. We may think it of some interest, however, that a comparatively new building in Paris was well-known to Tresguerras in distant Celaya. . . .

That was the culminating year — 1807. Tresguerras was at the height of his powers. He could look forward to an expanding life. Though he was not in accord with the authoritarian academy, his bridge and church spoke for themselves. Even though the period was not an active one in building, he could expect to be summoned for projects anywhere in central Mexico. He might even have commissions in the capital itself. Not so impossible now seemed that voyage to Europe, for which he had always longed.

But men live only as their times and places permit them to live. If the big fish disturb the pool even the minnows suffer. One would hardly think that the ambitions of far-off Napoleon Bonaparte would have forced Tresguerras to adjust to new ways of life. But they did.

In 1808 Napoleon seized power in Spain, and placed his brother Joseph on the throne. The event struck New Spain in a thunderburst. A people who had lived for generations under an established authority found themselves without authority, without a surely *de jure* government. There was no strong man to seize power, and there was scarcely even the conception that such a thing could happen. There were no organized political parties, but only factions. Local government, as at Celaya, might continue to function smoothly enough, but only for so long as some kind of central government was maintained. And what might be called the ruling class was fatally split between *Gachupines* and Creoles. As always in such a situation, things became incredibly complicated, but we need not go further in explaining them. Obviously the situation was ripe for revolution.

Immediately, in September of that year, came the first attempt at seizure of power. It was confined to the capital, and was abortive. There was no reason why the men of Celaya should be especially disturbed. Their most noble and loyal city was quiet and conservative, and would be likely to stick by king, church, and old regime, as long as there were such things to stick by. But *was* there a king?

Tresguerras undoubtedly continued with his work quietly. In this year there is even a likelihood that he was in Querétaro again for a while, executing some paintings at the Teresas church.

The next year passed quietly. There were, indeed, undercurrents and secret meetings, and what one man might have called "plotting" and another "political education." Querétaro, as it happened, was a center of such goings-on, and meetings were conducted behind the front of a so-called Literary and Social Club. Tresguerras may well have been involved, but there is no evidence, and we are not even certain that he was in Querétaro.

Then, in September, 1810, the top that had been clamped too long and too tightly on the now-seething pot suddenly blew off. Father Hidalgo raised his famous war-cry at the little town of Dolores, in the hills only thirty miles north of Celaya. Indian peons and mestizo ranchers flocked in, shouting for independence and death to the *Gachupines*. Hidalgo marched on Celaya with twenty thousand half-armed footmen, and four thousand ranchers on horseback.

This force far exceeded the whole population of the city. There could be no defense. Indeed, most of the inhabitants undoubtedly sympathized with Hidalgo's aims, and were ready to join the rebels. The *Gachupines* fled to Querétaro, many of the wealthier Creoles with them.

There is no indication as to what Tresguerras did. At least, we can be certain, his artistic occupations were considerably broken into, whether by physical or by psychological disturbance.

When Hidalgo entered Celaya, things went off much better than anyone had a right to expect. A few people were killed, but there was no massacre or general looting. Hidalgo and his men marched off to Guanajuato. There, as has happened so often elsewhere, they stained the cause of liberty by perpetrating a horrible blood-letting.

Then came risings in other places, and regular troops battling with half-armed Indians, and years of frightful civil war.

Celaya lay on a main road, but it escaped remarkably well. One day a passing general stood up two men in the town square, and had them shot for traitors — and one of them quartered. That sort of thing happened, but the town escaped general disaster. As to what Tresguerras did during this time, and what he thought, so little solid information is available that judgments have diverged. Writing only ten years after Tresguerras's death and having talked with people who had known him, Manuel Payno declared him to have been so devoted to the cause of freedom as to have written a hymn of praise at its triumph, and to have been so exuberant in his rejoicing that his fellow citizens thought he had gone mad. "Having the soul of an artist," Payno continued, "he understood what liberty meant for nations and for individuals." Quite the opposite has been more recently asserted by Francisco de la Maza and Jesús Rodríguez Frausto, who have critically considered the evidence of Tresguerras's own writings and a few of his official acts.

But the differences may not be irreconcilable. Throughout his life Tresguerras appears as a man who would avoid extremes. In a complicated and frightful period of political upheaval, such as Mexico had to experience, a man of moderation and good feeling is torn to pieces — sometimes literally, always spiritually. People were confused, factions shifted, ideas rose and fell, blood spurted in reprisals and counter-reprisals. During that long period, with all its ebbing and flowing, Tresguerras would have had second thoughts, like any other intelligent man. Rather, there would have been time for the series to go far beyond second thoughts, to hundredth-thoughts.

Some notes that he wrote in 1813 are of interest. That was a year of comparative calm, but much blood had flowed, and Hidalgo had been executed. In some way, Tresguerras had become the possessor of a book published in Italy about fifteen years before, a collection of Tuscan proverbs, translated into Spanish and illustrated. Perhaps merely as a pastime (there must have been little else to do) he wrote some comments on the illustrations, sometimes in prose, occasionally in verse.

As the date he noted "September of the year 1813 and of the American Revolution the third." Thus to write privately, under no compulsion, would seem to indicate that he accepted the rising under Hidalgo as, literally, an epoch-making event, and not as a mere insurrection. But, as might be expected in such difficult times, some of his comments seem to present a contradiction. Under an engraving "Force overcomes Justice" he wrote:

Yes, Force has overcome Justice . . . as we have seen in these our own days, unhappily, . . . when so many Europeans were killed by Hidalgo and his followers, most evilly aroused by hatred and vengeance. Oh, fatal and blood-stained insurrection!

Farther on, he wrote, to condense somewhat:

Surely, that project, inaugurated by Bonaparte and adopted by Hidalgo, cannot be considered merely the offspring of the devil, but — as it seems to me — it was the cursed idea conceived not by a single demon but by a whole council of

*them . . . so that hell itself has poured out on our America
whole vessels of evil, blood, and destruction.*

Such passages, certainly, do not suggest the devoted partisan of liberty. But neither do they necessarily indicate the
staunch supporter of reaction. Do we not, rather, hear in
them the eternally troubled voice of the liberal? He is ready
to write his date in the Third Year of the Revolution, but is
horror-stricken at what the revolution has been — wanting
his omelette, but shocked at the number of eggs that have
already been broken.

Also, the deepest note is not partisan, but humanitarian.
Most of all, he laments the bloodshed.

Tresguerras's political life, however, must be passed over
lightly — in part, because little is known about it; in part, because the artistic life remained always central. He held certain
municipal posts. In 1811 he accepted from the vice-regal
government the office of Procurador General of Celaya. This
appointment was probably more important-sounding than it
actually was, but still it made him a member of the establishment, and gave him a seat on the city council, a highly conservative body. As a member of it, he signed some documents
that may be construed as anti-revolutionary. In 1820 the city
celebrated victories of the established government over the
insurgents, and Tresguerras erected some commemorative
arches. But by that time no one had any very clear idea remaining as to which was the side of liberty and which was
the other.

In 1823 occurred an event which must have produced in
him mixed feelings. One of his first important works in Celaya had been the erection of the column topped by the statue of Carlos IV. Statues to kings were now out-of-date. The
column was moved to a new site, and erected there with a

Mexican eagle on top, and new inscriptions. Tresguerras, still a member of the city council, doubtless supervised the work.

In connection with this eagle one of the few anecdotes about him has been told. As the national emblem, the bird was represented as holding a serpent in its beak, and, in an awkward position, it seemed to be looking backward over its own shoulder. Asked why the eagle assumed this peculiar posture, Tresguerras replied, "So that it cannot see the enormities committed by our municipal authorities."

Doubtless some new construction gave point to the remark, but Tresguerras himself was a member of the city council, so that the story carries something of the pleasant and good-natured irony that was elsewhere, also, typical of him. . . .

In presenting the confused political theme, the story has run somewhat ahead of itself, and must now pick up the artistic theme, more central to the life of the man.

The descent of Hidalgo and his army on Celaya in 1810 had probably interrupted Tresguerras somewhere in the process of finishing off the Carmen church. Though it had been dedicated in 1807, what we may call the interior decoration probably continued for some years. There were altars to be planned and constructed, and murals to be executed. The work had the great advantage, in disturbed times, of being local and of calling for no great expenditure of funds.

In this period, also, he turned again to writing, the art which more than any of the others can survive and even flourish in troublous times. He composed two devotional books that appeared in 1818.

By this year things were quieter, and he could again take commissions in nearby cities. The celebrity of his works in Celaya had spread over all the region, and he had come to be recognized as the outstanding architect and engineer. Probably at this time he worked again in Querétaro, where much is credited to him.

But, until some meticulous historian of art and architecture publishes his findings, there is no way of knowing just what Tresguerras did, or when. Almost every town in the Bajío, and some as far off as Jalisco, claim specimens of his work. Some of the buildings ascribed to him are obviously much older, and fail to display anything of his touch. Possibly, of course, he may have done some remodeling or repair. But even if he merely walked by, one feels, the townspeople began to say, "He himself built it." The churches of Tresguerras have become like the beds where Washington slept.

Some work in Celaya itself is attested. The Franciscans employed him to refurbish their old church. The present portico is probably his — the severity of its classical columns relieved, in a way that seems characteristic of him, by the broken lines of the pediment. He built some small chapels in connection with the church. (In one of them he was to be buried.) He also planned and constructed new altars in neoclassical style, and "very elegant," as the Mexicans say. All of this work was on a small scale, and some of it was not so much architecture as interior decoration.

These were small matters in comparison with all that he had done during his five great years, but he could keep a little busy, and avoid the bitter taste of frustration. Most men, doing so much, would have thought themselves very busy and successful indeed.

At least, he could look back to great days of consummation. The church and the bridge still stood. He saw the church daily. He could see the bridge by a walk that was still not too long for a man who was vigorous, even though no longer young. . . .

Approaching his middle sixties, Tresguerras was old enough
to be displaying some amiable eccentricities, allowable in one
who was the most notable personage in the city — a place,
indeed, where the competition was not stiff. If you were one
of the few hardy travelers who visited Celaya, you were
shown, as the two principal sights, the Carmen church and
Tresguerras. As a matter of fact, they were very much the
same thing.

One of these rare visitors, in 1822, was J. R. Poinsett, the
South Carolinian, who is now endowed with only a faint im-
mortality because his name has been placed on the red
Christmas flower which he brought from Mexico. He was,
however, in his own times, an eminent man, and was just now
visiting the newly independent Mexico as a special envoy
from President Monroe.

He noted of Celaya, "The greatest curiosity in the place is
Don Francisco Tresguerras." He continued:

*He came to see me, and brought a manuscript, which he in-
sisted on reading. It was an essay on taste, and contained
some severe criticisms on his countrymen. He had read it
about half through, when, to my great relief, we were summoned to the window by the sound of music. It proved to be
a procession in honor of the Patron Saint of Celaya.*

First came a dozen young girls, fantastically dressed, on
horseback; then, the flag of the city, borne by three young
men; then two mule-drawn floats — the one full of fiddlers
who made "a terrible scraping," and the other with four children, representing the four quarters of the world. Finally
came a vast throng of people. Poinsett thought the whole
affair to be childish, and Tresguerras agreed.

The two then went to see the Carmen church. Poinsett, a
man of some artistic background, expressed proper senti-

ments of admiration, and especially praised a painting of the Virgin, Tresguerras's work — in rather patronizing fashion, describing it as "highly creditable."

Noting that some of the finest buildings in Querétaro, also, were of Tresguerras's planning, Poinsett characterized his new acquaintance:

He is devoted to the arts, and has contributed all in his power to improve the taste of his countrymen, without any other reward than the gratification of exercising his genius, and the hope of leaving monuments of his taste to his native city.

After dinner Tresguerras once more appeared — this time in old-fashioned dress, with cloak and sword! He took Poinsett to a shop in the arcades. There every evening — "nightly, throughout the year," as Poinsett put it, perhaps with exaggeration — a group of friends, including two priests, gathered to enjoy themselves. The guests sat around the counter, in country-store fashion. At the stroke of eight, one of the priests fell on his knees, and began to mutter prayers, the company joining in the responses. Afterwards, the Mexicans, suffering from want of visitors, overwhelmed Poinsett with questions, so that he himself was thwarted in his desire to learn about Mexico.

These years, for the aging Tresguerras, may have passed pleasantly enough. His wife still lived. She was no longer, certainly, that black-eyed minx whom he had painted. Whether she had grown fat (as most Latin women do) or had grown thin (as some of them do), we have no information. That he liked to spend the evening with his cronies rather than at home need not mean much. Age takes care of such things.

The children had grown up. The son was a priest, and so

there would be no descendants to bear the name. But there were grandchildren from his daughters.

To be the town's most famous citizen was pleasing. Like many artistic people, he enjoyed some adulation. He still played his flute with satisfaction. He had a faithful little dog that followed him around. He was getting old, but he was the kind of man who ages sweetly.

J. C. Beltrami, the Italian traveler, came through in 1825. He noted that Tresguerras worked "with the very greatest lack of self-interest, merely for the pleasure of having his universal genius serve his country in the beaux-arts." Nature, he declared, had endowed the architect with genius, and he had cultivated it, becoming equally outstanding as both painter and sculptor. Thereupon Beltrami was the first — at least, in print — to proclaim a not-too-happy epithet: "He is the Michelangelo of Mexico."

Beltrami's testimony, added to Poinsett's, would seem to make sure that Tresguerras, in his later years, worked without compensation, though as a young man he is known to have accepted fees. In the depressed period that followed the revolutionary wars the possibility of having an architect *gratis* may have helped stimulate building. In any case, Tresguerras was one, we can believe, who would rather practice his art without compensation than not to practice it at all.

In 1826, at sixty-seven, he was still vigorous enough to go off on a new adventure. There was a chance in San Luis Potosí, a hundred miles to the north, and about as far as he had ever ventured from home. People of that city had heard of the great architect, and they had some income from silver mines.

Tresguerras spent much of one year there. His principal work was a large municipal theatre. He also erected the chief altar in the Carmen church, doing the sketches and paintings himself. He put up a statue in the plaza.

Another of the occasional tourists of those times passed through in this year — an Englishman, Captain G. F. Lyon. Tresguerras, in the midst of his work at San Luis, called on the Englishman.

He still, at sixty-eight, maintained such a youthful appearance that Lyon put him down as "about fifty-five." Lyon declared himself "quite charmed with the good sense and taste of this gentleman," and praised his work both in painting and architecture.

He was at this time building a theater at one extreme end of the town, an altar-piece at the other; and painting besides, on a very large scale, for three or four different churches.

Lyon also expressed the opinion that, because of his years, "it is not probable that he will ever gratify his prevailing desire to visit Europe." Lyon could have been even surer if he had realized Tresguerras's true age.

Even after Tresguerras returned from San Luis, he kept busy for several years with comparatively minor works in and around Celaya.

In 1829 he reached his threescore years and ten, and he was definitely an old man, not only by Biblical standards, but by those of his own time and place. In fact, anyone could be considered a very lucky person who could live through all those epidemics and wars to reach seventy.

Some say that the best way to escape senility is to keep the mind busily at work. Tresguerras may illustrate the point. At seventy-two he was still engaged with what we may call a consulting job in connection with some work in Guanajuato.

Later, they told a story of him in these years. He still owned his little farm, a short distance outside of the city. A tenant worked it. If the story is to make sense, the farm must have lain somewhat to the west of the town.

Evening after evening, as it is told, the old man used to walk out toward the farm, his cape over his shoulders. As he walked, he played upon a small flute — and to walk and play at once shows him to have been sound of wind. Behind him followed his faithful companion, the little dog.

When he had arrived at a convenient spot, he seated himself comfortably, and looked back toward the city. The dome and tower of the Carmen church stood up high above the general level of low, flat roofs. He looked at the view with satisfaction, and gradually, as the sun came to its setting, the glint of the dome became almost luminous.

Then, if someone chanced to come by, returning from work in the fields, the old man would stop him, and point the church out, and then inquire what was the name of the architect. On being told, he would smile in gratification.

Now, certainly, this must have been all a little game. Not only did he himself know the name of the architect, but also, as he must have known, every passer-by knew both the name of the architect and the identity of the old man asking the question. Still, it was a pleasant game.

Life must thus have continued to be good. For one thing, he still lived in the same world, and did not face the strangeness and alienation that is so often the fate of the old. The yellow dome against the skyline had not been there in his childhood, but at least it maintained a tradition, and it still rose from the adobe houses, built along unpaved streets. He had lived through a period of rapid change in most parts of the world, where people had experienced the Industrial Revolution. But the old man had never seen a steamboat or a railroad train, and quite possibly he had never seen a steam engine of any kind. He had lived through a political revolution, but the social change had not been great. The *Gachupines* had vanished as a class, but Creoles, mestizos, and Indians continued, much as before. His religious faith remained.

In 1833, Tresguerras was approaching his seventy-fourth birthday. An epidemic of cholera raged that summer. On July 31, he went on his favorite walk again. It was the rainy season, but toward sunset the afternoon shower would have ceased, and the low sun, we can think, shone brightly against luminous clouds of white, set in the blue Mexican sky. The effect upon the view of the town and the church may have been more than ordinarily satisfactory. Yet, also, the view suggested the mournful thought that, within those houses, many people lay ill and dying of the cholera.

After a while the old man set out to return, but in different fashion from his usual one. He walked rapidly, hurrying, as if pursued.

A fellow townsman met him, and accosted him in astonished tones, "Where are you going in such a rush, my friend?"

"A good question!" said Tresguerras, calmly enough. "Death is pursuing us poor mortals with such frightening fury! And, as for me, only a few hours of life remain in this world."

"Bah!" replied the other, "you are still strong and well. Tell me! Where did you get that idea?"

"Friend," said the old man, "there is no time left for me to chat with you. Adios!"

He went hurrying on.

Perhaps he already felt the symptoms of the disease. Perhaps, as sometimes seems to happen to older people, he sensed in a subtle way that his hold on life had loosened.

He went home, added some codicils to his will, and died in a day or two.

OF THE FOUR individuals thus far put forward as having lived the good life, not one was without some advantage of birth, upbringing, and education. Even Joab received, we may suppose, what passed for an education in ancient Israel, and he could actually read, if the account is to be taken literally.

Still, each of these four is to be considered essentially a self-made man. The best-born of them, William the Marshal, was nothing more than a younger son of a minor baron.

Modern men and women are inclined to take this self-made quality for granted, and to consider that the real fruits of life can be plucked only by someone who has had to tend the tree. Just as, religiously, the difficulty of a rich man entering heaven is compared to the camel and the eye of the needle, so the comparison might here be as to the possibilities of the good life for one born at the very top of whatever social pyramid happens to be existing at the moment. Where would the challenge be?

But, in disproof, we may turn to one who was born a prince. He overcame that handicap, just as Tresguerras overcame handicaps imposed by various other limitations and misfortunes. He thus avoided the frustration and triviality which is the fate of most princes — as well as that of most people born to great wealth, and even of some of those, of whom David may be an example, who are born with such an abundance of ability and charm as to make life too easy at the beginning.

Again, we may think, this prince overcame his special

handicap much as some of the others did theirs, by means of the same helps. He was endowed with a favorable assortment of genes from his parents, and then those parents — and this is especially unusual for a prince — brought him up with proper training for the career that he was to follow, and so educated him. From there he went on his way, along the hard path of princes. For, certainly, that life is not easy.

His story shows it. Twice he faced the depths of tragedy. He found himself forced to renounce much that most men hold most dear. The great portrait of him in middle age, by Nuño Gonçalves, shows one who is grave and almost melancholy, and whose dark vesture in a company ablaze with color makes us remember another tragic prince.

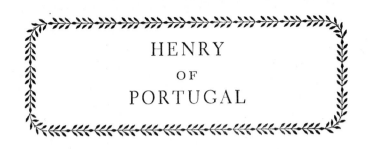

HENRY

OF

PORTUGAL

HE WAS BORN at Oporto on an Ash Wednesday, March 4, 1394. At his birth he was dedicated to Saint Louis, king and crusader. Also, as was fitting for a prince, the astrologers observed the sky and cast a horoscope, finding him born under the Ram, with Mars ascendant in the First House, and Sol and Saturn in significant positions. The interpretation was that the squalling baby would in his time accomplish large conquests and seek out hidden things.

There are those who like to conduct historical research on the principle *cherchez la femme*. Each great man, they wish to show, became great from the influence of a woman — mother, wife, or mistress.

In the present case there can be no argument. It was the mother.

She was a notable woman — this Philippa of Lancaster, Queen of Portugal. In the historical perspective she even seems more remarkable than her husband King John, though their contemporaries would have laughed at that idea, John being himself a very fair figure of a king and man, who had won the decisive battle of Aljubarrota and saved his country from the yoke of Castile.

Philippa was English — as English as Salisbury Cathedral or Chaucer's *Prologue*. In fact, she even has a connection with Chaucer, since she was the daughter of that fair and

good Blanche of Lancaster on whose death the poet composed *The Book of the Duchess*. On her father's side she was
a Plantagenet, daughter of John of Gaunt and granddaughter
of King Edward III.

Her father, in furtherance of his own political ambitions,
gave her in marriage to King John. Philippa doubtless took
it for granted. It was all in the long-established feudal way
of life. To be a queen was more than even John of Gaunt's
daughter had a right to expect, and her husband was vigorous and of a proper age, just thirty.

There were some drawbacks. Portugal was far off, and
probably seemed a little barbarous to the high-born English
girl. And John was on the barbarous side too. He had come
to the throne, only a few years before, by his own ability and
the breaks of the game, having begun life as a king's bastard.
(Well, such a story spoke for him as well as against him.)
He had lived in somewhat rough-and-tumble fashion, and
had two acknowledged bastards of his own.

Philippa, on her wedding day in 1387, probably had decided to reform her husband and to refashion the society into
which he was taking her — a common fantasy of brides. The
remarkable thing was that she did it. By all accounts, John
turned into a model and adoring husband, and the Portuguese court attained a remarkable decorum.

In fact, some might think that Philippa went too far. She
acted, at times, like an English Puritan, born two hundred
years before the term was invented. Perhaps a certain repres-
sion showed in the lives of her sons.

Whatever her own repressions, Philippa did not shun the
marriage bed or motherhood. In fact, she rivaled the grandmother for whom she was named, that Philippa of Hainault
whom the astute Bishop of Exeter, in the charming story,

chose to be queen because her broad hips predicted many sons.

Philippa of Lancaster was already twenty-eight when she was married, but in the next fifteen years she bore six sons and two daughters. The first two of these children died young. The other five sons and one daughter grew up to constitute one of the most admirable families in the long history of European royalty. In fact, few families, royal or otherwise, can match it.

The oldest son to survive bore the good Plantagenet and English name, Edward. This became Duarte on Portuguese tongues. Then came Peter, who was Pedro. The next was Henry or Anrique, and that was probably a name of the mother's choosing; one of her grandfathers had been so called, and her brother was Henry, known as Bolingbroke. The younger children were Isabel, John or João, and Fernando.

Edward, Peter, Henry, and John may fittingly be known by the English forms of their names, for they were proud of their mother's lineage, and knew about their English cousins — especially after 1399 when their mother's own brother became king, as Henry IV.

The two oldest boys even looked English, growing up tall and fair. Henry had more of his father about him — dark eyes and dark hair, this last with a tendency to stand up stiffly. Some traces of his mother showed in his fair skin, though it tanned easily. As a youth, he was tall, powerfully built, strong, and active.

Rarely have children grown up in such happiness. The mother must have possessed something like genius in family affairs. The five boys seemed set upon demonstrating the psalmist's text, "Behold how good and how pleasant it is for brethren to dwell together in unity." Father and mother, too, were joined in mutual love, and in love of their children. And there was the "well-beloved" Isabel, the sister. Edward, who wrote of it all in later years, declared, "Never was there any jealousy among us," and the record shows him right.

Education for boys was much along the well-established curriculum of chivalry — horsemanship and lancemanship. Everyone had to think in military terms because first a border war with Castile and then an uncertain truce dragged along. But Philippa would have seen to it that her boys learned the ways of the courtier, too. French was a second language still for English ladies and gentlemen. The New Learning was abroad throughout Europe, and a prince studied reading and writing, at least in his own vernacular, and even was likely to have dabbled in Latin. Naturally he was instructed in the doctrines of the church.

The two oldest sons even grew up to be a little bookish. They read several languages, and wrote readily and well — even, when they grew older, composing what may be called books. Such proclivity must have seemed a little odd to their father, though he may have been proud of their skills, at the same time.

Henry was less involved with books, and so we may account for his father's tendency to put more confidence in him. Legend has it that Henry was interested in mathematics, astronomy, and sciences generally, but such an opinion seems to be based chiefly on back-reasoning from his later career. There was little-enough available that could pass for science in fifteenth-century Portugal.

In another way, also, Henry was slightly set apart. In a large family there is likely to be a pairing off. Thus Edward and Peter were inseparable. As Henry grew up, they took him into their friendship, but there is such a thing as a third party, even among brothers — "beloved and treasured above all others" was Edward's way of addressing Peter in letters.

Next below Henry in the age-ranking was Isabel, but he could not associate much with her, according to the manners of the times. Under such a situation may have developed the later self-sufficiency of the man, along with his loneliness, and even a brooding quality.

Every obverse has its reverse. Philippa could not do so much for her sons without, in certain respects, doing too much. Edward, for instance, never quite escaped from his parents, and was writing, years later, that he still, even as king, regulated his life by respect to what he thought would be their wishes. Moreover, a fixed mother-image may account for Henry's never establishing an intimate relationship with a woman — or with a man either, for that matter.

Then, in 1411, came formal peace with Castile. The three older boys can only have viewed it with dismay. Here they were, just getting old enough to be in it, and suddenly that hope of martial glory had vanished, and they were not yet even knighted.

At the time of the peace Henry was seventeen — a fine lad, good at hunting, good at the tournament. And a black cloud of peace was settling over the land.

But peace also has its problems. Portugal was adjusted to the economy of a chronic war, and its cessation left all the fighting men unemployed, with nothing to do but to sit around the taverns and grow ripe for an uprising.

Besides one could now begin to think of a campaign against the Moors — a crusade, combining military glory and spiritual salvation. The memory of the Moors was vivid among the Portuguese, and the thought of a crusade still stirred youthful thoughts. Both to church and to state, the Moors were the hereditary enemies.

The Portuguese had defeated and conquered their own

Moors a century before, but others still held the nearby African coast, and their corsairs were a constant threat.

So, at the urging of his three older sons, King John began to prepare a great expedition. Security was excellent, and the objective was successfully kept from public knowledge. The surprise attack was scheduled for the summer of 1415, and it would be launched upon Ceuta, a rich Moorish city, lying just inside the Straits of Gibraltar.

Prince Henry was given extraordinary responsibility for one who had barely passed his twentieth birthday in that time of preparation in 1414. Even so early, he appears self-reliant and possessed of his father's confidence. The two older brothers remained under the father's eye, organizing the fleet and army based on Lisbon. Henry, however, was sent off to Oporto in the north, to oversee the almost equally great preparations at that city. He had older heads to advise him, and undoubtedly had instructions to do as they told him. Still, he was the King's representative, and the symbol of leadership.

In due course, Henry sailed his great fleet down the coast, and united it with the rest of the ships in the Tagus at Lisbon. The king took command; with him, as his second, the heir-apparent, Prince Edward. Prince Peter took over the vanward division of sixty ships; Prince Henry, the rearward division of sixty more. These were the large ships, as reckonings went in those times. Swarms of lighter craft were ready to sail as escorts.

Aboard, or ready to go aboard, were all the best of Portugal, along with adventurers and soldiers-of-fortune and crusaders from England and half the kingdoms of the continent — and none of them knowing where they were going.

The king offered to knight his three sons, but they declined, saying that they wished first to achieve some deed of arms. All was ready.

Then everything paused, and a hush fell. The queen lay dying.

In a scene of almost incredible sadness, Zurara, the chronicler, tells how the three tall sons came to her bedside. She had ready a new sword for each of them, and to one after the other, in proper sequence of age, she gave each son a sword, to be carried on the expedition. To each, in her weakness, she spoke briefly and nobly, commending him and the new sword to good deeds, each son in a different way. To Edward, it should be the sword of justice, since he would be king. Peter should devote his sword especially to that knightly duty of defending ladies. As for Henry, she gave him the sword, commending to him "the nobles, knights, gentlemen and squires." Then she said, "I give you this sword and my blessing — to be knighted with it."

Shortly, she heard the wind blow, and asked what wind it was, and was told it was from the north. Then that descendant of so many warriors thought of the ships lying ready, and said, "That is a good wind for your voyage."

The next day she died, the wife and mother. Even the hard, middle-aged King John was so stricken that the whole question of the sailing hung in uncertainty.

When the king rallied after a day or two, there was the question as to whether the ships had been allowed to get out of readiness, because of the delay. Prince Henry replied proudly that, as far as his division was concerned, the time required to depart would be long enough to raise the anchors and trim the sails.

So they left the Tagus, and ran before the north wind that the queen had heard. In a day or two they rounded Cape St. Vincent, the corner of the continent, and Prince Henry certainly looked at the high red cliffs without knowing how much of his life was to be involved with that place.

The great armada of vessels large and small, galleys and sailing-craft, moved on, exposed to all the winds of heaven and all the shortcomings of human nature.

Finally, however, the ships lay off the beaches of Ceuta, and things looked as if, in spite of some last-minute delays and false starts, the Portuguese had managed to take the city by surprise. King John laid his plan to feint with his right and strike with his left, and he granted a request that Henry had made at Lisbon — to lead that first attack. Some think that Henry was the favorite son, but it may be merely that he inspired more confidence, or even that he was the youngest of the three and so was expendable. Edward, as heir-apparent, had to be husbanded, and Peter was placed in command of the reserve.

Then, on the morning of August 21, the landing-boats splashed into the water. One squire had beaten the orders a little, and he hit the beach first. Prince Henry, raging at him, was close behind. They went up the beach in a rush, driving the Moors before them, and stormed right in at one of the gates.

Ceuta was a good-sized town with the usual maze of narrow streets. Once you were inside, your trouble had only begun. Henry and some of his men vanished into the town, and the king, coming up later, was told that his son had been killed. All the old warrior said was, "Well, that is what happens to soldiers."

But Henry could not have been happier, with a rough-and-tumble fight at each street corner. After a while Edward came up, and the two brothers fought together. The better-armed Portuguese were having much the better of it. Once the two brothers stormed up what seemed to be a dominating hill, only to discover, perhaps from the smell, that they had gloriously captured the city garbage dump.

In the end, everything was mopped up, without poor Prince Peter ever having had a chance. The king wanted to knight Henry then and there, but Henry would have nothing to do with getting in ahead of his brothers by the breaks of the luck. In due course, the ceremony was held, not as a battlefield promotion, but in all proper order, with the watching-in-arms all night in a newly dedicated church that just ceased being a mosque. Then the three sons were knighted in proper order, and each was girded with the sword that his mother had given him.

Now Henry of Portugal could hold up his head in comparison with his cousin Henry of England, who this same summer had won his victory at Agincourt.

The quick capture of the city had been so surprising that the Portuguese hardly knew what to do next. The king decided to garrison Ceuta and hold it in the face of all Islam. This would be a fine gesture, even if something of a military and financial hazard.

Then the great fleet sailed home on a fair wind, and took harbor at Tavira in the sun-baked southern province of Portugal, that takes its name from the ancient kingdom of the Algarve and faces toward the ocean and Africa.

There the king called his three sons before him. (Now there had never been dukes in Portugal, but Philippa's grandfather had been a duke, and so also her father and uncles, those princes sprung of Edward III, and Philippa must have thought that her sons too might someday be dukes, after the English fashion.) So, at Tavira, King John spoke out. His oldest son, he said, would inherit the crown, and so nothing need be done for him. But, as for Peter, he was created Duke of Coimbra. Henry was made both Duke of Viseu and Lord of Covilham. The king also gave him a kind of citation, "for the greatness of his effort in equipping the fleet at Oporto, and also for the dangers that he incurred, when we conquered the town."

Then the king and the princes left the fleet to march home overland, and receive their due plaudits.

The court, including Princess Isabel and the two young princes, came as far as the city of Evora to welcome the victors. There was a joyous family reunion, lacking only — as everyone must have been only too well aware — the mother.

There also they met Doña Mecia Coutinho, whose son had been one of the few casualties at Ceuta, killed at Henry's side. That prince, though he was later to win the reputation of being a man without feeling, was so overcome that he could not face Doña Mecia. He fled to his room to escape the scene when the mother must be informed, and he was so affected that she herself consoled him.

But Henry, though he could still make such displays of immaturity, had now come into manhood. Within the space of a few weeks, in his twenty-first year, he had been transformed from an inexperienced younger son into a seasoned warrior, a knight, a duke, and even a hero. There is, however, no reason to think he as yet had any vision of what his life-work was to be. That seems to have come over the course of the next few years, or perhaps — as legend prefers it — in some single moment of vision at some time in those years. As so often, what a man became was determined by events that were unrelated to the final end. We must attribute Henry's development to the duties that his father saw fit to put upon him.

Of the three elder sons, Edward was tied to his father and the court as the king-to-be. As for Peter, the king did not want, it would seem, to entrust executive matters to him. Peter had manifold virtues, and the king may well have loved him dearly without trusting him in public affairs. And, in the long run, the king was proved right. That left Henry, and he was, after Ceuta, altogether worthy of trust.

Immediately upon his return Henry went to Lisbon with the court. His new fiefs were in the North, and he must have expected to spend his time there and at Lisbon. He had no connection with the South.

But, early in the next year, which was 1416, the king appointed Henry to be governor of Ceuta. Just what the appointment involved is uncertain. Ceuta was under chronic threat from the Moors, but it already had, as its captain, the valiant Count de Menezes. Apparently, as governor, the prince was supposed to support the count with the resources of the kingdom. The only place from which this could be done was from the Algarve in the south.

Henry was largely in the Algarve after this appointment. Supply ships had to be sent to Ceuta, in convoy because of Moorish corsairs. Henry kept dispatching expeditions to raid the Moorish coast. Even so early, though not yet for exploration, he was sending his ships out.

A crisis flared in 1419. The Moors came down in such strength that the gallant count called for help. Henry got a fleet together and sailed over, young Prince John with him. They found, however, that the garrison had handled the affair successfully. Henry, his fleet all ready and nowhere to go, was for making a try at Gibraltar, which the Moors still held. But orders from the king forbade it, since the capture of Gibraltar would have irritated the Castilians.

In this year Henry's connection with the South was still further strengthened by his appointment as Governor of the Algarve. About the same time he was made Governor of the Order of Christ.

This order had succeeded to the Templars on their dissolution in Portugal, and it had inherited the wealth for which the Templars were famous. The order had continued the tradition of the military monks, but King John now finally secularized it. With the secularization, the members were relieved of their vows of poverty and chastity, so that Henry's continuing celibacy cannot be thus explained. Possibly, however, the tradition of the order was of some influence.

Thus, at the age of twenty-six, Henry held an enviable position. Even Edward, as long as his father lived, lacked independence of action. Peter was eclipsed, and decided to set out on an extensive journey throughout Europe. He asked Henry to go along with him, and they remained good friends. But Peter had to go off alone, for by now Henry had too much else on his mind.

For one thing, on the last expedition to Ceuta, he had had to settle down for three months of what amounted to garrison duty. What do you do in such a case — especially if you are not involved with women? Henry could spend some time in religious observances, and in inspecting his troops and ships, and in a little practice at sword-and-buckler perhaps. But, with an active mind like his, he set about gathering information — first of all, for strategic reasons. Ceuta had plenty of Moorish captives and slaves, and along with them were Negroes, who had first been captives and slaves of the Moors, and then had exchanged masters without its making much difference to themselves. They could all be questioned, through an interpreter if necessary. *What is the name of your country? How many days' journey? What direction? Are you Moslem, or something else? Do you know of any Christians living there? What does your country produce? Is there gold? How about ivory and spices?*

Gradually, after the dust of lies and fanciful tales began to settle, you had a little idea of what lay to the south. First came the mountains of the Moors, and then the great desert, lacking people, crossed by caravans of camels. Then, still further, very shadowy, there came vaguely into view a land of a great river (was it a branch of the Nile?), and grass and trees, inhabited by Negroes, having cities, producing gold and ivory.

Though he was rated as the sober one among the three elder brothers, Henry was not dull. And who could hear such tales without a kindling of the imagination?

The coincidence of timing, as well as it can be established, seems so close as to make likely that the residence in Ceuta brought about the first voyage of discovery, though it was directed west, not south. Typically for Henry, the sober one, it was really a voyage of rediscovery, for there was plenty of evidence that certain islands were out there somewhere.

"I was blown out of my course by a storm!" That is the hoariest of seamen's excuses, to account for being anywhere you were not supposed to be. It is a poor bit of water that cannot blow up some kind of a storm at need.

Quite possibly, Henry had asked his father's permission. That was a mistake. The king was past the time of adventuring. Even the glorious capture of Ceuta had proved to be something of a mistake, and little more than an added expense. Portugal had too few rather than too many people. Why discover more lands?

But these things may be managed. After the return from Ceuta two of Henry's squires volunteered for some service that would bring them renown. Their names deserve recording — João Gonçalves Zarco, and Tristão Vaz Texeira. Henry sent them, ostensibly, on a somewhat extended reconnaissance along the Atlantic coast of Morocco. They ended up by sighting one of what came to be known as the Madeira group, and that means that they were blown off their course by — well, say, four or five hundred miles. Of course, it may have been an unusually bad storm.

This voyage of the two squires began a new age. From it the tradition of exploration runs right on, without break — and now we are working for the moon.

What was new about this voyage, and what ties it even more to the present "scientific exploration," is that it was followed up. That was the great new feature of all the Henrician exploration. Daring voyagers there had been before — Hanno, Pytheas, and others. But the results were lost, and the stories became mere legends, until we are scarcely sure whether there ever was a Hanno or a Pytheas. But of Henry we can say, "Perhaps he did not discover as much as some others, but what he did, stayed discovered."

Though the dating is a little uncertain, there seems to have been a second voyage of discovery, and then the actual colonization, on the main island of Madeira, in 1420. Thus was begun the amazing westward expansion of Europe that was not to end until it had swept clear across the Americas.

In the next few years Henry continued to govern the Algarve and to watch over Ceuta, and he also sent ships southward along the Moorish coast, though for a long time they did not get far enough to accomplish anything that could be called discovery.

In that direction, beyond the cities of the Moors and only fifty miles off the coast, lay the Canary Islands. You might say that people had always known about them. A tradition had even descended from antiquity. By Henry's time the Castilians had planted colonies on three of the islands. The others were still held by the natives, called Guanches, an interesting and mysterious people, neither Moors nor Negroes, good fighters.

According to vague reports — but likely enough — Henry
sent a scouting expedition as early as 1422. He began to argue
the Castilian title to the islands, on the ground that occupa-
tion, not mere discovery, gave the rights. On the other hand,
"Peace with Castile!" was the basis of Portugal's foreign
policy. Still, the Canaries were far off and strikingly unimportant, and there was little likelihood that the king of Castile would think them worth a war. So either Henry's father
allowed the southward probing, or else Henry merely went
ahead without bothering to report to Lisbon.

Apparently he sent ships southward every year for twelve
years. Twice at least, he sent forces to attempt conquest,
though he left the Castilian-held islands alone. But both
these expeditions came to nothing, because of obstinate re-
sistance by the Guanches, and difficulties of supply.

All that was really accomplished was that the Portuguese
seamen became familiar with that coast and those waters.
At first they had known Africa only as far as the unimportant
cape that they called Não. Though it was probably an Arabic
name, it was the same as the Portuguese word for *no* or *not*,
and there was a rhyme to the effect that anyone who went
further would *not* return. Cape Não was a five-hundred-mile
run from Lagos in the Algarve. But, to get to most of the
Canaries, you had to sail beyond Cape Não, and the Castilians must have been doing so regularly. So the Portuguese
horizon rapidly advanced about two hundred miles farther,
to within sight of a headland called Bojador. That name
looks like an Arabic word put into a Spanish form. The
Portuguese might have taken it vaguely to mean The Bulger,
or possibly The Restrainer, or even (as the name goes in some
other parts of the world) Cape Turn-again. Whether or not
they took it as a name of bad omen, they did not want to go
beyond it. The seamen told stories of what would happen to

any ship that went beyond Bojador. There was even a story of one expedition that had done so, more than a hundred years before — two Genoese ships that had vanished without trace.

Back in the Algarve the prince must have pooh-poohed such tales. But he was sitting safely in Portugal, and running no risk of being eaten by the fishes or starving on some desert shore. One thing, it is, not to believe a story, and another thing to order a crew to sail into what they think to be certain death. If they should just happen to meet with bad luck, how long would it be before you could get another crew to sail so far?

So the prince bided his time. He was a good bider. Standing there on the line between the Middle Ages and the Renaissance (though, of course, he did not know it), he had something of the medieval mystic left in him, and to such a man time does not matter much. Besides, there were practical difficulties. An advance base in the Canaries would help greatly, but it was proving hard to get. In addition, there was his father. Old now, King John still ruled, and he was not going to have any son of his giving Castile a reason to break the peace.

We cannot, however, think of Prince Henry as brooding, day after day, on the cliffs of Cape St. Vincent, and looking southward. Though exploration may have already become his most basic interest, he still had multifarious duties. Lisbon and the court were only a hundred miles to the North, and Henry, still a young man and known as a hard rider, could make that in two days, and doubtless often did. Beyond Lisbon lay Viseu and Covilham.

Certainly in the late twenties he must often have ridden North, for in those years an epidemic of marriages struck the family. So far, John was the only one to succumb. In 1425 he had married his half-niece on the illegitimate side. She seems to have made him a good wife, and John continued unimportant in the story — a clean-cut fellow, who probably enjoyed romping with the children, and hot mulled wine after dinner.

In September, 1428, great ceremonies were held for Edward in Coimbra. It was a fitting royal marriage, the bride being Leonor, sister of the King of Aragon.

Though Edward had produced an illegitimate son, he had generally been shy with women, and had written of their virtues with awe. Now, during the days of preliminary festivities, he proceeded to fall in love — but properly, with his fiancée. Henry was there, though for some reason, probably illness, King John was not. This meant that Henry reported to his father in a letter, about the only one to be called personal that still survives. Henry wrote a good letter, with touches of humor, and it makes us put him down as a normal young man and a dutiful son. Though he himself was no hand with women, he was amused at the diffidence of Edward, who visited his Leonor several times a day, but never got up courage to kiss her. We should note, however, that Henry qualified, "As far as I know." It is an honest phrase to write, allowing that Edward might have been more enterprising in private. It also shows Henry as the realist, and even the scholar. The man who went to that trouble to qualify would not accept unearthly terrors beyond Bojador unless someone showed him evidence.

There was much else in the letter of entertaining suggestion. Henry had enjoyed a boar hunt, and he approved the technique of two pages in a bullfight. He recorded that Edward praised the dancing of Leonor, as well as her singing and her playing on the minicord. Edward's admiration was the important matter. Henry did not state whether he himself joined in the praise.

On September 22 the heat was severe, the ceremony was long, and the bride's costume was heavy. At the end she fainted. Henry wrote, a little cavalierly and in no-nonsense fashion, "We dashed water on her, and she came to."

The consummation of a royal marriage is a matter of state. So, after the couple had been properly bedded, Henry wrote in all assurance, "The Lady Infanta is now wholly your daughter."

Peter, back from his long travels, had returned for the wedding, so that it was a reunion of all the children. His turn came next, and in 1429 he married another peninsular girl, daughter of the Count of Urgel.

In the same year it was Isabel — and high time, for she was thirty-two. Politically speaking, it was a brilliant marriage; in some other ways, not. She went as third wife to Philip, the wealthy and powerful Duke of Burgundy. Though she was not the genius that her mother had been, she did well in a situation far from easy.

The time was ripe also for Henry to be married, but there is no suggestion that he ever considered it, or that his father considered it for him. Politically, they both may have thought it unwise. Too many families of royal birth could cause trouble in a kingdom, as anyone could see by taking a look at England and their cousins there, where troubles had already been plentiful and more of them seemed likely to arise.

Alone, after the weddings, Henry went back to the Algarve and his main business of life. Yearly the ships went to the Canaries, and their crews saw Bojador off to the south. At a deeper level, things were moving a little, and Henry was certainly helping them on. Shipmasters were getting confidence at sailing out of sight of land, trusting more to compass and astrolabe. Ships were being tried out, and improved. The new caravels were showing themselves very good at sailing into the wind. With their fore-and-aft rig, they could do better than the old cross-wind course, getting around to almost forty-five degrees. Then, too, sailing routes were being explored. On the return voyage from the Canaries you should not hug the coast. Instead, you did better to steer north, and pass boldly out of sight of land. Making the Madeiras, or their latitude, you could catch a westerly right back to Portugal.

Some think that out of this new sailing route came the next discovery, that once again a shipmaster, blown far off course, finally saw breakers spouting, or what looked like a cloud but did not move. Again, it is a long way to be blown by accident, and very likely the discovery, or rediscovery, came because someone was told to go and look.

In one way or another, one of Henry's captains got to the Azores. The date may have been as early as 1427 or as late as 1432, but a few years are not worth an argument. Again — and this is what is important — the first voyage was followed up, and eventually the whole archipelago was surely fixed in the corpus of geographical knowledge.

All this represented a long step into the west. From the Azores to Newfoundland is not very much farther than from Portugal to the Azores. In a way, it was unfortunate that something now happened to open the way to the south and to take Henry's attention away from the west.

On August 15, 1433, King John died. He had reigned, greatly, for forty-eight years, until attaining the ripe age of seventy-six.

Edward succeeded to the throne without incident. Much as all the sons had loved and admired their father, they must have felt a certain sense of relief from the hand of age.

Now, instead of being restrained from Lisbon, Henry was probably urged on. Edward, and Peter too, were active, intelligent, young, and inquiring. In the very next year after the king's death — and such time-linkage can hardly be coincidence — a ship sailed south.

Zurara, the chronicler, preserves some of the details. . . . One of Henry's squires was Gil Eanes. He was a native of the Algarve, born in Lagos, a good seaport which was coming to be Henry's seat of activity. Thus born, Eanes must have been a seaman by inheritance. In 1433, while the king was still living, Eanes had made a voyage to the Canaries. Such voyages had been routine for the last twelve years. Doubtless Henry would have been glad to have one of the captains reach beyond Bojador, but there is no evidence that he put pressure on them or gave anything that could be called orders. Now, with a new king at Lisbon, it was different.

Bojador was still there, and men told of all its host of terrors — shoals, boiling seas, a blazing tropical sun that made human life impossible, monsters of the deep. To pass it, the sailors said, meant to lose soul with body, for it was as good as committing suicide. One is amazed that an unimportant point of land, not even a notable landmark, could have affected the minds of seafaring men, necessarily bold by profession, so that it blocked exploration for a generation. We forget the power of superstition. Besides, the equatorial horror had support from classical writers, such as Ptolemy, and from fathers of the church, such as Augustine.

Prince Henry did not believe those stories. He took Gil Eanes aside, and told him. But, if Zurara is to be trusted, Henry did not, even then, give orders. Instead, he said, no matter what risks Eanes might take, the reward would be commensurate.

Eanes sailed, and Henry waited. Who could be sure? After all, should he doubt Ptolemy and Augustine? He could remember the two vanished Genoese ships. Only reason and common sense sustained him. How could any sharp line be drawn at that one cape?

Then Eanes was back. He had passed Bojador!

He had not gone very far indeed — about as far as you could spit over the lee-rail with a stiff breeze. But he had brought the ship close ashore, and launched a boat and landed. He deserves to be remembered, this squire of Lagos. It was much like landing on the moon.

He discovered, as he told Henry, neither men nor trace of them. But he found some scant wild flowers growing in the desert, and he picked a few and brought them home, as if from some other planet. They were of a kind known in Portugal and called Our Lady's roses, and he showed the withered flowers to Henry.

It was not much; it was almost nothing. But it was a little step forward, and with Henry there was never any step backward. Ahead lay all the unknown globe, and eventually much more!

All the brothers had taken mottos in French. Henry's was *Talent de bien faire*, that is, "Desire to do well." It suits him, but sometimes one thinks that it might better have been "The very next year." Always there is about his actions a continuing urge, the repeated effort — never pressed too hard, but always pressed a little farther. Again one thinks of the mystic to whom the years are nothing. That does not excuse anyone from the desire to do well, but still there is time. The man dies, but the mills of God grind on.

So — and it *was* the very next year — Henry sent Eanes again, and Afonso Gonçalves with him, in two ships, and they sailed farther, though not very far. They said, when

they returned, that they had gone fifty leagues beyond Bojador. Such voyagers had no accurate way to reckon dis-
tances, and they generally exaggerated. That is no matter.
They found the country still deserted and desert, but they
discerned tracks of men and camels.

Then — naturally, the very next year — Henry prepared
to send Gonçalves again, and now, as prince, he gave orders
that the ship was to sail as far as it could. Even so, there
seems to have been no pressure, and the captain could decide
for himself how far that would be. Besides, Henry envisioned
no mere reckless voyaging. Gonçalves was also to explore the
land, and endeavor to capture a native, from whom information could be obtained. Since war with the Moors was
chronic, this unfortunate native could be considered a prisoner of war.

Most curiously of all, Henry assigned to the expedition two
horses and two sixteen-year-old boys to ride them. These
horses were to be used for expeditions ashore, and this is probably the only exploring expedition ever so equipped. Such
trouble and expense shows how greatly Henry was concerned
with the interior, not merely with the seacoast. Probably,
because the ships themselves were so small, the horses were
mere ponies and the boys were the equivalent of jockeys.

So Gonçalves sailed still further — by as much, this time,
as five hundred miles. At one point he put the horses and the
boys ashore. Riding light, with lances and swords but no
armor, they scurried off, twenty miles upcountry. They found
only a desert, but finally met a few miserable Moors. In high
spirits the boys closed in, and skirmished, and one of them
was wounded in the foot.

When they came back and told the story, Henry must have
loved it. It was just what he would have liked to do at sixteen. But he was past forty, and his life too full of responsi-

bilities for him to be going on voyages. Besides, as prince and duke, he was far too valuable to risk capture by the Moors. His ransom would have bankrupted the kingdom.

Thus his life was shaping up — to send out his captains, but himself to stay at home. The southward exploration, we can hardly doubt, was beginning to be the great passion of his life.

Already he was becoming inexplicable to his contemporaries — much more so to them, indeed, than he is to us today. Since his time the desire for knowledge, whether you call it "scientific" or not, has become respectable and commonplace. In Henry's isolated Portugal, the conception hardly existed. But the three older brothers all seem to have had an infection with the peculiar madness of wanting to know. Possibly Edward and Peter were even worse touched than Henry, but he, the practical one, did something about it.

In still feudal Portugal, Henry was a strange fellow. So it is that Zurara, writing his chronicle, thought it necessary to have a whole chapter explaining to his readers just why in the world Henry was doing it. This is a task that Zurara himself was not equipped to perform. He was a public-relations man with the job of presenting a far-out mathematician or a theoretical physicist. He started out, like a medieval theologian, to give five reasons, and then added a sixth. Now, when a man has to use the shotgun method, obviously he does not really know the reason.

Of course, Henry himself might have done the same thing, and doubtless his motives were mixed. Men's motives generally are. We can think it true that he wanted to have better observations of the southern sky to further the study of astrology. Also, he wanted to outflank the hated Moors strategically, and to establish contact with the kingdom of Prester

John or any other Christian realm that might remain isolated somewhere in Africa. He wanted to break the Moorish monopoly of the trans-Sahara trade in gold and ivory and spices. He wanted to spread the Christian faith. But, in the essence, Zurara seems to come closest to the truth with the simple reason that he gives first, that is, that Henry "wanted to know what land lay beyond the Canaries and a cape called Bojador." To put it even more briefly, "he wanted to know."

Five hundred miles in two years! And the whole world was only about twenty-five thousand miles around, as the astronomer-astrologers believed. The two sets of figures, put together, seemed to say that Henry's ships, within his reasonable expectation of life, could reach out for ten thousand miles, and, in fact, get to India or almost any place as yet imagined.

But other winds were blowing, besides those that took ships down the African coast. Henry's "desire to do well" felt other responsibilities and pressed toward older outlets.

No other great man's life has been so much tied up with brothers. This time, it was Fernando, the baby of the family.

He was that, not only in years, but also, it would seem, in immaturity of character. How could he well escape it, being the youngest of five brothers? He was, indeed, like Henry in some respects. He never considered marriage, and was highly religious. But he lacked Henry's practical touch, being even more extreme in religious practice and devoting much of his interest to alms-giving and other good works.

His wise old father, King John, had let him go his way, and that was probably the best thing to do. His brother Edward, having become king, considered the family honor, and made Fernando the Master of the Knights of Aviz, a religious-military foundation like Henry's Order of Christ. Fernando took it seriously, and got the idea of leading his knights in a crusade against the Moors in Africa. His father would have told him to go back to his praying, but Edward acted like the considerate gentleman that he always was. He even called what amounted to a family council. Henry supported Fernando, thinking it time to repeat the success of Ceuta, now receding into history. John considered both sides, balancing inexpediency against honor and getting nowhere. Peter opposed the whole idea. Edward himself was really in opposition, but he yielded, probably swayed by the thought that this would be a crusade.

So it was 1414 over again, with the armorers banging on their anvils, and the recruits marching and drilling. But this time there was no security.

Henry was in command, the obvious choice. But even he was no experienced general. He had fought well at Ceuta, but he had never commanded an army in battle.

On September 13, 1437, Henry and Fernando with army and fleet appeared off Tangier, and found the city well garrisoned and the defenses in excellent repair. Besides, from escaped slaves they must have learned the ominous news that the war drums were beating all through the hills, as the tribesmen mustered.

Remembering the poor showing of the Moors at Ceuta, Henry need not have been alarmed. He did the right thing, by attacking at once, before Moorish reinforcements could arrive. The attack was beaten back. In the following days everything went from bad to worse. Henry, as general, made some mistakes. A month later, the Portuguese had been cut off from their fleet and penned up in a hastily entrenched camp, and were surrounded by a well-organized Moorish army, augmented by hordes of tribesmen, howling for Christian blood.

But Salat-ben-Salat, the Moorish commander, knew that

the Portuguese had some fight left in them; also, he may have feared his own uncontrollable tribesmen. The terms that he offered were hard, but not so bad as being slaughtered or surrendering unconditionally to be sold into slavery.

The Portuguese could keep their arms and return to their ships, but Ceuta must be surrendered. Salat-ben-Salat would give one of his own sons as a pledge, and he demanded in return one of the Portuguese princes. Henry offered himself, but it was no time for chivalry. The Portuguese leaders declared that he was too valuable and that the surrender of their commander would be a double disgrace. So Fernando, the baby, was given up.

As the army moved back toward the beach, the wild tribesmen swarmed in. The Portuguese fought their way through, but some men were cut off and killed.

The ruined army took refuge in Ceuta. At last, tragedy had struck at Henry. He remained in Ceuta, almost as if ashamed or afraid to return home.

The disaster shook Portugal, and reverberated through Europe. Then came negotiations.

By attacking after the capitulation, the Moors had broken the treaty. So Henry claimed, with some right; though Salat-ben-Salat claimed, also with some right, that he had no command over the tribesmen. As for Ceuta — did Henry, as field commander, have any right to surrender crown property and an important national holding? The king must decide. And would not the surrender of the city and its churches be a betrayal of Christendom?

The argument did not help to get Fernando back. As for his Moorish counterpart, the well-haremed Salat-ben-Salat merely declared that he was not much concerned, for he had plenty of sons. Fernando did not help by writing pitiful letters about being forced to wear chains and do hard and menial garden work. There was not as much iron in him as in his brothers. One misses the voice of the father saying, "That is what happens to soldiers." But Prince Fernando had never been physically strong, and harsh treatment broke him down rapidly.

After some months Henry returned, but his days were bitter and barren. No ships sailed south. His younger brother languished in Fez. Argument continued, but Ceuta was not surrendered. The days had passed — if, indeed, they ever existed — when national utility and prestige could be readily sacrificed for the person of a royal prince. On the other hand, Ceuta was unprofitable, and Portugal might really be better off without it.

Then, early in September of 1438, bad news came to the Algarve, and Henry went spurring off again on the road to the North. He did not make it in time. On September 9, King Edward had died. The circle of the brothers was at last irrevocably broken.

Edward had been a king, conscientious and honest, but neither skillful nor fortunate. He had reigned only five years, but he helped nothing by his dying or by his manner of it. He left to his people, as his heir, young Alfonso, his six-year-old son. He also left a will, appointing his wife to be regent.

He had fallen in love with Leonor at the time of their marriage, ten years before. So, apparently, he had remained. We are accustomed, romantically, to praise such men, but it might be better if kings did not love their wives — as, indeed, few of them have been noted for doing.

A six-year-old boy for king, and a foreign woman for regent! Moreover, she was a woman who was not notable for either wisdom or strength of character.

The burghers of Lisbon, insulted and shocked, were up in arms, almost literally. Prince Peter, the king's oldest uncle, was their candidate for regent, and he had the support of most of the responsible leaders throughout the country. Henry might well have made a better regent, but he was bearing the onus of Tangier, was younger than Peter — and, besides, he undoubtedly did not want the post.

The kingdom had enjoyed stable government for half a century. Now everything was open for intrigue at court and factional strife.

Henry, kept from his ships, stayed in Lisbon. He put forward a compromise measure, pleasing nobody greatly and showing no high statesmanship on his own part. Peter was at the center of controversy. Even John was pulled into it.

But the three brothers, though they might differ on policy, remained one in love and mutual confidence. When factional plotters carried false calumnies from one prince to another, seeking to set them at odds, the brothers only laughed.

What was really needed, one imagines, was for one of the princes to have stepped in with a well-planned *coup d'état*. But the sons of John and Philippa had been reared in an atmosphere of love and reason. (They were what would now be called "nice guys," and there is a cynical proverb that such people finish last.)

After a while, however, Peter got practical control of affairs, to the great relief of most people. Among them Henry must have been included. His was another task, and he could now turn to it again. The troubles over the regency were much less profound, in a personal way, than those over Fernando.

One speaks of a man burying himself in his work, as a means of living through a time of sorrow. So it may have been with Henry. Less than two years after the black day at Tangier, he had already been engaged with plans for colonizing the Azores.

As for ships, some of them may have ventured south even

in these bitter years. If so, they did nothing special and set no new mark of discovery, and so they are not recorded. Only in 1441, after a lapse of five years, did the persistent Henry get on with the work.

That year, two ships sailed from Lagos. They were under independent command, but sometimes acted in company. When the first ship came back, Henry had interesting news. The ship had not advanced any further south, but the crew had made some captives. These were Negroes, or largely of Negro blood. So, at last, Henry had been successful in outflanking the Moors and getting to what lay beyond. One of the Negroes, a chief, could talk the Moorish language, and so could give information through an interpreter. Arrangements were made to return this chief, for a ransom.

Then the other ship came in, and it bore what may have been even better news for Henry. This captain had pressed on to the south — not much farther, only about a hundred and twenty-five miles. But the achievement showed that things were moving again. The farthest headland that this crew had seen they had named White Cape, because of its light-colored rock or sand, and it is still, in Spanish form, Cape Blanco. There, though no one knew it as yet, the coast of Africa ceases to trend southwest, and falls away almost due south. Henry's ships had really begun to sail around the continent.

The next year, a ship took the Negro chief back, and so much time was spent at that and at trade that there was no advance. Still, much happened that was wonderful, and Henry at times must have forgotten his pain at the thought of Fernando in hard captivity. The ship brought back captive Negroes who had been exchanged for the chief, and also a little gold dust, an ox-hide shield for a curiosity, and some ostrich eggs. These last had kept fresh, and they were served at Henry's table — the chronicler commenting smugly that no other Christian prince could have a meal like that!

Then came 1443, and still another voyage. This captain, returning, told of adventures among some coastal islands inhabited by Negroes. Best of all, he had nosed his way around the White Cape, and gone a little farther still, though only about seventy-five miles. But, year by year, it added up.

In this same year, the pathetic Prince Fernando died miserably in Fez. A new blackness of tragedy closed in around Henry.

Also at this time, Henry himself took an action that showed, symbolically at least, how his life was shaping up. . . . So far, during his long periods of residence in the Algarve, Henry had probably stayed at or near Lagos, which was the convenient port for his ships and an established town. Twenty miles to the west and south was the jutting corner of the continent — a double-pronged corner, with Cape St. Vincent reaching to the west and Sagres Point to the south, the two being in full sight of each other, three miles apart. They are much alike — sheer red cliffs topped by level uplands, treeless and heath-grown, eternally windswept. Either cape could be chosen as *ultima Europa*. Henry — and it seems natural — chose the one reaching to the south. In this year, 1443, he obtained right to the land on Sagres, intending to live there himself and to build a town, to be called Vila do Infante — that is, Princeton.

The site was inhospitable, scarcely offering goat pasture. The nearest village lay five miles inland. There was a cove where two or three ships might find shelter, no real harbor.

But the place had its beauty, of sea and surf and sky and cliff and heath. A man, wounded by tragedy, might find his solace there. Withdrawn almost as to a hermitage, he could do his penances and hear his masses and bring his soul to peace. Perhaps most important of all, he could look out upon the sweep of untrammeled horizon.

The practical thing would have been to remain at Lagos. Henry was practical enough, but he did not live by bread alone. Sagres, symbolically, was the place for a man who still yearned for things that lay beyond Bojador.

The next year was 1444, and a good one. Zurara, in telling of it, shows himself both the pedant and the snob, as a court chronicler could hardly escape being, though he also shows himself a humanitarian, such as we would hardly expect in that century.

The common people, Zurara declares on the authority of Titus Livius, object to great enterprises at the beginning, but are eager to share in success. In this year the common people of Lagos suddenly decided to get in on a good thing. They assembled and armed no fewer than six caravels, put them under a captain named Lançarote, and applied for permission to make an expedition down the African coast. The prince granted it readily, and arranged for each ship to carry the cross of the Order of Christ, thus making a crusade out of it — though it really was intended for nothing better than a slave-raiding expedition.

Here again, as so often, what happened in connection with Henry pointed to the future. All this was nothing but modern capitalism raising its head. These were the first of the both glorious and infamous Merchant Adventurers. Behind these enterprising men of little Lagos came the Hudson's Bay Company, the East India Company, the Virginia Company, and all the others. They changed the world.

In only a matter of weeks — so harmless had Bojador come to be — Lançarote's fleet was back, with 235 captives. These were of mixed Moorish and Negro blood, but were not Mohammedans, so that there was the very slightest justification on the grounds of prosecuting the ancient war. There could be religious justification, for the enslaved heathens could be converted and their immortal souls saved. Moreover, the Portuguese were not hypocritical in this matter, but saw to it that the captives were baptized. Once Christian, they received some kind of freedom, and they soon intermarried with the local peasants and were absorbed.

But, when the ships returned, there was what can only be called a slave market at Lagos. The prince was there, mounted on a great charger, and he took his just share of the captives, being too much a man of his time to be concerned with the ethics of it. (But Zurara lamented their fate.)

As a result, some historians have become bitter against Henry as a proponent of slavery and the initiator of the slave trade. That is nonsense. Slavery and slave-raiding had been going on for some thousands of years. What Henry accomplished was to give them a new chance. For, as all of that shows again, the only way to be sure of doing nothing wrong is to do nothing at all.

Henry, indeed, would have been much moved by the religious argument. In fact, however, he did not like the whole business. He always thought in terms of the long pull, and this slave-raiding brought only short-term profit. It turned the tribes hostile, prevented peaceful penetration, obstructed trade, and even made exploration difficult. This great expedition, for instance, had not pushed any farther south.

So this same year — perhaps using the profit from his share of the slaves — Henry sent other expeditions out, and he found Dinis Dias, a man after his own heart. Dias was a gentleman no longer young, and he was living comfortably in Lisbon, but his heart was stirred to do some great deed. Henry gave him a ship, well-equipped.

In due time Dias came back, and told his story. . . . Without ever lowering sail, he passed clear beyond Bojador. He kept on, past Blanco, farther than anyone had gone before him, along hundreds of miles of southward-trending coast. He went beyond the desert and even south of the grassland and the last traces of the Moors. He came to a land of great rivers, and green tropical forests, where Negroes lived. At last, his ship lay off a long point jutting far to sea, to the westward — high land, rich with verdure. He called it Green Cape, and it is still Cape Verde.

Then he steered back northward, his ship riding high — and we might say, proudly — for she bore little booty except new knowledge, and that is not a heavy cargo. But that was the import that Henry most desired, and he gave great rewards to Dinas Dias.

Though Dias did not know and Henry could not guess, the ship had gone to the westernmost point of Africa, for at Cape Verde the continent reaches out a little further than at Cape Blanco. Beyond Cape Verde the coast runs away southeast and then east.

It was a year to cry the triumph of age. Henry and Dias together, neither of them young, had taken the exploration seven hundred miles to the south in a single season, as far as all the youngsters had been able to do in all the years preceding.

Then — curiously, as it seems to us (and how often we write thus about Henry!) — there was no follow-up the next year with any far-flung voyage.

One can give reasons, but they do not sound altogether convincing. . . . First, Henry was colonizing the Azores. The peopling of Madeira had been a great success, and that island was producing timber, abundant crops, and wine. Henry had introduced sugar cane from Sicily and wine grapes from Crete. So the next step, westward to the Azores, was now justified.

Such an enterprise took money, and Henry was chronically short of funds. Plantagenets were brought up to despise trade, and to consider that money only existed to be bestowed on worthy followers. In spite of his large income from several sources, Henry lavished his rewards in true princely fashion, and was regularly in debt.

Others moved in to profit from his discoveries, and along all the Guinea coast the traders and slave-raiders were busy. They worked along a little farther, a few of them realizing that Henry liked to hear such news, and would be generous. But the advance beyond Cape Verde totaled only seventy miles in 1445, and two hundred and fifty in 1446.

Also, about this time — perhaps a year or so later — Henry established another "first," by beginning to build a fortified post at Arguim, a hundred miles beyond Cape Blanco. Though called a fort, it was rather what came soon to be known as a "factory," that is, a trading post with good enough defenses to make it safe against attack from the local tribes. In the next centuries these factories spread around the world. A few of them were destined to grow into some of the world's great cities, and others — like Jamestown and Arguim itself — were to lapse back into trees and brambles.

There may have been a more deeply seated reason why the advance slowed down. Henry was religious, almost to the point of being superstitious. Sometimes, he may have thought that God did not wish knowledge to be revealed too rapidly. Each step, rather, should be made deliberately; each advance, consolidated. Besides, in spite of everything, Henry was himself a landsman. Mere mapping of the coast of Africa was not enough. He wanted to explore inland. So his men went feeling their way up the big rivers that were discovered south of Cape Blanco. Also, Henry collected information from captives, and opened up avenues of trade.

In 1447 there was no advance at all, though there was plenty of trading, and some slave-raiding, and much useful exploration in detail along the seven-hundred-mile coast from Cape Blanco south to Cape Verde.

Those years, from 1441 to 1447, had been good ones, in spite of the memories of Tangier and the miserable death of Fernando. There had been the great voyage of Dinis Dias. In many respects these years constituted Henry's period of greatest fulfillment.

As to his personal life at this time next to nothing is known, and that very lack of knowledge is significant. We know so little, doubtless, because there was little of interest to tell. Legend fills the picture with some details — untrustworthy on the whole — of the lonely, brooding figure on Sagres, sending his captains out, consulting gravely with the astronomers and cartographers and mathematicians who formed his School of Sagres.

There is one certain little foundation stone of truth in all this. Clear back at the time of the first voyages to Madeira, Henry had brought from somewhere a learned Jewish cartographer and maker of nautical instruments, known as "Master James." Henry, with his practicality, would certainly have seen the importance of reinforcing his rough shipmasters with skilled technicians and with scientists, in so far as one may use that term in a fifteenth-century context. Two or three of these gathered together might be said to constitute a school, and we can imagine the prince in a somewhat amateur way, discussing problems of exploration with them. But Henry was not "the Navigator," that designation having been put upon him only by his nineteenth-century English biographer, R. H. Major. Even today the Portuguese do not know him by that title.

In fact, Henry might well have been insulted by being so called. Navigators were people to be hired. A great feudal lord was above such mechanical arts.

So the School of Sagres cannot be supported by evidence, and without it there is little possibility of establishing Henry as the first great modern patron of scientific research. On the other hand, there is no possibility at all of proving the contrary, and perhaps there really was some kind of crepuscular institute of science under his patronage.

At least, he was a patron of the University of Lisbon, bestowing upon it some valuable properties in the city. Here again, we cannot maintain that he was supporting science, for he actually endowed a chair of theology. Still, any man who supports a university shows some interest in the activities of the mind.

Henry had been known as a personage throughout Europe ever since the brilliant day at Ceuta. Partly his family connections, but also his chivalrous deeds, won him the Order of the Garter from Henry VI of England.

He maintained, apparently, agents for information, and probably for trade relations, in many countries, as chance-preserved notices make clear. There is mention of a certain man from India who was in Henry's entourage. Once, when a captain brought back hot news of a war in far Africa, Henry replied that, yes, he knew about it already. And how do we know that the prince kept an agent in the seaport of Galway in Ireland? Why, it turns out that a captain brought a lion back from Africa, and Henry sent the beast to his man in Galway, "because he knew that nothing like it had ever been seen there."

In spite of all his troubles, one thinks that Henry had some good times out of his explorations — what with wild-flowers, and ostrich eggs, and live lions being brought back.

As to the man himself, during these great years, we must work mostly by deduction. He was a prince and feudal lord, governing the Algarve and the Order of Christ. He must therefore have had numerous administrative officers. More-over, he had been reared in the tradition of royal dignity, and he was lavishly hospitable in entertaining any notable visitors who came to him, either from Portugal or from foreign lands. No guest departed without a gift.

But these guests might have wondered at the other face of their host. They drank wines fit for a prince's table; he drank water. They ate rich food; he, during almost half the days of the year, ate Lenten fare. They slept softly; he passed many of the nights in toil. They, men of the world, knew the pleasures of the bed; he lived, and had always lived, a man alone.

Those guests probably missed a certain gaiety; there was lack of feminine charm. Their host observed the services of the church meticulously. His talk was calm and restrained; "a lewd or unseemly word," wrote Zurara, "was never heard from his lips."

The prince of these years, it must have been, that men re-membered later — the lord no longer young, but still in his vigor. They remembered a man of such self-control that the self-control itself was terrifying. Anyone in displeasure sensed the fires beneath. But all that the prince ever said on such an occasion was, for dismissal, "I commend you to God. May you prosper."

He was not a man for punishments. People even blamed him for rewarding those who scarcely deserved it.

And always there seems about him a little mystery, as when

Zurara wrote of his procrastination — certainly a common frailty. Zurara admitted that this quality could merely be the result of phlegm, but then added that it might have been purposeful, "for some reason clear enough to him but not realized by others."

The "palace," of which there is mention in these years, was probably at Lagos. Often — and more and more as the years progressed — the prince spent his time at the village of Raposeira, only five miles from the cape. There he lived simply, in some kind of country house. Slowly, perhaps held back by lack of ready funds, the building of the town on the cape continued to advance.

Those were the good years, while Peter was firmly established as regent. But, in 1446, the young king, Alfonso V, had attained his fourteenth birthday, and by a ludicrous custom was ceremoniously proclaimed of age. He therefore was no longer required to be subject to a regent. Apparently a little frightened, he retained Peter in charge for about a year, and then intrigue and faction got the upper hand. The intriguers were in, and Peter was out. Soon the intriguers took the offensive, and Peter's whole position was threatened, even his life.

John had died in 1442 — as respectably as he had always lived, of some undistinguished fever. The least colorful of the brothers, he may well have lived the happiest life.

He had, however, been far from a nonentity, and now, in a time of emergency, Peter and Henry were the only ones remaining. Their relationship had been good. As Zurara wrote of those two, after the dark days had come, "Certainly, there was always great love between them."

But, as Peter and the king fell into enmity, Henry was caught in that old-time tragic dilemma, the conflict of loyalties. He found himself torn between brother and brother's son, between allegiance to king and country and to his nearest of blood.

Some historians have made it a contest between tyranny on the king's side and justice on Peter's side, with Henry — temporizing, at best; treacherous to his brother, at worst — allowing justice to go under.

Almost anyone would agree that Peter was much wronged. But such situations are never simple, and the bond of loyalty to the king was an overwhelming one for Henry. Besides, there was the practical side. Even if Henry had gone over to Peter in open revolt, the two of them together could not have matched the king's power. Peter, in fact, was acting like a madman. Perhaps his father had been right all the time about his second son's impracticality. When, at length faced by the hard choice — accept imprisonment, leave the country, or fight — Peter obviously, should have chosen exile, and played for time. His sister in Burgundy would have received him; his cousins in England would have welcomed his return. He was a prince and duke; factions would shift; Henry's solid influence would make itself felt. But Peter, like the boyish knight-errant that he sometimes was, chose to fight against impossible odds, and thus to drag his faithful men with him.

Then, for a moment, Henry stood aloof, a choice still open. At that moment, the skilled intriguers who surrounded the king played the right card. Henry received a summons to join the court. If he refused, he was in open revolt. If he obeyed, he could no longer be free to join Peter.

There really was no option. Henry was not ready to aid Peter in his wildness. Besides, at court, Henry would have access to the king, and might bring his nephew to some gentleness and reason. His influence, added to the queen's, might swing the balance. The queen, Peter's daughter, was still a child, of negligible weight in such a situation, but the king loved her.

It was not to be. In the bright days of May, 1449, Peter's little band drew near the king's army. Henry was with the king.

On May 20, at Alfarrobeira, there was an almost accidental encounter. At the beginning, Peter (not even in full armor) took a cross-bow bolt in the heart. Among those who died on the field was that paladin of Christendom, Peter's closest friend, Alvaro Vaz de Almeda — Count of Avranches, Knight of the Garter, hero of Agincourt and last man off the beach at Tangier. Lesser men of Peter's following were slaughtered bloodily in a vindictive pursuit.

Henry, his military spirit kept under control for once, took no part in the fighting. As he rode southward, a second darkness of tragedy for a brother had enveloped him. Only he was left, of the five. Out of all the children of John and Philippa — those who had grown up together in such harmony and happiness — he and Isabel, "the well-beloved," still remained, and she was far off in the North.

Henry, in that tragic May time, had passed his fifty-fifth birthday. If not old, he was certainly no longer young. In the South lay his home; in the South, his work. The southward-pointing headland of Sagres was the symbol.

In these last years — now, if ever — the man of legend appears in reality. A prince of something-more-than-human stature, calm and impassive, stands upon the ocean-girt promontory, and with far-seeing eyes gazes at the horizon.

In these years Henry performed two more acts of duty to his family, both of them the more trying because they stirred the old embers of tragedy. . . . Fernando's body had been publicly exposed in Fez, but his faithful men had managed to get possession of his heart and lungs. When these men were finally ransomed, they brought the relics to Portugal. In 1451 Henry took the pitiful remains to the great church at Batalha, which served as the family mausoleum. In 1455, the king permitted an honorable burial to the remains of Peter. The body was disinterred from where it had been unceremoniously dumped. Henry, once more, made the melancholy journey to Batalha. As the only surviving brother he must have looked upon the tombs with a sense of resignation.

As always, he returned to the South. The town on the point was still a-building. He spent most of his time at little Raposeira. It was sunnier and less windswept. From there he could easily ride over to the point, see how the new town was advancing, and look out for any sail of a ship riding the westerlies back to Lagos harbor.

He still had his dukedom and his governorships, and must have been a busy enough man from day to day. In spite of the legend, he did not press the exploration very hard. Perhaps it was for lack of ready money, and because of the sense of his accumulating debts. Perhaps it was the realization that he had already accomplished two great objectives — to outflank the Moors and to open the trade with the trans-Sahara kingdoms. Perhaps it was approaching old age, and the voice that comes to a man, "I have done enough."

Yet he was not idle. He continued to push the establishment of the factory at Arguim. He set himself strongly against slave-raiding, and encouraged peaceful trading.

Also, once more, he put energy and money into trying to make good a footing in the Canaries. Certainly the Castilian possession of these islands, right across the southern sailing route, was a constant menace, and they would have been important as an advanced base for Henry's caravels. Over the course of the years he tried everything — Papal intervention, purchase, conquest from the Guanches. Nothing would serve, not even, as he finally attempted, conquest from the Castilians.

In this last, what is most interesting, again, is the foreshadowing. Portuguese and Castilians, in 1450, fought in the Canaries without embroiling the home countries, just as, for instance, in the next century, Elizabeth's sea dogs fought Philip's *hidalgos* in the West Indies while England and Spain still kept the peace at home.

But the Castilians held tight. Henry's luck was never in the Canaries.

Finally the buildings on the point were in a good enough state of completion for him to live there, at least part of the time. Some of his documents are thus dated. But probably there was never much in the way of a town. Only the scantiest of ruins remain — most notably, what seems to be a compass-model or wind-rose, a hundred feet or more in diameter, crudely build of stones laid in position. No one is really sure that it is of Henry's time, though that seems likely. No one is sure either just what use it may have had, and that is rather characteristic of Henry also, for there was always a touch of the mystic about him and a little of the mysterious about how he worked.

In spite of all the complications in these years, some captains went exploring, and the results must have been pleasing to Henry, even if they were not spectacular.

One of the captains was Diogo de Teiva. In 1452 some of the Azores were well enough colonized to serve as a base for further exploration, and de Teiva sailed from Fayal. He steered southwest through four hundred miles of empty ocean. No one can get excited over nothingness, but at least the voyage explored a new area of the earth's surface. On his way back, de Teiva veered northward, and discovered the two most westerly islands of the Azores group.

In 1453 the prince sent two captains south, with the old formula of instruction, to sail "as far as they could." Except for Dinis Dias, no captain had ever been optimistic as to how far he *could* sail, and sometimes the crew may have made difficulties. These captains of 1453 perhaps went a little farther, but not by much.

In 1455 it was the turn of Alvise Cadamosto, a noble Venetian who had entered Henry's service. He got to the River Gambia, two hundred miles beyond Cape Verde, no farther than others had gone before him. Complaints from his crew, or so he reported, brought him back. In any case, he did some valuable exploring, in more detail than had been done before.

He sailed again in the next year, with three caravels, in company with Antoniotto Usodimare, a Genoese. It would seem that Henry was getting tired of his Portuguese captains and their excuses. But the Italians failed to do much better. They did, however, name Cape Roxo, that is, Red Cape. So there was White Cape and Green Cape and Red Cape, as you sailed down the coast, and these names still stand.

Moreover, driven out to sea, in one voyage or another, the Italians discovered the Cape Verde Islands.

But, by this time, the armorers were beating on their anvils again. Exploration had to wait.

In all his life, in fact, we can think of Henry as a man subject to duties which ranked in a kind of hierarchy. At the top, though anyone would hesitate to arrange them in order, were his commitments, all more-or-less connected, to his family, to Portugal, to God and the church, to the crusade against the Moors. Only after these demands had been satisfied could he devote himself and his resources to what may have been his own chief interest, exploration.

After two years of preparation for war the new and magnificent expedition sailed from Lagos on October 14, 1458 — 220 ships and 25,000 men. Henry went with it, on his fourth military invasion of Africa. On the first one he had gone as an untried young man, under the command of his father. On the second and third expeditions he had been in command, each time with a brother under him. Now he was sixty-four, of the older generation. His nephew, the king, aged twenty-six, was in command, but Henry was still very much in charge. Also on the expedition were two other nephews.

The king took a lingering look at Tangier, but Henry advised against any attempt there. He had barked his knuckles once against those walls. So the fleet sailed to the small city of Alcácer, and everything went off like a repetition of Ceuta, forty-three years before. Henry, despite his age, directed the attack, and after a respectable struggle the Moors surrendered to lenient terms.

Once more, Henry returned to the Algarve, and to his own still-half-built town. Yet, this time, there was not so much to which he could sail back. The brothers were gone. He had no wife or mistress, and never had known such solace. He had no children, though he had adopted one of his nephews, and lavished much love upon one who seems to have been a very ordinary prince. Between Henry and the young king must always fall Peter's shadow. As for the exploration, his slow-burning but continuing passion for over thirty years, he may at last have realized that the time of any great new discovery, for him, had passed, and that the earthly destiny, "to seek out hidden things," as predicted in his horoscope of so long ago, had now been fulfilled.

Yet, even after the return from Alcácer, he sent off a ship or two, giving the captains the old orders. Now, finally, the prince was really living at the new town that he had built at Sagres. So he, the lonely watcher, might literally have seen those ships sail and return.

And — this is pleasing at the very end — they brought good news. The record is hazy, yet it seems that in 1459 a staunch captain, Pedro de Sintra, did sail farther yet, past the White Cape and the Green Cape and the Red Cape, and more than three hundred miles still farther. There he and his men saw a mountain ashore, and they heard, as the story runs, the thunder grumbling among the gorges like the roaring of lions; so they called it Lion Mountain, and now it is Sierra Leone. The turn-again point for that voyage was within eight degrees of the equator.

There was nothing very startling in it. This was not an opening of the route to India or any contact with Prester John. Still, it was pleasant news for the old man on Sagres, that someone had sailed still a little farther on.

In the autumn of 1460, only two years after the return from Alcácer, he knew that it was time. He summoned Ferao Salgado, his scribe and public notary, and dictated his will. It was a long document, almost like a final autobiographical statement. Even after finishing the will proper, the prince continued to give various instructions.

In an opening paragraph he identified himself by name, title, and office, and stated that he was still in control of his faculties. In a second paragraph he commended his soul to God, to "my Lady Saint Mary," to Saint Louis "to whom since my birth I have been entrusted," and finally to all the saints and angels. In a third paragraph, he instructed that his body should be laid, with that of his father, "in the Monastery of Saint Mary of Victory," but that there should be no elaborate funeral, only the simplest of rites. He then bequeathed his properties, including his rights in the islands of Madeira, and "Guinea, with its islands." He mentioned especially "Prince Lord Fernando, my much esteemed and loved son," though only a son by adoption.

In the instructions that followed the will he listed sixteen churches, both on the mainland and in the newly peopled islands, of which he was the founder.

Within two weeks after the dictation of the will, the end was at hand. He lay at Sagres. In those last moments, that lonely man on that lonely promontory was perhaps no more alone than anyone else must be at that final moment. Then, on November 14, 1460, he set forth at last on his own voyage, far beyond Bojador.

Yet, more than with most men, something of his spirit lingered, and in the next few years sent men on across the sea. When Prince Henry died, Diogo Cáo was a young boy, and he was to sail far past the Congo. Old enough to be playing with toy boats was Bartolomeu Dias, who was to see the Cape itself. From the hillside at Genoa, young Christopher Columbus already was looking at the ships.

INTER-CHAPTER V

EVERY MAN who impresses his contemporaries develops a legend — or, as we say, a "public image." After he is dead, he is remembered chiefly in terms of the legend, and it may continue to develop, as long as his memory remains vivid.

A legend goes to extremes, making a man, for instance, better or worse than he really was. Also, a legend simplifies, so that the necessarily complex and hard-to-understand man-of-reality becomes the massively simple and transparently understood man-of-legend.

So, after five hundred years, most people think of Prince Henry of Portugal, if they remember him at all, as the Navigator, a vast and serene and over-awing demi-god, standing upon the southwest corner of Europe, sending his ships out, and saying to each successive captain, "Sail farther still!"

Indeed, few men come closer than he does to justifying a legend. As far as a human being may well be, he was vast and serene, and he did live at the southwest corner, and he sent his ships out, and sometimes, at least, instructed his captains to sail farther.

Still, he did more than just that, and he was much more complicated. So let his story stand.

As for the last one of this series, we return again to the pattern of the self-made man. He was born, indeed, under more restricted conditions than any other of the series — in all the economic and cultural poverty of the American frontier. Thus beginning, he proceeded to live in a way that might be taken as a textbook demonstration of the American dream. Fill the portrait out, here and there, with some imaginative touches, and we might well have The Great American Novel.

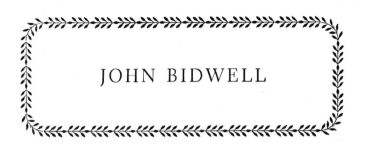

JOHN BIDWELL

I_N THAT Biblical story, young Saul went to look for his father's asses, and found a kingdom. Someone else found the asses.

Young John Bidwell did perhaps a little better. He went to look for a horse and a mule, and found, if not a kingdom, something that was close to being one. Also he found the horse and the mule. . . .

In 1843 the Sacramento Valley in California was theoretically Mexican, but it was, practically, Indian country. In fact, as Bidwell recalled years later, it still looked "as new as when Columbus discovered America."

Because of a necessity which need not be recounted, that young man had recently been forced to borrow a horse and a mule from a certain Manuel Vaca. Bidwell had taken them to Sutter's Fort, where Sacramento now stands, the last northern outpost of what might optimistically be termed "civilization." Though he had kept the animals picketed, they had disappeared, apparently by human agency.

Now, one of the unalterable rules of the universe is that a horse or mule, once lost, becomes highly valuable. Vaca demanded seventy-five dollars as compensation. This was exorbitant, and even ridiculous. It totaled three months' salary as paid by Sutter to Bidwell.

Since Vaca was not a person of great power or influence, Bidwell might easily have paid him a reasonable compensation, and then told him to go whistle for the rest of it. There was not even a court where Vaca could have sued. But Bidwell was a highly conscientious young man. Also, he was peaceably inclined. Besides, it was spring, and he may have had itchy feet.

Probability suggested that the animals were in the possession of a party of Americans who were heading north, on horseback, for Oregon. Bidwell decided to ride after them, and recover the spoil. Sutter lent him an Indian *vaquero.* The "wild" Indians were generally harmless, but a man should not go alone. On the first day, from isolated ranches, Bidwell picked up a German immigrant known as "Greasy Jim" Brueheim, and a Danish immigrant named Peter Lassen, who was to leave his name printed large on the map of California.

There was no trail. The four of them rode north, across the grass-grown plain. They pressed hard, having to overtake. Even so, they paused now and then, not able to resist an encounter with a grizzly. Game was constantly in sight — deer, elk, antelopes, bears.

About the end of the second day they came to a place where a little stream, "clear, cold and sparkling," flowed along, embowered among sycamores. Away from the water the great oaks, spaced far apart, stood majestically, park-like. Beneath the trees bloomed thousands of wildflowers, and farther off, the grass stood luxuriant — two, three, and four feet tall. Lifting the eyes a little, you saw the foothills to the east, and farther off the peak that would bear Lassen's name. Higher still, stretched the dome of the sky, blue and beneficent as it can be in that valley in March. There John Bidwell found his kingdom.

He never forgot the place, though some years would pass before he came into possession. Next day, he and his companions rode on, and sighted the Oregon party, encamped on the opposite side of the Sacramento River.

The stream was coming down deep and swift with melting snow. Bidwell had no horse that he trusted to swim it, and his companions wanted no part of that crossing. But Bidwell was not to be turned back. Having only a small hatchet for a tool, he improvised a raft of brush and branches, building it up so that it looked, he confessed, like a load of hay. He did not think that he could manage it in the current alone, and he persuaded one of the local Indians to accompany him, for a payment of some beads and a cotton handkerchief.

They hopefully pushed the raft off with willow poles, but it soon began to submerge, as it soaked the water up. The current swept them downstream, and they were up to their middles in cold water, only knowing they were on a raft because they could feel it beneath their feet. In imminent danger they drifted down about two miles, and then managed to get to the opposite bank. Bidwell walked to the camp.

Here, as might have been expected, the men of the other company, a rough frontier lot, refused even to display their horses for his inspection. By luck, however, three of the men turned out to be old companions and friends of Bidwell's. Two years before, in 1841, they had all come across from Missouri together in the Bartleson Party, the first group of immigrants to reach California overland. These three had for Bidwell all the feelings of comradeship, of men who together had endured long hardship and faced death. They declared that Bidwell should at least have a chance to locate the animals that he described, and about a hundred horses and mules were driven in. Bidwell soon found his animals. But, at this point, most of the men in the company merely said that he could not take them. Then, suddenly, Ben Kelsey, one of Bidwell's friends, took the matter into his own hands. Anyone might be ready to classify Ben as a ruffian, but at least he would stand by an old comrade, and he was, as Bidwell put it, a "resolute" man.

Since no one wanted to fight Ben Kelsey, Bidwell got his animals. He swam them across the river, and started back on the hundred-and-fifty-mile ride to Sutter's. . . .

So much space devoted to a seventy-five-dollar episode may seem biographically unwarranted. But, during this expedition, Bidwell first became enamoured of the region which was eventually to become his famous Rancho Chico. Moreover, the incidents display not only the manner of person that he was at twenty-three, but also what he was throughout life — active, ingenious, a lover of the land, courageous, and conscientious, almost to the point of compulsion.

Some might also wish to add "lucky." Indeed, Bidwell would have been the first to agree. He sometimes declared that his whole life had been shaped by chance — a statement that outraged his wife, who held to her own opinion that his success was the obvious result of his unsurpassed good qualities. . . .

He was born on August 5, 1819, in the western tip of New York, four miles from the Pennsylvania line and four miles from Lake Erie. From that spot the lake was in view, and he remembered that, as a child, he conceived it to be a blue border running around the earth, across which the ships passed, being held to the perpendicular surface by some force that he did not understand.

He remained on that farm until he was ten years old — an age, if the theories are true, at which his character was already shaped. He remembered much about it, and his reminiscences read like a classroom demonstration of that early American way of life which is now buried deeper than Mycenae or Troy.

He remembered making sugar from the maple tree; going to school, a mile and a half, when the snow along the road was higher than his head; seeing a bear caught in a log pen; going to "borrow fire" from a neighbor; from the age of seven, being set to do his chores; going to a "show" at the village, and seeing a monkey and a zebra.

When he was seven, a steamer was to be launched on the lake. His mother did not want him to go, but he went anyway. "I did not know the way, but I found it. I inquired the way and got along." (Of much of his later life, too, he might have said the same.)

He remembered his mother, with love — "as good a mother as can be," he wrote once, and that was a strong statement for a naturally reticent man. She was a Baptist, and "a great hand to study her Bible." But she did other reading also, and he remembered her as "well posted."

The father was hard-working, not educated, a man with a strong sense of family. He believed in discipline, and could even be severe, but the boy seems to have cherished no resentment. Still, in later life, he wrote, "I resemble my mother more perhaps."

Both parents were of the stock of New England. In the ancestry there were pioneers, first settlers, and a Revolutionary grandfather.

The father may have lacked skill as a farmer and a sense of good management. The family remained poor, but poverty was taken for granted. Probably they were no worse off than their neighbors. Food was good and plentiful, and the boy grew up tall and strong. He never cared much for hunting, but he enjoyed fishing. He had brothers and sisters for playmates. By and large, the childhood must have been satisfactory.

Probably the worst that can be said about such an early

American upbringing is that it tended to stint the emotional and artistic life. Everyone "made do" with what was available. Even the folk arts were scarcely cultivated. Because of poverty, as he remembered — but also, it may have been, because of this cultural pauperization — the family never gave presents on birthdays or other holidays.

Only through reading was there contact with the thought and movement of the greater world. From his early years a love of learning glowed within the boy, a persistent spark, never to be extinguished. Opportunities for schooling were pitifully small — a three-month term in the winter, in some one-room schoolhouse. An incident that he remembered serves as illustration both of the poverty of the American frontier and of its ingenuity. The teacher wanted to illustrate the properties of light, but had no lens. He then went out into the winter day, got a piece of ice, and shaped it to serve for his purpose.

Three months of school, nine months of work around the farm — that was the routine. A few winters, as he remembered, he was not able to go to school at all.

Yet he was quick to learn, even under those conditions. As he wrote, with customary restraint, "When I was nine years old, I was a pretty fair scholar for a boy. I remember that I came out at the head of the class in spelling."

Then the family began to "move," again the American pattern. They worked westward, naturally. They spent a year or two in the northern tip of Pennsylvania, and then a short time in northeastern Ohio. In those locations, life continued as it had in New York, and the boy grew to be fifteen. He was beginning to do much of a man's work, and to think of himself as at least half a man.

In 1834, the family moved on, to southwestern Ohio. After a year or two there, the boy began to be on his own. In the new location there was no good school available. In the region that they had recently left there was a school, and he still had a contact, because an older half-brother had remained there. In January, 1836, the sixteen-year-old left home, and set out to walk the three hundred miles through eighteen inches of snow. Perhaps the weather improved, as he went along, making sometimes thirty miles a day.

At Kingsville, Ohio, he found an academy, with an excellent teacher, a graduate of Amherst. There Bidwell enjoyed his longest more-or-less-continuous schooling — a year and a half. Under this master, he studied "natural philosophy," which was some philosophy with a little physics and astronomy thrown in. He also studied chemistry, and made some beginning in Latin. He worked at algebra and surveying on his own, remarking in later life, "I used to be tolerably fair in figures." Grammar and correctness of language were his special interests.

During this period, he supported himself by working at various jobs, such as helping in a sawmill.

In the autumn of 1837, just eighteen, he returned home, but scarcely to do more than to touch base. By now he was pretty much of a man. Moreover, by the standards of the time, he was "educated."

During the next two seasons he taught school, in southern Ohio. What one of his pupils chiefly remembered of him later was that he kept discipline without the customary use of the switch.

During the months when school was not in session, he worked, either on the home farm or elsewhere. He was trying to get a little money ahead, having developed the ambition, extraordinary for that time and place, of going to college.

In the spring of 1839, however, he decided to see a little of the world, and he went west, as normally as the sun. He had seventy-five dollars and what extra clothing he could carry in a knapsack. He intended to be gone a month, and to return and go to college. *Dis aliter visum.*

He took a look at Iowa, and then went on into northwestern Missouri, close to the Indian country. Being short of money, he taught a term at school — in the summer, for a change.

The region was recently open for settlement; the soil was rich; the people seemed friendly. That fall, he purchased a claim on 160 acres of land, though he was not of age. As a strong and active young man — able to teach school or do anything else — he would have had no trouble supporting himself for a few years, while he got his farm into working order. He might have become a prosperous Missourian. His love of learning ruined that prospect.

In the summer of 1840 he discovered that he lacked some necessities which he could not obtain where he was. He set out for St. Louis. The necessities were books.

Low water on the river delayed his return, and he arrived to find that his claim had been jumped. The claim-jumper was a rough character, and Bidwell, being still underage, could not enforce a legal case. He was on the world again, and foot-loose. Then he met Robidoux. Such a conjunction of circumstances as this would make him write in later life that his career had been determined mainly by chance.

This Robidoux had been to that far-off and little-known and even mysterious land called California. Moreover, he enjoyed telling stories about what an earthly paradise it was, where chills-and-fever were of such rarity that, when a man was so taken, people came from miles around, out of curiosity, to see him shake. What footloose westward-yearning American could resist such stories? Times were bad in Missouri, that winter of '40-'41, and the fever-and-chills raged mightily. The California fever raged equally, and for a while it looked as if Missouri was going to be depopulated. Young Bidwell went about, helping to organize the Western Emigration Society. People even signed a pledge to go, and "it took like wild fire." Soon there were five hundred names.

Then reaction hit just as hard. When Bidwell, who was never a man to go back on his word, appeared at the rendezvous in May, only a few men with one wagon were there.

Eventually, others arrived, and they all set out with a dozen or so wagons — the first party of emigrants to try for California. They began the epic story of the covered wagon. Their journey is a famous one, but here we are concerned only with the participation of one young man.

This is properly the Bartleson Party. That it is sometimes called the Bidwell Party is the result only of the fact that Bidwell later came to be a prominent man. In 1841, though he had had something to do with the organization, he was not a leader. The company included several men of marked ability, and Bidwell was merely a young fellow, not skilled as a hunter or trail-finder, with no particular qualifications for leadership.

Yet, as the hard weeks passed, in mountain canyon and by desert spring, he proved himself. He always did his share conscientiously at such chores as standing night guard. In an alarm about attacking Indians he kept his head, and did not panic. When his oxen disappeared (everyone thought, taken by Indians), he followed their trail overnight, doggedly and boldly, and brought them back.

Bidwell teamed up often with "Jimmy" John, about his own age. They were good friends, and much alike, but there was a basic difference. John was without fear to the point of recklessness. Bidwell showed himself courageous, but always with a touch of good sense.

At one desperate moment in the Sierra Nevada the two were given the task of scouting ahead. John's recklessness almost brought disaster, and he ended up by losing contact with the company. Bidwell went back, and guided his comrades to safety.

Bidwell kept a diary during the trip. Somewhat rewritten and edited, it still exists in a printed version. It is not much, as diaries go, scarcely more than a log book. But, as all writing must, it displays the man. We note his modesty; he is rarely his own hero. He displays an esthetic feeling for the country. On the same day he wrote "a most beautiful landscape," and "a beautiful little lake," and "a most beautiful defile, beautifully watered by a small rivulet." Before decrying repetition of words, remember that scrawling in a small notebook by the light of a campfire does not encourage subtlety of language.

Most of all, he noticed vegetation. He could even be a little pedantic, writing, "sage, or rather it ought to be called, wormwood." Especially, he knew his trees, recording often the particular variety — bur oak or white hickory. He noted the last appearance of hackberry trees as the party entered the desert country.

In each of the wagons, one would guess, there was some special treasure that the owner cherished, either for sentiment or for profit. One man carried grain alcohol, which was a good article of commerce among the mountain men. Another carried a lump of "lead," which others believed to be a plated lump of gold which he had stolen and melted down. Bidwell's wagon carried books.

Eventually, one bad morning in the desert, the wagons had to be abandoned. Even so, Bidwell kept one book, when they put packs on the oxen. It was not (should we regretfully report?) his Testament. It was an atlas of the heavens. In eminent danger of death, across the burning reaches of the deserts and up and down the roughest mountains, he took that book into California.

Half-starving, not even knowing where they were, they struggled through the pathless and rugged Sierra Nevada. October 31 brought their lowest point. That morning Bidwell ate for breakfast all that he could find available — the lights and windpipe of a coyote.

Then they emerged from the mountains and found game. At last, trail-weary and almost destitute, the company straggled into the first California *rancho* on November 4, 1841.

A few days later, lacking a passport, separated from his companions and friendless, Bidwell found himself thrown into a Mexican jail, his only company a few Indians. At least, he would consider that he had reached bottom. A few days later still, Fortune's wheel had turned a little farther, and he was free, a passport in his pocket. (He treasured that passport, and preserved it for the rest of his life.)

Just what Bidwell had expected to do, once arrived in California, he never stated. Probably he had no clear idea. He knew, in fact, very little about California.

In 1841 the opportunity lay toward the north. There the amazing Swiss, John Augustus Sutter, was establishing his empire at New Helvetia. The Americans generally called it Sutter's Fort, and it would eventually take the name of its river, and become Sacramento.

To New Helvetia young John Bidwell took his way, passing on the trail through certain adventures by flood and field which in a less crowded story might well be made the content of a chapter.

Between Sutter and Bidwell there was an instant *rapport*. Each took to the other, and their references, one to the other, were always in high terms. "My most faithful servant and partner," wrote Sutter, years later, "I liked him from the beginning."

Sutter needed men of all kinds to work and administer his vast holding. For him, Bidwell was an answer to prayer. He was even one of the best-educated men in California. Sutter hired him at twenty-five dollars a month.

Board and lodging were thrown in, such as they were. Board consisted of tough beef three times a day, though by great effort Sutter managed to have wild duck for Christmas. Lodging consisted of a bed and blanket, somewhere in a corner of the fort.

Bidwell was soon sent off to his post, which was in the settlement that the Russians had just abandoned on the coast. Sutter had bought from the Russians all the movable property. Bidwell's responsibility was to ship this miscellaneous material, by water, to New Helvetia.

He could feel he had almost rounded the world. Here, on the Pacific Ocean itself, he was handling Russian goods that had been brought all the way across Siberia. Some of the old weapons bore French markings, and Bidwell concluded that they had been captured from Napoleon on the retreat from Moscow, twenty-nine years before.

He spent almost a year, thus, dealing with the leavings of the Russians. It was all new experience, and he enjoyed himself. Probably he had his book along, and could do some observing of the stars. Always the farm boy, he dried some apples and peaches, and made some cider. He carefully observed the country roundabout, especially its vegetation. He got his diary ready for publication, and added a description of California, though he had to admit that he did not as yet know it very widely.

One or two of the statements in this description seem inspired by his own private oracle — for example, "the best

part of California, I am told, lies high up on the Sacramento."
So also he wrote that with foresight, "your produce and economy would not fail to make you a vast fortune."

March of 1843 arrived. The job was liquidated. He went
back to Sutter's Fort. This was the occasion on which his
horses were taken, and he rode north to recover them. . . .

Back at New Helvetia with his horse and mule, Bidwell
remained in Sutter's pay. There was, indeed, little choice of
employer, and Bidwell was not yet ready to be on his own.
Besides, Sutter's star was in the ascendant, and gave every
indication of rising still higher. To be his right-hand man
might well mean to be an important person.

Sutter now put Bidwell in charge of the Hock Farm, a subsidiary establishment twenty miles up the river. There Bidwell, with the usual staff of Indian and half-Indian *vaqueros*,
had charge of a thousand head of horses and five thousand
head of cattle. He also was entrusted with building a large
ranch house of adobe brick.

It was a frontier post. There were plenty of Indians about,
but they were of the inoffensive Californian type. Bidwell
got along well with them. Grizzly bears were plentiful in the
thickets along the river. He shot an enormous one within
fifteen feet of the house.

Though it was not an important period, Bidwell learned
about running a California ranch. Also, he must have per-
fected his Spanish, for this was the only language of commu-
nication. He did not content himself, in the usual frontier
way, with mastering a collection of nouns and some set ex-
pressions. Instead, as he put it later, he memorized the whole
grammar. He also learned to speak fluently.

Sutter was well pleased with everything, including the new
house. But, in the summer of 1844, Bidwell left Sutter's employment, amicably. He went off locating land grants in the

Sacramento Valley, putting to use some of his skill as a surveyor.

He also applied for some land of his own, undoubtedly having Sutter's recommendation. On July 26, 1844, he was given the grant of Ulpinos, provisionally. The land lay down-river from New Helvetia, and much of it was low and marshy. To have the grant confirmed, Bidwell had to become a Mexican citizen. He had no objection to that. Like most Americans, he must have believed that California would soon be independent, like Texas, or would be part of the United States. So a brief period of Mexican citizenship did not make much difference.

Fortunately, one of the older regulations had now lapsed, that is, that any landowner must embrace Catholicism. Bidwell, though he was not much of a Protestant at this time, was always anti-Catholic, partly by his early training, and partly by his dislike of authoritarianism. Moreover, he was conscientious, and would hardly, like many Americans, join the church hypocritically, merely for the land.

In October, Sutter and Bidwell went off together to the capital at Monterey. There Bidwell was naturalized, and on November 20, the grant was confirmed.

There was more to this than meets the eye. The governor was not giving a land grant out of the goodness of his heart, and his admiration for an upright young American. Governor Micheltorena, an appointee from Mexico, was in a weak position with the native Spanish-Californians, and revolution was threatening. He was building up his strength by attaching the foreigners to him.

Indeed, revolution flared immediately, and Sutter took the imprudent step of getting involved in it. He at once organized a small "army" of about a hundred of his Indians and an equal force of foreigners, mostly Americans, whom he was able to collect. On January 1, 1845, this force left New Helvetia. Bidwell went along, serving as Sutter's personal aide or secretary.

The combined forces of Micheltorena and Sutter moved south, the headquarters of revolt being in Los Angeles. The march was slow, because the governor, unromantically, was suffering from piles, and had to ride in a carriage. Late in February they approached Los Angeles, and then occurred what is in California history the famous "battle" of Cahuenga. It is, in fact, the very model of what a battle ought to be. There was a lot of galloping hither and yon, and some long-range artillery firing, and a casualty list of, traditionally, one mule. Bidwell attained the distinction of being captured twice in the same battle. There were Americans on both sides, but they sensibly decided not to shoot at each other.

In the end the governor was overthrown, and both Sutter and Bidwell found themselves prisoners. Sutter was confined, though not arduously. Bidwell was allowed to wander around as he would. He also earned Sutter's further gratitude by doing all that he could to alleviate the situation.

Before long, Sutter patched up a peace with the new regime, and he and Bidwell got back to New Helvetia about the end of March.

After this taste of military experience, if it can be called that, Bidwell signed a year's contract with Sutter, to act as his bookkeeper and general manager, at fifty dollars a month. In northern California things were looking up. The first covered wagons had made it across in '44, and other parties came in '45. There was increased activity around New Helvetia, with much coming and going. Bidwell was at the center of things.

He kept the books. He held the unpleasant job of seeing

that people paid their bills. He went off, occasionally, to scout for timber and mill sites in the foothills.

In his middle twenties now, he was a serious-minded, quiet young man. He was not boisterous in the usual frontier way, and he was scarcely even hail-fellow-well-met. He made some friends, though not many. He made no enemies, even though he had to collect the bills.

He chewed tobacco, after the backwoods fashion of the time. He was a smoker. He did not drink, except occasionally, when the social situation forced him. He was not a gambler or an easy spender, but still he did not save any money. Whether or not he became involved with any of the Indian women is not in the record. Quite possibly he did not. He had a certain reputation for primness.

He wore pistols, after the custom of the country. But he never had to use them or even to so threaten. His quiet manner seemed to be enough.

One of the recent immigrants was a huge ruffian from Texas, named Kinney. He merely appropriated seventy-five of Sutter's mares, and put his brand on them. Sutter himself was cowed. Bidwell undertook the job. As he told, years later:

I had to go pretty well armed, but went quietly. I told him that he had to bring every one of those mares down and rebrand them. I stayed there until it was done. . . . It was quite an undertaking, as I had no assistance. . . . Nobody else would go near him; yet I had to do it; yet he never threatened me and I did not threaten him; only I told him he had to give up the horses.

At some time Bidwell lived for a short period on his Ulpinos grant. He was so horribly plagued by mosquitoes that he became ill, and he decided to have nothing more to do with the place. He managed to exchange it for a grant called Colusa, fifty miles up-river from New Helvetia. But it, too, was low-lying, and did not appeal much to Bidwell. He still kept in his mind, as an ideal, the delightful tract of country that he had seen by the fine little stream, when he had ridden north after his horse and mule. Unfortunately, the land there had already been granted. Still, he made an advance in that direction. On May 14, 1845, Edward A. Farwell gave to Bidwell his power of attorney for all his interests in California. Farwell, in bad health, was returning to the states. He held the grant of five square leagues of the land that Bidwell coveted. Since we may assume a *quid pro quo*, Bidwell's acceptance of this responsibility must have meant that he obtained some rights or privileges to the land.

On April 1, 1846, Bidwell's contract with Sutter expired, and he went into business by himself, for the first time. There was a salmon-run up the Sacramento, and Bidwell set off to catch and salt salmon. It might have paid off, but California was to be no place for peaceful enterprise in that year.

In June many of the Americans went into revolt against the Mexican government, in what California history knows as the Bear Flag incident. Bidwell already had a stake in the country, and probably did not favor this violent action by his compatriots. Indeed, the whole affair was a dubious one. Bidwell was not really involved until toward its end, and never in an important way.

Just at this time, however, came the news that the United States was at war with Mexico. This was a different matter. Bidwell, like all the rest, sloughed off the recently acquired Mexican citizenship, and entered the forces of the United States. Commissioned as second lieutenant, he was shipped off to the south of the state. At this time, however, there was no fighting. The Americans occupied California, rather than conquered it. The Spanish-Californians had never liked Mexico and Mexican rule anyway, and saw no point in dying for that republic. They would just as happily (or unhappily) be ruled from Washington as from Mexico City.

In August Bidwell found himself acting as magistrate for the district of San Luis Rey, between Los Angeles and San Diego. The duties were not arduous, and the population was small. Bidwell had chiefly to negotiate between the Californian ranchers and the local Indians. The former claimed the services of the latter, under the prevailing system of what is sometimes known as debt-peonage. Under American law — and generally having a sympathy for Indians — Bidwell refused to recognize the claims of the ranchers, and he naturally became extraordinarily popular with the Indians.

Within a few weeks the Californians in general decided that they really did not like the Americans. The Americans had been, to say the least, untactful. So the Californians rose in what the Americans called a revolt, though how people defending their own country can be said to be in revolt is difficult to determine. The Californians took over, and the American troops were penned up in a few towns.

For a while, neither side came near San Luis Rey. Bidwell organized a force of his friendly Indians. He had no firearms for them except a small rusty cannon. Instead, he had three or four bayonets and some spikes that he had them put on long sticks for spears. Some of the Indians supplied their own bows and arrows. So Bidwell became probably the last American officer to command an army equipped only with spears and bows, and he may well also have been the first one to do so.

At the approach of Californian forces, Bidwell told the Indians to go back to being peons, and he himself retreated, hastily, and alone, upon San Diego.

After that, it was not quite so much comic opera. To get supplies, Bidwell made a hundred-mile sea voyage in an open boat from San Diego to San Pedro. He got his supplies, and then, on the voyage back, he was caught in a storm and had to throw them all overboard to lighten the boat. He passed a night in imminent danger of being drowned.

The Californians occupied San Diego, and the Americans withdrew to their ships. Next the Americans, growing stronger, landed and occupied the town again. Then, one day, the Californians set up a small cannon on a hill, and began firing into the town, to the great annoyance of the Americans. A dozen of them decided to do something about it, though they appear to have been directed less by orders than by a kind of spontaneous impulse. As Bidwell put it, "twelve of us started for the hill." The Californians stuck to their cannon, and fired three times as the Americans came swarming up. Fortunately the aim was high, for one well-directed blast of grape-shot would have wiped out half the assailants. When the Americans were within fifty feet, the Californians finally bolted.

This incident was probably more serious than it appears to be in Bidwell's narration. His conduct may have earned him a reputation.

Gradually the American forces, army and navy, built up at San Diego, and on December 29 they marched on Los Angeles. Bidwell, promoted to major, acted as quartermaster for the whole force.

There was no fighting worth the mention. In a few weeks the whole country was pacified again, and the volunteers could be mustered out, leaving the regulars in charge.

In the fine California spring of 1847, Major Bidwell, aged twenty-seven, rode north among the green hills of the coast country. In some way he had acquired eleven horses, and he drove these ahead of him. At Carquinez Strait he swam the horses, and that in itself sounds like something of an adventure.

Thus returning, like so many civilians who have gone to the wars, he began to pick up his life where he had left it off. He had gained some experience, and some self-confidence, and a new title. It was a title-conscious society, and he was called "Major" thereafter.

During four years he had known the upper Sacramento Valley, and he had always remembered that fine country with its oak glades and rich grassland. The stream had a name now, though a commonplace one, being called Arroyo Chico, which is merely "Little Creek." Farwell, for whom Bidwell possessed power of attorney, held a grant just to the south — the usual five leagues. The Mexican governors had been liberal with land. It was one thing of which they had plenty. William Dickey, also a friend of Bidwell's, held a similar grant north of the stream.

As yet these holdings offered little. You could raise cattle, but you were far from any market. You could exist at the subsistence level, on cattle, game, and whatever crops you cared to raise. To hold the land you had to make some improvements, such as a house and corrals.

Bidwell put up some kind of house on Farwell's grant. More remarkable, he rode south, clear to his old post at San Luis Rey, there to get trees and vines for planting. The dream seemed about to become real. He began to dig a ditch for irrigation.

In January, 1848, Bidwell was still living there. But this was no ordinary January. In this month the water sluiced through the tail-race of Sutter's mill, and John Marshall picked up his gold. Again, the dream receded. In '46 it had been war; in '48 it was gold.

In March Bidwell rode south again. He was going to the country near San Francisco Bay to pick up some fruit trees, though it seems the wrong time of year to be planting them. At New Helvetia they told him about the gold. In fact, he was the first to take the news of it to San Francisco.

He could hardly have been human if he had resisted the temptation. Returning, he made a quick visit to Sutter's mill, and saw the methods of mining. Gold, he reasoned, could just as well be found farther north, in the country nearer his holding, where he had explored for Sutter in seeking timber. He organized a party, collected supplies, and then set out with his partners. They found gold, at a place on the Feather River, which has ever since been known as Bidwell's Bar. The find was important, for it more or less proved up as gold-bearing all the country that lay between that point and that of the original discovery, sixty miles to the south.

Bidwell and two partners worked there through the blazing hot summer. In some way, he managed to hire half a dozen Indians as workers, either bringing them with him, or negotiating with some of the local tribesmen. He always had a good touch with Indians. They had no interest in the curious yellow stuff, and were willing to work, when they felt like it, in exchange for some kind of article that appealed to them more.

There was gold in workable quantities, but apparently Bidwell never had the luck to strike a real bonanza. At the end of the season, as well as can be estimated from his vague statements, he was about $10,000 ahead of his expenses. That would have been a fortune in '47 and it was still a good amount of money in '48. But, at the rate prices were rising, he could tell that it was not going to be very much money in '49.

He spent the winter in the mountains. When the rains came and the river ran high, there was no possibility of working at the gold, but he probably had to stay there to protect his claims.

The winter passed miserably. He fell ill, and developed a cough. Besides, a man is never happy when he feels his world going to pieces around him. Gold-seekers — "a heterogeneous mass of strangers," as Bidwell, the by-now-old-time Californian, described them — came pouring in. They were submerging the old California of the far-flung ranches, and the land as it was before Columbus landed. Already, in the spring of '49, Bidwell was looking back to that time with nostalgia, as the period when "we were a law to ourselves," and when there was a rough-and-ready but manly code of honor. Ironically, at the very moment when all the world was setting out to reach California, Bidwell was intending to leave it, discouraged by his long winter illness. On April 5, with good foresight, he wrote to a friend, "we may expect, from what has already passed, the greatest confusion, resulting in the perpetration of the most horrid outrages and crimes, etc., etc., etc., etc., etc."

He got over his despondency, and stayed. Actually to have left California at that moment would have been defeatism to the point of insanity. But gold-mining was not for him. He stayed at Bidwell's Bar that spring, but engaged more as a trader than as a miner. Then, that summer, came the culminating event of his life.

He had already been accumulating some capital. The Colusa grant, though he had never settled there, had acquired some value, and in this year he sold it for $2000. He also had his mining profits of 1848, and had probably increased this amount in the first months of 1849.

On July 6, 1849, he purchased, for $1785, half of the Rancho del Arroyo Chico. This was what had been Dickey's original grant, which Bidwell had wanted ever since 1843.

In 1851 (the price having risen to $9000) he was to purchase the rest of the ranch, and so it can best be described as a unit.

The conventional five-league grant totaled about 22,000 acres, slightly less than the usual American "township," six miles on a side. But a grant was never surveyed with accuracy, and could be laid out in such shape as the grantee preferred. Arroyo Chico, thus, was a broad band running east-west. At its west end you started from the Sacramento River, a navigable stream. Riding east, you crossed a belt of low, level "black lands," as good an agricultural tract as you could expect to find outdoors, and amounting to about four thousand acres. Still further east, you came to the "red lands," which were the first roll of the foothills and good for grazing. The southern boundary of the ranch was Chico Creek, a perennial stream, with possibilities for a watermill and for irrigation. Along the stream the heavy growth of oak and sycamore offered timber for local use. The black lands were grass-grown, awaiting the plow without the labor of clearing.

That summer, on his own land, at last, Bidwell built himself a cabin of oak and sycamore logs. Since there was little labor to be hired, he probably built it mostly with his own hands, thus again, in his almost incredible way, conforming to the conventions of the American Dream.

From this time on, he seems to have had no thought of leaving California. The opportunity was fantastically good, for a man with both land and working capital. The ranch was close to the mining region, which was filling up with thousands of miners. They were producing gold in quantities that the world had never seen before, and they had to have supplies of all kinds, especially food. There was no abundant source of food, and by the ordinary law of supply-and-demand prices went skyrocketing. Especially needed were wheat and cattle.

At Arroyo Chico, there was only one problem — production. Bidwell had to meet it, at first, almost with his bare hands.

That fall, after the rains came, he managed to get a sowing of wheat in. He did it, as he wrote, "after the manner of the Mexicans." That would mean the use of improvised wooden plows.

When the grain ripened, it had to be cut by hand, with sickles, without even scythes and cradles available. Then a herd of wild horses was driven in, and milled about on the level ground where the cut grain had been heaped. Behind the horses ran Indians, "almost as wild," to keep the horses running. In a short time, the pounding hooves threshed the grain out. Then followed a long and laborious process of winnowing the grain by hand. . . .

During this decade of the fifties, the strands of life were three — the ranch, his Indians, and his public service.

After that first crude year, the ranch developed, under the influence of high prices and a ready market, with a rapidity that is almost commonplace for gold-rush California, but can scarcely be equaled anywhere else at any period. Probably there was never again a year like that first one. Even in 1851 there would have been scythes and cradles, though the prices paid for them were fantastic.

In this same 1851, Bidwell was able to send a gift of fruit trees and vines to a friend on a ranch fifty miles off. The friend returned the favor with "ten fine hens, well-cooped." Other letters tell of the acquisition of sheep, and of dairy cattle, bought from covered-wagon emigrants who had driven the animals across the plains.

In 1852 he wrote of having cut so much timber that he needed an ox team and wagon to haul it. He had to have timber to build fences, and a bridge across the creek, and a new house. The original cabin burned in this year, and he erected a large and substantial building of adobe, in the old California fashion. It was two-storied, and had timbered galleries around it. In 1853 he was so far ahead of basic production that he was supplying seed to other people. In this year, also, he built a flour mill, and began to produce his own finished product.

By 1854 everything was in full swing. His mill was running, and was producing flour by the ton. His nursery was producing. He was selling grapes. A threshing machine had replaced the wild horses of five years before.

All this production was being supplied in an economy which created constant demand and an abundant supply of gold. The profits were enormous. Instead, however, of merely exploiting a situation for all it was worth financially, Bidwell developed into an experimenter, a man with a deep love of the land and of all that it could produce.

Horses, cattle, and sheep ranged the red lands. With these he strove for better breeds, and he developed his dairy products. Soon he introduced hogs.

His black lands produced wheat as their staple crop, with some barley and a little corn and oats. But his real love was for horticulture. As early as 1855, he was producing grapes, peaches, apples, quinces, pears, and figs. Soon he planted English walnuts, and introduced the first almonds into California. He set about propagating ornamental trees and shrubs. In the middle-fifties a description summarized, "The princely mansion is surrounded by extensive lawns. The estate is probably not surpassed in California."

Such a leap into riches, and power, has corrupted many a man. But Bidwell was not corrupted, as is shown by the treatment of his Indians.

When he had gained possession, a small "tribe" was already there. These Me-choop-das numbered about a hundred, were inoffensive, and existed at a very simple level of culture. By Mexican law and American custom, they had no right to the land, and, generally speaking, no rights at all. Indian-shooting was a common practice. If not shot, the Indians rapidly disappeared by starvation, disease, and cultural shock.

Bidwell, almost alone among early Californians, treated the Indians with humanity, and gave them protection. Though they were not especially pleasant neighbors, he moved their *rancheria* to within a hundred yards of his own house, so that he could protect them. He gave them employment on the ranch, both men and women, though inevitably their culture collapsed under the pressure of advancing civilization.

Bidwell wrote proudly of what he had been able to accomplish,

I seem to have a sort of intuitive insight into the Indian character. . . . I have never justified any abuse or the wrong treatment of the Indian. I had for them a regard, a sympathy — knowing that their lands had always been taken from them without any compensation.

He even underwent personal risk, as he wrote, quite casually, in a later reminiscence:

*There was a fellow who was making himself too familiar
with some Indian woman I had working for me. I lost my
temper for once, and seized a willow stick and wore it out on
the fellow's head. He went out, got his revolver, and shot at
me, but missed. I can't stand any nonsense about men that
way.*

The Me-choop-da tribe came to be known as "Bidwell's
Indians." On several occasions he managed to protect them,
with difficulty and at hazard to himself.

The problem, indeed, was the essentially insoluble one
that always occurs when a primitive people is overwhelmed
by civilization. The story of "Bidwell's Indians" is largely a
sad one, and it could not have been otherwise. But Bidwell
himself acted with honor, responsibility, and good will. At
least, the Me-choop-das survived.

In addition to paying them for their work, Bidwell allowed
them to live in their village, to glean in the fields, to collect
wood. They continued to follow many of their old practices.
They preferred their own primitive houses, dug out in a shal-
low circular hole, and then roofed across into a low dome.
They kept their ancient and often noisy ceremonies, wailing
for their dead, as they always had.

In the old days the Me-choop-das had suffered from raiding by the fiercer mountain tribes. In the early fifties these
raids continued, and the mountain Indians made no distinction between Me-choop-da and white man, as far as lifting cattle was concerned.

A bold raid of 1852 resulted in the loss of some of Bidwell's
cherished dairy cows, and he organized his only expedition
against Indians, recruiting some Americans and about thirty
of the Me-choop-das. He insisted, however, that the thieves
should be arrested, not shot at sight, as the usual custom was.

Partly as the result of this restriction, things went badly. An American was killed by an accidental shot, and the Indians escaped. Bidwell was adversely criticized, in the light of the results.

Throughout the fifties, Bidwell devoted much time to public affairs, in spite of his many other activities. He was a member of the senate in the first legislature. In May of 1850 he left San Francisco on a quick trip to Washington, by the Isthmus route, being entrusted with conveying a 125-pound block of gold-bearing quartz as California's contribution to the Washington Monument. In the east he again saw members of his family, and indeed he never lost these contacts throughout his life.

In 1851 Bidwell was a delegate to the Democratic state convention. In 1855 he was the Democratic candidate for the state senate, but lost the election. In 1859 he acted as chairman for the Railroad Convention held in San Francisco.

In 1860 Bidwell founded the town of Chico, on some land that he had acquired just to the south of the creek. He laid it out with an eye to the future and in a public-spirited manner. The streets were wide. One block was set aside for a plaza — an early California touch. Sites were reserved and donated for public schools and for churches. At first, Bidwell gave a lot to anyone who would build on it. As a result the town grew prosperously.

During these years he was twice involved in steamboat accidents. Once a boiler exploded, and he was almost killed by a piece of flying metal. He carried the scar on his forehead through the rest of his life. The other accident displayed more of his own qualities. His steamboat collided with another and began to sink. Panicked passengers began jumping overboard. Bidwell stepped on deck, coolly judged the interval available, returned to his cabin for his clothes, and then dressed on deck, as the boat continued sinking. When the deck was down to the level of a boat that lay alongside, the fully-dressed and fully-collected Bidwell merely stepped across to it.

As the tension of the sixties approached and the Democratic party threatened to split, Bidwell came out strongly as a Union man. In 1860 he went to the Democratic convention at Charleston, as one of the eight California delegates. The delegation was under the domination of Senator Gwin, representing the Southern faction. Bidwell, always independently minded, broke with his colleagues, and cast the only California vote for Douglas.

In California the Civil War brought almost as much confusion and stress as it did in states nearer the conflict. Since many of the Union men went off from Chico to join the army, the sentiment became prevailingly Southern. As Bidwell wrote, "Sometimes thirty or forty men would go by hurrahing for Jeff Davis." Troops had to be brought in to get matters under control. Even so, Bidwell received a warning to leave town. At this time, the old-time frontiersman boiled up. "I replied that I intended to stay at home. If they attacked me, I expected to kill one man, which one I couldn't tell, but intended to stay at home." He stayed.

In 1863 Leland Stanford, Governor of California, appointed Bidwell to be brigadier general of the militia. Though he fulfilled his duties, the new general never had to fight a battle. There were, however, two lasting results. A post to control the Indians was called Fort Bidwell, and it still exists as the most northeasterly settlement of California. Also Bidwell ceased to be "Major" and became "General."

In 1864 the traveling editor of the *Springfield Republican*, Samuel Bowles, stopped at the ranch, where he especially enjoyed the melons. As to the forty-four-year-old owner, he commented, "General Bidwell still seems a young man, is fresh and handsome and of winning manners."

Also in 1864 Bidwell again went east as a delegate, this time to the convention of the Union party. After participating in an enthusiastic endorsement of Abraham Lincoln's candidacy, Bidwell went on to Washington. As a titular general and a figure in state politics, he was in a position to expect a favor, and he asked to go to the front near Richmond. Created a bearer of official dispatches, he visited General Grant, whom he greatly admired.

In this same year Bidwell ran for Congress, largely on a platform of unionism. He was elected, by a majority in his own district considerably greater than Lincoln's.

In Congress he served honorably, but with no more distinction than would be expected of a freshman member. In a personal way, however, the two years' residence in Washington was highly decisive. For one thing, he had to leave the ranch in charge of a manager, who proved inadequate. Bidwell found himself involved in heavy debts. Also, some exposure to Washington society made him more of a man of the world. Finally, he met Annie.

During many years, naturally enough, Bidwell had been thinking of marriage. Even a name or two floats vaguely through his letters. In 1851 his friend and former patron Sutter had, in Germanic fashion, made a negotiation about his daughter Eliza. In a long letter that suggests considerable embarrassment, Bidwell had declined the offer.

During the course of some Congressional duties, however, he came to know Joseph C. G. Kennedy, Superintendent of the Census. Later, Bidwell was entertained at the Kennedy home, and met the family. He soon found himself, in spite of his long years of bachelorhood, becoming highly interested in one of the daughters. At this juncture he went off for a three months' tour of Europe, but he found this great adventure to be something of a failure, for he was always thinking of the girl, and fearing that "someone would gobble her up" during his absence.

The passport description of that year is worth quoting as a set description. Height, six feet; forehead, high; eyes, gray; nose, straight; mouth, small; chin, ordinary; hair, dark brown; complexion, fair; face, long. But let no one be deceived into thinking that the "ordinary" chin, whatever that may be, indicated a man lacking in determination.

Back in Washington, Bidwell soon proved himself a highly awkward but none the less effective wooer. As a charming story runs, Annie found herself praying one night, "O Lord, give the general a wife worthy of him — some other person — O, no, Lord, do not do it! Let me be his wife!"

There were parental objections to having a daughter exiled into the wilds of California. Naturally, these were overcome. On April 16, 1868, at the age of forty-eight, the rugged frontiersman married a well-bred and carefully-reared girl of twenty-nine.

The Kennedys were a family of some prominence, and Bidwell himself was well-known. The list of wedding guests was impressive enough even to impress Bidwell himself, so that he expanded his diary entry a little. It read:

Our bridal day! — rained hard and thundered in the morning. The President, Gen. Grant, Lieut. Gen. Sherman — and several foreign ministers attended our wedding. Left for N.Y. at 7 P.M.

From New York they took the steamer, returning to California by the now well-developed Isthmus route.

Annie was a pretty and charming girl, devoted to her husband. Just how the passport authorities would have classified her chin must remain uncertain. But she, like her husband, was not lacking in determination. She was what, those days, was described as "a strong-minded woman." She was full of good causes and of good works — a Presbyterian, a believer in teetotalism and votes for women. Her influence upon her husband was tremendous, though there is no reason to doubt that his influence upon her was equally strong.

Because of her, it may be said, he became a Presbyterian and a Prohibitionist. But in neither action did he have far to move. Since childhood, he had been a Protestant in feeling, even though not a church member. He had scarcely been a drinker at all, and several years before his marriage had given up the making of wine, and pulled up his vineyard of wine grapes, not wishing to be involved with anything approaching the liquor-traffic.

In that charming mixture of sentimentality and formality that the Victorians so often displayed, he called her "Precious," while she addressed him as "General."

There were no children, but that in itself may have worked to have made the bond even stronger.

Annie took to the ranch naturally, from the very beginning. Undoubtedly her General deserves much credit, for he was used to transplanting delicate and exotic seedlings. "His character," she wrote, years later, "was a continual and fascinating surprise to me."

In the first place, he had provided "the Mansion," which was enough to surprise anyone, and certainly to delight the heart of any bride of the sixties. Several years before, Bidwell had put himself into the hands of a San Francisco architect. While yet lacking a mistress to care for it, he had built a twenty-five-room house — solid and magnificent, as they built in those days, and yet not lacking in dignity, grace, and beauty. Unsentimentally, he had torn down the adobe.

The Mansion, as it has always been called, stood a hundred yards from the babbling creek, surrounded by broad lawns on which were growing newly planted ornamental trees.

They settled down there, and the years began to flow over them. They were richly lived years, often eventful.

First of all, there was the pageant, continually presented, of the land itself, as it burgeoned in the spring, and ripened in the summer, and lay dormant in the fall, and again grew green beneath the winter rains.

Every year the General kept his diary. He was no sprightly Pepys, nor any Thoreau or Emerson, full of insights. The entries were the hasty jottings of a busy man. But the pages were crowded with memoranda of life and growth, such as the picking of the first strawberries and the ripening of the cherries.

The ranch itself produced like Egypt in the years of the fat kine. All kinds of livestock flourished, including honey bees. Yearly the wheat and barley flooded the granaries. The General used the most modern American machinery. But more and more he loved his fruit orchards, and his groves of nut trees, and his vineyards. He saw California, eventually, as a vast orchard, made fruitful by irrigation. He loved to experiment, introducing casaba melons and "Egyptian corn."

The payroll of the ranch was never less than one hundred, but doubled for harvest and fruit-picking, and now and then touched a peak of five hundred. The workers were predominantly American, including schoolchildren on vacation in the summer. But there were a few Chinese and half-clad Indians, the Indian women with their babies on back boards.

Along with the primitive Indians, mechanics were manipulating the latest in farm machinery. As early as 1869 Bidwell was having sent from New York large quantities of that newly developed product, which he noted as "gasoleine," though it was probably more like what was later known as kerosene. He must have been using it for some kind of lighting or heating.

The ranch was the chief interest of both husband and wife. To systematize their love of plants, they studied botany. During one day's drive in the foothills, he identified seventy species, giving for each the scientific name.

In addition to farming, he maintained and enlarged the flour mill, continued with the nursery, added a cannery and a fruit-drying establishment, and produced some of California's first raisins.

Curiously, he never managed to get out of debt, and this worried him, although from a modern point of view it could merely be considered as a moderate bonded indebtedness. But he was always a man whom loose ends bothered, and the floating liabilities troubled him in a kind of moral way. "I am ashamed," he said once, "to think I got into debt." At the same time, he and Annie always lived amply, and even splendidly.

One little show-off trick he enjoyed. At the time of wheat harvest he would send a man out in early morning to get the first sack that came from the combined harvester. This grain would be rushed to the mill and ground into flour, and it, in turn, was rushed to the kitchen at the Mansion. Then, at eight o'clock breakfast, he would quietly remark to the current guest, "These biscuits this morning were growing in the field."

He employed a manager, and for some years one of his own nephews held the post. The manager freed Bidwell for much of the daily routine, so that he and Annie could go off when they wished. But the General was never away long enough to lose the feel of things. He liked to be out and around the ranch, often eating lunch in the fields with the men. He enjoyed doing a little work himself, setting out more shrubbery, swinging an ax when a tree had to be got down.

He was, however, much less likely to be felling a tree than to be tending or planting one. If one stood where a new fence was being constructed, his standing orders were to swerve the fence. He carried walnuts in his pockets, and when he saw what looked like a vacant spot, he made a planting.

Such a large land-holding demanded constant attention and activity. A not-untypical entry in the diary runs:

Events: Building Indian chapel — making levee — Cutting wood in Flume field — making concrete side walk at P.O. corner — Drove to Prospect ridge, Mr. & Mrs. Parry with us.

They were not isolated, especially after 1870, when the railroad reached Chico. In fact, there was a constant stream of visitors, and the entertainment, though lacking in alcoholic beverages, was lavish. In the long dining room of the Mansion, twenty people easily found places. The General thought nothing of cutting one melon after another and sending them back until he found one that suited his taste.

One famous visit, in 1877, was from the botanists Asa Gray and Sir Joseph Hooker. John Muir joined the party. With him as guide, they all went off for a luxurious camping trip, to botanize around Mount Shasta. The General climbed halfway up the mountain, thinking it not a bad accomplishment for a man close to sixty. He weighed over two hundred, these days.

Even more notable for celebrities was a visiting party of

1880, including President and Mrs. Hayes, and General Sherman.

But the Mansion did not cultivate snobbery. Many of the visitors were members of the Bidwell or Kennedy families, and others were local people. One visitor was a policeman from San Francisco, who happened to have done a good turn for Annie.

Once in a while the General called for his charger, and Annie helped him into his shining armor, and he rode off brandishing his bright sword. He went to battle for some good cause, but he was always defeated. He could hardly have expected to win. He could join neither the Republicans nor the Democrats, and the backing of some splinter-group was not enough. In himself he lacked sufficient charismatic quality. Tall and black-bearded, dignified and even handsome, he might be called a good leader, but not a great leader. Besides, he was an amateur against the professionals, and the amateur does not win — especially he did not, in those days, when the professional politician was at his zenith.

In 1875 he ran for governor on the ticket of the People's Independent party. His candidacy must have frightened the professionals a little, for they unloosed on him a full blast of vituperation from their newspapers. Because of Rancho Chico, he was called a land-monopolist who was hypocritically opposing monopoly. He was even attacked as being still a Mexican citizen — the editors apparently hoping that if enough mud was thrown some of it would stick.

Bidwell had always been an individualist, and in his later middle age, with Annie to back him, he became something of a rebel. In the light of what happened in later years, one would put him down as an early liberal and progressive. He was a trust-buster (or, at least, so wished to be) twenty years before Theodore Roosevelt. He fought for the Australian ballot, women's suffrage, income tax, national parks, prohibition, and a rationally controlled immigration.

As for "civil liberties," he might not have even recognized the term, but the idea was deep within him. Every man deserved decent treatment; that was part of his basic creed. His continued protection of his Indians, along with much else, showed it.

During these years Annie began to take the Indians over. She had tried from the beginning, but she lacked her husband's natural touch, and the women and children shrank back from her and were silent. Only after several years did she begin to win their confidence. Naturally, she worked toward Christianizing and civilizing them. She built them a little church of their own. She tried to get them to live in wooden houses — that having become a symbol of American life. She found that the women were quick at sewing, and so she trained them as seamstresses. Soon they had a brass band, and were celebrating the Fourth of July. Underneath, they remained Me-choop-das, and kept on having a medicine-man. Still, they knew that Annie was their friend, just as the General had been for so long.

The years at the Mansion, however, did not all flow by as in a pastoral idyll. Much of the interest in Bidwell's life lies in the way in which it displays the preposterously quick shift from the frontier period into modern civilization. Some of the shift was merely mechanical. His diary recorded the coming of the railroad, the telegraph, the electric light, and the typewriter. But there are other symbols. One might be the contrast of the prancing wild horses of the first harvest, and the smoke-belching steam threshers of the later years. Another symbolic pair of pictures might be the young man of '41, making a starving meal on the lights and windpipe of a coyote, and the portly middle-aged man, gormandizing over his melons. So also, in the sixties, in the attacks upon his Indians, we see the lingering frontier. But in the seventies and eighties the violence sprang from modern problems of capital and labor.

The railroad barons had imported Chinese by the thousands. After railroad building slowed down, these laborers went on the market. Bidwell employed a few of them around the ranch. Times were hard after 1873, and many American workmen, half-starving, turned against the Chinese.

On March 13, 1877, five Chinese were murdered at Chico. Employers received curt anonymous notes, such as that which came to Bidwell, "Sir: Get rid of your Chinese help within the next two months or suffer the consequences. Let this be enough."

The old-timer met that challenge by telegraphing to San Francisco for ten Winchester rifles. (It was a small town, and he could be sure that the content of his telegram would not be kept secret.) He retained his Chinese workmen, and helped to organize some local counter-measures. Eventually the murderers were arrested, and convicted.

"I go on the principle," he said, "that every man has the right to what his industry and intelligence can earn for him."

Another crisis flared in 1886. On March 1 came a note:

Get rid of your chinese help now or youl see fire over your head when you least expect it. We positively mean business and dont you forget it. last call, last notice.
Anti Chinese Club Com of Chico

A boycott was declared against Bidwell. One of his barns, containing $10,000 worth of hay, went up in flames one night. The flour mill was forced to close. Bidwell, for once, was backed to the wall.

He wrote some public letters trying to placate the boycotters, and explaining that he really did not employ very many Chinese. He even discharged some of them, but the boycott was forcing him to discharge many workmen, and the Chinese may only have gone along with the rest.

Bidwell attended an anti-Chinese convention in Sacramento, with the avowed intention of opposing the movement. When he took his stand on the platform to speak, the crowd rose in a pandemonium of name-calling, shouting, and cursing. Maintaining his dignity, Bidwell stood with folded arms for half an hour. He was not able to speak.

One editor came to Bidwell's support, in words that are revelatory:

We have thought him prim — have thought that he had created a moral standard too high for a mere mortal to reach, but he has hewed to the line thus marked out as nearly as ever man did.

But the ruin of Bidwell would have meant that the town lost its chief payrolls. Local opposition to the agitators developed, and the situation quieted.

Throughout the long anti-Chinese agitation, Bidwell steadfastly opposed unlimited immigration and advocated control, but he also stood for the right of the individual Chinese to work as he saw fit. . . .

In 1887 occurred an event both shocking and ironic. . . . Annie, marrying her Californian so many years before, must have feared that she was exposing herself to a life of violence. There had, indeed, been some violence, but her General had passed unscathed through everything. Now, in supposedly sedate Washington, her father — irrationally and by the hand of a fanatic — was brutally murdered. . . .

In the eighteen-eighties Bidwell's individualism had so

estranged him from the major political parties that he became a Prohibitionist. Undoubtedly Annie's influence had much to do with it. In thus moving, however, the General was not becoming a man with only one fixed political idea. He sought the party not merely because of its opposition to the liquor-traffic, but also because of its being a party of protest, about the only one available at the time.

On the Prohibition ticket he ran for governor in 1890, and two years later he was nominated for president. His careful letter of acceptance offered something about the liquor problem, but more about women's suffrage, regulation of public utilities, income tax, and other ideas that have become basic in the modern United States.

He did a little speech-making in 1890, but in the presidential campaign of 1892 he did not take the field actively. In any case, it was all a gesture — futile, except in so far as it showed that someone was still maintaining some ideals. In the presidential election he received 264,123 votes. . . .

After that year, he rode no more upon crusades. At seventy-three he began to accept old age. He had always lived actively, and continued to do so, but he had been ill on numerous occasions, and his constitution was by no means of granite.

Annie, though so much younger, had been seriously ill in 1888. Bidwell began to withdraw from his business affairs, as much on her account as his own. The manager took more and more responsibility for the ranch and the subsidiary projects. Some land was rented out.

In earlier years they had traveled considerably — to Yellowstone, to Washington, to Europe, to Alaska. Now they grew content to sit at the Mansion, or to drive in the vicinity. An observer noted that the General never hurried. He took things a bit easy, with a regular nap after the noon meal.

Year by year there was more a touch of the magnificent and legendary about him. A newcomer wrote of "courtly General Bidwell," driving to meet a train in his fashionable barouche, behind a highly groomed, well-matched team.

He kept his early western love of horses. With his typical broad-mindedness, however, he once declared himself also to be extremely fond of mules. White-bearded, he went joggling about the ranch on a mule named Jenny.

The trees that he had planted twenty-five years before grew high around the house now, overshadowing it. In front of the house stood a tall magnolia. He once listed more than a hundred and twenty ornamental trees and shrubs growing in the grounds. There was also an enclosure, with tame deer.

Along the creek, however, the native growth was allowed to maintain itself, so that it remained much as it had been, with oaks and sycamores, when he had first seen it in 1843. All that was done there was to clear out dead wood, which was thriftily sold for firewood in the town. Trails and bridle paths were maintained. Fancifully, out of *Paradise Lost*, he and Annie named it Vallombrosa. There were a few deep holes in the stream, and after a lapse of thirty years the General had begun swimming again.

Thus he advanced into his seventies, and the century into its nineties. He still kept his diaries, a new volume each year, but the handwriting began, progressively, to show touches of shakiness.

Always he kept his love for the outdoors. He said once, "It is even now a luxury for me to camp out and eat my dinner with the men on the farm." Every summer he and Annie still took a camping trip into the nearby mountains. They went in leisurely and in a somewhat luxurious fashion, with a carriage and a good team of horses. In these years he began

keeping his diary in a new fashion, which sometimes gives it
a curiously modern style. Thus, on a camping trip, he noted
for August 1, 1896:

Met
2 fine bay horses on the summit grade.

Brought
*Bucket of snow from Summit to Prattville, which we reached
about 6 P.M.*

Camped
about half mile above Prattville — Dugout spring.

In his early years he had shown a passion for education and
books, but during the period of his ceaseless activity he had
enjoyed little opportunity for such interests. As Annie
once put it,

*The General is not a great reader in the sense of reading many
books, but he never reads a book unless he has his books of
reference ready at hand.*

As evidence of this continuing attempt to extend his
vocabulary, one finds written on a back page of one of the
diaries, "Dendrite — arborization. Atavism — return to
original type."

In his later years he apparently enjoyed his books again. A
visitor found him ready to quote, not only the Bible, but
Wordsworth and Tennyson as well.

He never lost his interest in education. He attended the
county institutes whenever he could. Besides giving the
original land for the new Normal School, he served on its
board of trustees. He was appointed a regent of the
University of California. Because of business pressures, however, he resigned without serving.

Like most men who are living an active and satisfying life, he had done little looking backwards, and during many years he seemed almost to have forgotten his early adventures. In 1864 he had crossed the plains and mountains by stagecoach, and later he traveled there by railroad. On these occasions he traversed much of the route that he had followed in 1841. Old memories must have stirred, but he made no such notes in his diaries. Once, as the train followed the Humboldt River across Nevada, his whole entry was: "Breakfasted at Carlin — dined at Battle Mountain — supped at Humboldt." He had thus, between breakfast and supper, clicked off a hundred and fifty miles, across the country where in early October of 1841 he had expended a week in hard and sometimes desperate marching.

As time went on, people began coming to him for interviews about the history of California and with suggestions for him to write some memoirs. At first he had poohpoohed the idea that he would have anything to contribute, but later he came to like it. He left some long and interesting statements, and contributed some articles to *Century Magazine.*

Here and there, in the interviews, he would leave off discussing Sutter and Frémont, and make a comment on himself. "I delight," he said once, "in rambling and climbing over the mountains." And, again, on human beings in general, "I believe, as bad as we are, we are growing better." And still again, "Yes, I think I have always had a longing to go into a new country, and sometimes I wish there was another new country for me to go to even now — some place that I might explore."

Once the interviewer got a few words out of Annie, and she talked about her husband, not about herself. Her comments are worth recording, "He is never tedious . . . He is firm as a rock . . . He is always kind to other people. . . . It is beyond my conception that a man can keep so quiet, and yet feel as deeply as he does. . . . He never likes to walk on level ground, is very fond of climbing."

In August, 1899, he was eighty. Soon he saw the new century in.

The handwriting in the diary, that spring, was curious. The shaky lines indicated a failing body, but the large letters were well shaped, showing a stalwart mind still in control. He kept active. White-bearded, but still erect, he went about the ranch. He talked with his Indians, knowing them individually. He was patriarch of the whole region, known and respected by everyone. He had also become a kind of living legend, one of the last links with the heroic and almost mythic pre-Gold-Rush years.

People told strangers, and told their children. . . . He crossed the plains, way back; first settler here, planted the first crops. *Tough old codger — you couldn't ever scare him!* He took care of the Indians, founded the town. *Pretty nearly everything you see around here, he did it first.* He gave land for the Normal School; without him this place just wouldn't be. *They don't make them like him any more.* Not stuck up, either; always speaks to you.

He began to record, once again, the cycle of the year — 1900. On January 20, he noted cardamine and buttercups. On January 31, the first almond tree was in bloom.

There were callers, as always. There were dinner guests, though not so many as there had been a few years before.

Often, these days, he wrote of work near the creek. He was having a new trail cleared out in Vallombrosa. On April 3, he wrote,

Up creek — Reuben, Harry and William Conway with me. Made cottonwood log heap. Callers: Mrs. Kitchen — book agent. Weather: Cloud and sky — fresh and airy.

Next morning, he was up at four o'clock, read until six, and drove off to the work at eight. On getting out of the wagon, he said, "I feel just like a boy."

He worked for a while with cross-cut saw and crowbar, and then suddenly fell prostrated. He died that afternoon.

Throughout California, men spoke of the passing of an era. In their low houses, the Me-choop-das wailed for their friend.

AFTERWORD

◇—◇—◇—◇—◇—◇—◇—◇

THERE IS a good rule-of-thumb for the writer, "Don't state; demonstrate." Relying upon this principle, I need not analyze minutely the ways in which the six men of the present project achieved the good life. If the demonstration has not already been effective, a mere statement certainly will not be.

The original quest of this inquiry, however, was the nature of the good life itself, and into this we may make a further exploration, with the six men supplying a background.

First of all, I must allay suspicion of too great naïveté on my own part by admitting an autobiographical factor. Obviously, I must have chosen the six because my life-experience had exposed me to them, and because I had achieved with them some kind of identification. In fact, during the course of working on the project I talked with various people, and one of them countered by suddenly saying, "Why, George, you have lived the good life yourself."

In reply, I found myself caught in a dilemma. Out of modesty — and out of real inability to judge in my own case — I could not admit the contention. On the other hand, to deny it strongly seemed ungrateful to my family and friends, and to a society which has perhaps treated me better than I deserve, and has at least enabled me to live.

But, as to the autobiographical element here, anyone trying to judge will certainly be caught in one fundamental problem. To what extent, on the one hand, do these six represent what I am? To what extent, on the other hand, do they represent what I should like to be?

To be sure, every book has an author, and so is to some extent autobiographical. No book can rise above its author, any more than water above its source.

These six — and I have chosen them — were not perfect. This is not merely to admit that they were human. On the contrary, rather strong cases can be made against some of them, and even have been so made. Joab was likely to be a little quick with his favorite stroke beneath the fifth rib. Prince Henry has been attacked as the founder of colonialism, and for much else. Schliemann, at times and in some respects, was a downright unpleasant person. As author, I have not tried to gloss such matters over. I have still tried to make the demonstration of the good life, as seen in totality.

These six were all men, not women. Basically, that limitation may be autobiographical. Also, there was a technical problem. Few women are adequately recorded in the documents available, the world having been, in general, make-oriented. Theoretically, I should have been glad to include a woman, and at least I can point out that several fine ones have played supporting parts. Some of them might well have been, themselves, candidates for admission to the study, if enough material had been available upon them.

Here one would include the Countess Isabel, the second Madame Schliemann, and — most certainly — that mysterious mother of her sons, Zeruiah. So, also, Philippa of Lancaster lived greatly, and Annie Bidwell passed long years of satisfaction and fulfillment. In fact, we begin to think that where a man experiences the good life, there also you may find a woman with him, though where is cause and where effect can be no easy matter to discover.

In addition, I would have done better — or, at least, have made my list more representative — if I had chosen some men of civilizations, nations, and races besides those that are now included. Again, I must chiefly plead the limitations of the finite author. I am necessarily of a particular race and civilization, and my background of training and work, circumscribed by the modern need of specialization, has failed to bring me into close contact with certain regions and cultures. Besides, there is the problem of language. As it is, I have had to read widely in five languages, and to dip into two or three others. And, in general, one cannot do good work in biography without being able at least to read the language of the one who is the subject of inquiry.

Some limitations also arise from the fact that six is a small number, scarcely sufficient as a base for broad generalizations. In looking back over the list, for example, I am struck, and almost horrified, by the universal demonstration of activity. Anyone might ask, "Is there no place in the good life for contemplation?" There is a touch of the brooding mystic in Prince Henry and a certain quietness in Tresguerras. But, by and large, they were men who wanted to be doing things.

Quite possibly, this too is a limitation of the author. At some unconscious level, I may see the active man as my hero. I myself have done a good deal of work in my time, though temperamentally I am slow-moving. I have sometimes thought of myself along with those inhabitants of Hamburg, as described by Thomas Mann, who were at once phlegmatic and energetic.

Still, the activity of the group may result chiefly from limitation in numbers. If I had included six more, some of them might have been of a contemplative type.

Also, looking back over the stories of the group, I miss lightness and humor. I blame the sources. The Bible, for instance, is notoriously a humorless book, and its writers would not have recorded Joab's witticisms, if he made any. The Marshal undoubtedly had a good sense of humor, and several of the anecdotes display it. He enjoyed his practical joke on the burghers of Rouen, and one imagines him a man with a hearty laugh. But, except with professional humorists, a man's jokes seem to be interred even before his bones. . . .

But what positive qualities do the six display? May we from these deduce any qualities of the good life?

They all — I may maintain as a beginning — seem to have been men with what we may call a sense of goal. They knew what they wanted, and they strove for it. One goal attained, or having become impossible, they went on to something else. I would maintain the generalization that a man who does not know what he wants is unlikely to attain the good life. Schliemann, during his middle years, provides a demonstration.

This sense of goal, however, must not be interpreted to mean that the men were overcome with ambition and narrow-mindedly pressed toward a single end, neglecting all else. On the contrary, they were men of breadth, and enjoyed many contacts with life. Even Prince Henry, who was perhaps close to fanaticism, was very much a member of a family, and was warrior and statesman, as well as far-seeing patron of exploration. The others all knew the warmth of family life, granted that we do not know much about Joab. Schliemann was equally outstanding as money-maker, linguist, excavator, and scholar. In addition to being knight-at-arms and royal administrator, the Marshal established a notable family, enjoyed a bit of joking, and loved music. Tresguerras is obviously the most outstanding in his versatility. Besides practicing all the arts, he served as a municipal officer; he married for love; he enjoyed his club of friends; he was inseparable from his little dog. The man who is most likely to attain the good life, we might conclude, is not the specialist or the fanatic, but he who establishes and preserves many different holds upon life.

At the same time, breadth and multiplicity of interest do not mean superficiality. In connection with the six men in general, a most striking impression is that they were deeply committed. They lived hard; they gave themselves, day by day, year by year. They were not half-hearted. In old age, not one of them had to look back and think that life had passed him by. *Talent de bien faire* was Prince Henry's motto; a general motto under which all of the six might have approached life would have been *Take and use me.* Each one, nearing the end, could feel that he had lived hard, and even that, according to his capacities, he had lived to the limit.

All of the six, I believe, were men of responsibility. In modern jargon, they were "mature." A sense of responsibility seems chiefly to be bred into someone by early training. When such a person emerges into early adulthood he knows that he is essentially on his own, and that he also has some obligation for his family, for his community, and even for his nation. Some people develop a sense of responsibility for mankind.

Such feelings may not be reasonable. Some families and some nations are not deserving. Schliemann's father, for instance, may not have warranted the support that his son gave him. Sometimes a tragic conflict develops between the early-established sense of responsibility and the later-developed sense of logic. When responsibility to others becomes a dominating principle, the result may be a saint, but scarcely a man who has reached the goal that we have here set. Besides, as a universal goal, this kind of sainthood would be

self-defeating. There have to be some sinners for the saints
to work over.

Certainly, however, there must be a degree of responsibility. The individual has to recognize the need to care for himself — economically, if in no other way.

Among our six, responsibility is least marked in Schliemann. Throughout much of his life he was something of a
buccaneer, not even owing loyalty to any nation. But he did
not reject his family ties, and he maintained honest business
relations. As one passes in rapid mental review the lives of
the five others, responsibility seems to have been a highly important quality.

Inevitably, "responsibility" mingles with "loyalty" — a
difficult word and a dangerous idea. "Joab remained loyal to
David," we may write, in full consciousness that nearly everyone will accept the statement as a fine compliment to Joab.
But there is always the problem of higher loyalty. Perhaps
the tribesmen of Israel would have been better off if Joab,
one morning, had taken the kingdom over.

At the one end stands the individualist and egotist who
rejects responsibility; at the other end, the saintly laborer for
the good of others. The positions of our six lie somewhere
in between.

These men all possessed courage — that primary human
virtue, without which the other virtues are of little value.
Even Schliemann, who was not always heroic, showed stark
courage when he went forward after his shipwreck. As Zurara
wrote of Prince Henry, "His heart knew no fear, except the
fear of sin."

Possessing courage, each man was also — sometimes by
profession, otherwise, as occasion called — a fighter. Joab
and Schliemann, indeed, may possibly be put down as in-
clining to be quarrelsome. The same, however, can scarcely

be maintained of the Marshal and of Prince Henry, even though they were of the professional warrior class. Though Bidwell's experiences in fighting the Mexicans are not especially important, he quickly reacted for his own defense, even with the threat of firearms, during the Civil War and during the troubles over the Chinese. Tresguerras, who seems the most peaceable of them all, vigorously composed his satires in reply to Suasnávar.

Along with courage, in natural association, go self-reliance and individualism. The Marshal, refusing King Richard's attempt to gloss the matter over, replied boldly during the famous interview at Fontevrault. Joab, more than once, indulged in the dangerous practice of speaking his mind to the king. Bidwell in his later years espoused several unpopular causes.

Yet, basically, these men were not rebels. Thinking independently, some of them found themselves, at times, in a minority. In general, however, they were able to function freely within the already-established society.

All of them were men of sufficient ability and strength of character to make their ways in the world. They possessed a considerable physical vigor, though Schliemann and Bidwell were often ill.

They kept a larger view of life — the stability of a kingdom, the exploration of a continent, the planning of a church and a bridge. They were not content with eating and drinking day by day; they looked before and after.

Religion — perhaps with the exception, in opposite directions, of Schliemann and Prince Henry — they accepted as part of a way of life.

They attained, as old age approached, what we may call an integration of character. As discontent is natural to youth, so is smugness to middle age. The two qualities seem to lie as two poles of human adjustment. These men seem to escape smugness, and attain balance. They lost the discontent of youth, but they moved forward still, as age permitted. If we may quote, "The kingdom of God is within you," these six, in their later years, seem to have achieved that kingdom.

Highly remarkable is the long period of activity, and even of high achievement, that each of them enjoyed. Prince Henry — aided, indeed, by his high birth — became a noted soldier at the age of eighteen, and remained a leading figure of his times until his death. The Marshal received a high appointment when he was in his mid-twenties, and continued steadily, attaining a full course of honors, until he finally, past seventy, became Regent of the kingdom. Schliemann had accumulated a fortune when he was in his early thirties, and he did not flag until he fell upon the street in Naples at sixty-nine. The records of the three others are comparable, or even better.

Thus they completed the cycle of human life. They seem to have accepted the finitude of man's years. There is no suggestion that they fought hopelessly to be young. Rather, they matured and aged, until the end came. Yet they stayed alert. In his seventies Bidwell was still planting walnuts.

Old age, we may say, was kind to them, though such a statement really means that each of them remained the same man, as he left youth behind. Not one of them knew senility. By maintaining such activity as old age permits, they also maintained active minds.

Finally, death also was kind. Only the Marshal lay for a while in pain. Prince Henry weakened rapidly. Joab took death quickly, as he had given it. Schliemann, Tresguerras, and Bidwell were stricken and died within hours. Are such fates only that matter of luck, of which Schliemann and Bidwell spoke so often? Or is there an influence of mental attitude?

Did these men attain happiness? Is the good life also the happy life? That may be questioned — at least, with Prince Henry. Some even argue that life cannot attain fullness without a mingling of tragedy.

If these six are to furnish our guide lines, the attaining of the good life is bound up with a sense of goal, with full commitment, with the acceptance of responsibility, with courage, with long-time fulfillment, and with a final and resultant integration of spirit.

SOURCES
❖❖❖❖❖

TEXTUAL

William the Marshal. The great biography is the primary source, and a magnificent one. *Histoire de Guillaume le Maréchal* (ed. Paul Meyer, 1891-1901) is the only edition available, although another one, with English translation, is in process. The Meyer edition is in Old French, with a somewhat unsatisfactory synopsis in modern French. Also very valuable is Sidney Painter's *William Marshal* (1933), which finely supplements the original biography.

Schliemann. In the preparation of such a brief sketch as this one I have not attempted to work with all the voluminous materials still in Athens, which include 60,000 letters. Even published material is, if anything, overabundant. Of basic importance are his own writings. Those purporting to be autobiographical, however, are often unreliable, when checked against contemporary letters, etc. For this reason I have not relied much upon *Selbstbiographie,* and *Schliemann's First Visit to America* (ed. S. H. Weber, 1942), and I have exercised caution even with *La Chine et le Japon.* Of very greatest value are the three volumes of his published correspondence, edited by Ernst Meyer. There are several biographies, all of which seem to me to get too much involved with the gold-seeker, and to miss a great deal about the whole man. The best of these, I should say, is Emil Ludwig's *Schliemann* (1931). It publishes some passages from original documents which are not elsewhere available.

Joab. A Biblical concordance supplies the sources of data. Joab receives mention in biographies of David and in histories of the Hebrews, but there is no special study. Laurene Chinn has written the novel, *The Unanointed* (1959); I find myself in only partial agreement with the interpretation of character there offered. Controversy is involved about the manner of Joab's taking of Jerusalem; anyone wishing to investigate might begin with Hugues Vincent, *Jerusalem de l'Ancien Testament* (1956), p. 632.

Tresguerras. Materials on his life are scanty, and some of them are in local publications which are difficult to find outside of Mexico. I am especially grateful to Sr. Jesús Rodríguez Frausto for his gift of the copies of *Publicación del Archivo Histórico de Guanajuato* ("Biographias," 85-90), which contain his basic work on Tresguerras. Also of great value has been the edition of Tresguerras's *Ocios Literarios* (1962) edited with introduction and notes by Francisco de la Maza, and including the *Carta Autobiográfica* and a bibliography. But even with these aids Tresguerras's life is not fully recorded. Especially lacking is a critical study of his architectural and artistic work. At present, one has great difficulty in even knowing what he produced. Luis Velasco y Mendoza, *Historia de la Ciudad de Celaya* (1947), contains some biographical information, and is valuable for background. The works of Rodríguez and de la Maza can be consulted for scattered biographical references. Sacheverell Sitwell, though without adding to the biographical data on Tresguerras, records his judgment that the Carmen church is "not only the best church of the nineteenth century, but, also, the last good church ever built." (*Spanish Baroque Art*, 1931, p. 78.)

Prince Henry. Of numerous biographies I have found most useful: Elaine Sanceau, *Henry the Navigator* (1945?), Vitorino Nemesio, *Vida e Obra do Infante D. Henrique* (1959), and Carlos Selvagem, *Infante Dom Anrique* (1960), the last two available only in Portuguese. The older standard English works by Major and Beazley are now outdated, and, besides, deal more with the exploration than with the man. A more recent valuable study of the exploration is Edgar Prestage, *The Portuguese Pioneers* (1933). Important, in any study of Henry, is the work of Gomes Eanes de Zurara, especially *Crónica do Descobrimento e Conquista de Guiné*, which I have used chiefly in the French translation (1960), edited with excellent notes by Léon Bourdon and Robert Ricard. J. P. Oliveira Martins, *The Golden Age of Prince Henry the Navigator* (1914), is strongly anti-Henry. A little may be gathered from the accounts of Alvise Cadamosto, Diogo Gomes, and João de Barros.

I have made no reference to the theory of Henry's having had an illegitimate daughter. The idea seems to be completely exploded by the evidence produced in the note (pp. 50-51) of the edition of Zurara mentioned above.

Bidwell. Rockwell D. Hunt, *John Bidwell* (1942), presents much valuable information, but I have worked chiefly from the original documents. These are amazingly voluminous, and are to be found chiefly in the California State Library, and in the Bancroft Library of the University of California. I have been unable to examine all this material minutely, and did not think that such an examination was necessary for the writing of my brief sketch. Bidwell's diaries in MS extend from 1864 to 1900, with a few breaks in the early years. There are printed versions of his 1841 diary (latest edition, ed. Francis P. Farquhar, 1964). There are numerous letters, and much miscellaneous material. Bidwell's articles in *Century Magazine* (1890) have been partially republished in *Echoes of the Past* (1928) but do not contain much biographical information which is not available elsewhere in more detailed form. Of great importance are two biographical statements by Bidwell, now in the Bancroft Library, especially the one entitled *Dictation* (#802). Also of value are his reminiscences as published in *Out West* (January to August, 1904). Both Hunt and Farquhar list other biographical items. An account of the Bartleson Party is presented in my *California Trail* (1962).

SOURCES

<><><><><><>

ARCHEOLOGICAL

The development of archeology should have sensitized scholars to the reality that many important sources are not
textual. I myself find it of importance to visit places where
the subjects of my inquiry have been active. With my six
men, I have been able to do so, except with Joab.

I followed the Marshal in the summer of 1965, first picking up his trail in Kilkenny. Thence it lead to the narrow
streets of Lincoln, where he fought his last battle. At Striguil, high-set on its cliff above the Wye, one gets the best
sense of his power as a feudal lord. One wall was built in his
time. The trail led on through Marlborough in the still-
pleasant countryside of southern England, where he spent
his boyhood, and beyond that to Runnymede, and the Tower
of London, where he took refuge in his illness. His tomb, in
the Temple Church, is still impressive, with his recumbent
effigy upon it. In France, there is the chateau at Chinon,
where Henry II died. Not far away is the abbey of Fontevrault, which was the scene of the fateful interview with
Richard. Rouen has grown out of recognition since the Marshal's day and so has Neufchatel, which was Drincourt, where
he fought his first battle. But at Tancarville one can still see
the castle courtyard, where as a teen-ager he went through
his schooling in chivalry. Finally, there is the badly ruined
castle at Longueville, where he brought Isabel as a bride.

Though I have never been to Troy, I have followed Schliemann a little at Mycenae and Tiryns, and have seen his stately house in Athens.

Perhaps more than any of them, Tresguerras is part of his local scene. I have been to the Bajío several times, and in December, 1962, I spent some time there, especially looking at his works. The great church still seems almost as new as it would have been in his time. In 1962 the main toll highway ended just a little to the east of the River Laja, and the traffic funneled across the old bridge. Just as it had stood the summer floods for a century and a half, so it took, without sign of strain, the pounding of the speeding, heavy trucks. But one of the stone ornaments had been knocked off, as if the modern world of machines and power could not tolerate the simple pleasure-giving curves of an earlier world. Even the landscape of the Bajío, as I have tried to indicate in the text, seems to suggest something of Tresguerras's spirit.

As for Prince Henry, a bout with some infection kept me from getting to his tomb at Batalha, but I went to Sagres, where one still gains some sense of the man. When I was there, it was so much more pleasant a place than crowded Lisbon that I began to think that Henry may merely have preferred it for that reason.

Bidwell is a man of my own country. I have even followed much of his 1841 trail, and managed to get to the isolated but beautiful hot springs which he described with gusto in his diary for September 21. The Mansion still stands in its grounds, taken over as a State Park. Vallombrosa also is a park, and looks much as it did in Bidwell's time, except where it has had to suffer being leap-frogged by a freeway. I saw Bidwell's Bar for the last time in February, 1966; it will soon be beneath the water of a huge dam. Fort Ross, Sutter's

Fort, and even the Hock Farm can still be visited. Many photographs and other memorials exist. His passport of 1841 is in the State Library; his authorization to visit the Army of the Potomac, in the Bancroft Library.

ACKNOWLEDGMENTS

SEVERAL of my colleagues at the University of California have read the manuscript in whole or in part and have aided me with valuable comments. I wish particularly to thank Darrel A. Amyx, Walter J. Fischel, James D. Hart, Charles W. Jones, Josephine Miles, and Lesley B. Simpson.

I wish also to express my gratitude to others, in various parts of the world, who have generously contributed their time and troubled themselves in various ways to help my project. I remember especially Karl Aschenbrenner, Justino Fernández, V. H. Galbraith, W. H. Hutchinson, Constantino Patrides, Jesús Rodríguez Frausto, and Gutierre Tibón.

To the staffs of the Bancroft Library and of the California State Library, I gratefully acknowledge much assistance in the study of Bidwell. The Inter-library Loan Service of the University of California made diligent search for obscure materials on Tresguerras.

To three members of my own family I am especially indebted. My wife has traveled with me, exploring this subject, in various parts of the world, and she has also read the manuscript as it progressed, and provided much wisdom toward its completion. My cousin, Robert Wilson, was my traveling companion in Portugal. My granddaughter, Anna Evenson was with me in England and France, and was the first to spot the almost obscured ruins of the castle at Longueville.

Berkeley, California
August 13, 1966

305

DATE